STYLE CHECKLIST

For all are as below ask:

How **important** or insignificant is this to people in this play (world)?
How **polarized** or uniform are they in their views?

Time
How **rapidly** does it move for most people?
How **conscious** are they of time passing?
How do they **record** or note time?
What is the dominant **tempo/rhythm**?
Do people **focus** mainly on the moment, on whole lifetimes, the future, the past?
In what **point in history** is the play set, written, performed? How do these interact?
How far does the audience or play **move** out of its own time?

Space
How is it **defined** and viewed? Is literal, spiritual, philosophical, or abstract?
How large a **bubble** do people carry around?
How do **personal** spaces alter? How flexible?
To what degree is **privacy** respected?
What are attitudes towards **invasion** and force? How is space **violated**?
How do these beliefs **translate** into audience proximity, and movement patterns

Place
Is the **setting** rural, metro, coastal, inland, protected, exposed, confined, open?
Age? Is it new or old?
What **influence** does terrain, flora, fauna, weather have?
Does the place have a specific or generic **character**?
How aware are people of **other** places? How **provincial** is their perspective?
Are they **citizens** only of this spot or of the world?
What is the **relationship to nature**? To what extent is the environment altered or accepted?

Values
What are the **beliefs** most widely **shared**? What ideals?
What are the **traditions** and how large is the commitment to them?
How is **friendship, family, trust** and **community** defined and how are these **bonds broken?**
What is the predominant **mood**?
Who are role models, heroes, **idols?**
What are shared **fantasies** and ideal futures?
How do they define **sin**, consequences, forgiveness, ethics, justice?
What gets **attention**? What holds it?
Value placed on **money**? Uses for it?
What is the place of **God** and the church in life? Are these two ever confused?
What kind of **humor** dominates? What role has laughter in society?
How is **fear** defined? What are its sources and how to people cope with it?
How and to what degree is **emotion** expressed? How suppressed?

Structure
Who **leads** and who follows?
How easy is it to bring about **change or justice**?
How absolute is **authority**? What is the voice of the individual?
What is the government **system**?

How is **daily life** ordered?
How is **family** defined? How are **etiquette** and rules set?
How much emphasis is on **education**?
How are **groups** created and identified? Which are most powerful?
What **professions** dominate and how is **work** viewed?
How is **information** gathered and spread?

Beauty
What is the **look, most aspired to**, in this group?
Who are the contemporary **ideals** of perfection?
What part does **fitness** play in physical attractiveness?
What is the relationship between beauty, health, and **comfort**?
Which **colors, textures, silhouettes** are favored?
How important is **fashion**? How fast does it **change**?
To what degree is **nature** altered in order to create a thing of beauty?
How is **taste** defined?
What are favored modes of **artistic expression**?

Sex
How significant to the collective **consciousness** is sex?
What are considered **turn ons** and **turn offs**?
Which **areas of anatomy** are revealed, concealed, emphasized?
What are sexual **stereotypes?**
How is **sexuality communicated?**
How is **seduction** defined?
Is the **emphasis** on the act or the chase? On pleasure or procreation?
What is the standard **courtship ritual**?
How much tolerance for **deviation**?
What are the accepted attitudes towards **infidelity**, towards **promiscuity?**
What **degree of suppression or expression** of sexuality occurs?

Recreation
What is most people's idea of **fun?**
What would be an **ideal social occasion**? An enjoyable day?
What is the **participation** level? Are they doers or watchers?
Intellectual life? Thinkers or mindless hedonists?
What are common **shared** hobbies and **pastimes?**
What are differences between **sexes?**
Consumption? Favored and coveted meals, drink, drugs?
What is the relative **importance** of recreation in life? The standard view of
indulgence?

Sight
How do all the above manifest themselves in the way the world looks, in **shapes,
angles, light, shadow, patterns of movement?**
In **clothing**, furnishings, props, hairdos, and jewelry?
What is the pattern of **movement** and **contact** and its significance?

Sound
How does it come out in **speech** and **nonverbal** communication?
To what degree are **listening** and **speaking** prized?
What **vocal quality** is most desired, rewarded, emulated and for what reasons?
Is there **standardized** pronunciation or great variance? Which part of pitch
register is employed?
Is the **word choice** vague or direct?
What is the role of **music** and **dance** in life?

STYLE FOR ACTORS

"Style is a journey from tourist to native. It is living in the world of the play, not just visiting it."—from Chapter 1

Anyone who has ever struggled with capes, fans, swords, doublets, and crinolines should make *Style for Actors*, second edition, their constant companion. Robert Barton has completely updated his award-winning handbook for the twenty-first century with contemporary references and up-to-date illustrations. This is the definitive guide to roles in historical drama.

The past is a foreign country, and this outstanding book is concerned with exploring it from the actor's point of view. Specific guides range from Greek, Elizabethan, Restoration, and Georgian theatre to more contemporary stylings, including futurism, surrealism and postmodernism.

Barton takes great care to present the actor with the roles and genres that will most commonly confront them. His analysis moves from entire genres to specific scenes and characters. A huge resource of nearly one hundred and fifty practical exercises helps a new-found understanding of style to make the leap from page to performance.

Robert Barton is Professor Emeritus of acting at the University of Oregon. As well as writing a regular column for *The Voice* and *Speech Review*, he is the author of *Acting: Onstage and Off*, *Voice: Onstage and Off* (with Rocco Dal Vera), *Theatre in Your Life* and *Life Themes*. The first edition of *Style for Actors* received the Theatre Association's Best Book award.

STYLE
for Actors

A Handbook for Moving Beyond Realism

Second edition

Robert Barton

Routledge
Taylor & Francis Group

NEW YORK AND LONDON

First published in 1993 by
Mayfield Publishing Company
1240 Villa Street
Mountain View, California 94041

This edition first published 2010
by Routledge
711 Third Avenue, New York, NY 10017

Simultaneously published in the UK
by Routledge
2 Park Square, Milton Park, Abingdon, Oxon OX14 4RN

Routledge is an imprint of the Taylor & Francis Group, an informa business

© 2010 Robert Barton

Typeset in by Bembo and Futura by
Florence Production Ltd, Stoodleigh, Devon

British Library Cataloguing in Publication Data
A catalogue record for this book is available from the British Library

Library of Congress Cataloging-in-Publication Data
Barton, Robert, 1945–.
  Style for actors: a handbook for moving beyond realism/
  Robert Barton.—2nd ed.
      p. cm.
  Includes bibliographical references and index.
  1. Acting. 2. Drama. I. Title.
  PN2061.B295 2009
  792.02′8—dc22   2009000702

ISBN10: 0–415–48572–X (hbk)
ISBN10: 0–415–48573–8 (pbk)
ISBN10: 0–203–87387–4 (ebk)

ISBN13: 978–0–415–48572–2 (hbk)
ISBN13: 978–0–415–48573–9 (pbk)
ISBN13: 978–0–203–87387–8 (ebk)

Printed and bound in the United States of America by
Edwards Brothers Malloy on sustainably sourced paper

CONTENTS

CONTENTS

ILLUSTRATIONS

In loving memory of Carrow and Billie De Vries who showed me what a family could be as well as the joy of a life surrounded by books.

PREFACE

This book is a guide for the actor who is ready to move beyond contemporary realism into the less familiar acting territory of historical periods and genres. At the introductory level, actors learn to perform in a familiar world. This book is about performing in new worlds.

Great emphasis is placed on tools rather than on rules. The guiding assumption is that it is more important for an actor to know how to ask questions, since answers change from production to production. This book attempts to prepare actors for a variety of directorial approaches, without restricting their choices. Although style is an extraordinary challenge, there are many right ways to meet it.

The book strives for a tone that is personal and empathetic, addressing readers as human beings, with respect for their own inherent wisdom. It attempts to connect frankly with the person who has to go out there (sometimes struggling with panniers, feathers, fan, cape, sword, doublet, and couplet) and *do* it—the actor.

The text is distinct in that:

1. Style is presented as situational, flexible, and ongoing, rather than as a set of laws. Actors are encouraged to approach each new production freshly, without preconceived notions of stylistic conventions.
2. The styles included are those most performed. Far more space is devoted to the works of Shakespeare and Molière than those less likely to be encountered in the actor's entire life, such as miracle plays and Roman tragedy.
3. Interviews with imaginary persons from each historical period—a Greek seer, an Elizabethan noble, a Restoration courtier, a Molière actor and a Georgian merchant—convey the ways in which beliefs support and change acting.

4. Familiar styles are used as bridges to less familiar ones, with music, clothing, language, and "stylized" encounters, such as courtroom trials and marriage ceremonies, serving as lead-ins to performing the classics.

5. A ten-step investigation into the periods through time, space, place, values, structure, beauty, sex, recreation, sight, and sound allows the actor to look at a play the way an anthropologist might look at an undiscovered country and to investigate it with the same urgency.

6. What the actor is most likely to be asked to do in production is always favored over what was believed to have been done in the original productions. The world each playwright creates is favored over the one in which he may have been living.

7. Period or classical styles, which strike young actors as remote, receive far greater emphasis than do contemporary styles, which always have the advantage of starting in familiar territory.

8. Improvisation is offered as a primary means of entering each period. Actors have a chance to explore a style within a strongly defined context, while momentarily free of text, by participating in the nearly one hundred and fifty exercises.

9. Issues often omitted when style is addressed, such as translations, eastern theatre, musical theatre, scansion, and displaced plays (those written in one period but set in another, such as *Amadeus* and *Les Liaisons Dangereuses*), are included if they are likely to involve the actor.

10. A list of scene suggestions for workshop and showcasing accompanies the discussion of each historical style. A full annotation of all the scenes in the plays of William Shakespeare is included.

Part 1 is called "Finding style." The text begins with two chapters about style in daily life: recognizing it, analyzing it, and using it to understand one's own experiences. Chapter 2 also presents ten categories for examining and entering a world—in the theatre or outside it. These ten categories are carried forward through the remainder of the book and are presented in a checklist format on the inside front and back covers. Chapter 3 analyzes the differences between a limited contemporary realistic actor and one who comfortably performs the classics to determine what characteristics all good style actors share.

Part 2 is called "Achieving style." The next four chapters address periods most produced on Western classical stages: Greek, Elizabethan, Restoration, Molière (neoclassic), and Georgian (eighteenth century).

Part 3 is called "Exploring style." Chapter 8 deals with scripts written in one time but performed or set in another. It also addresses varieties of translation, adaptation, and edition and offers a system of connecting any script to the audience for which it is being presented. Chapter 9 surveys the genres (the Isms, from Romanticism through Postmodernism) that define today's theatre. The final chapter examines personal style, both in performance and in life, so that the text ends as it begins, with the actor's examination of self.

USING THIS TEXT

The book strives to be equally accessible to the individual practitioner working alone and to those who are part of a training program, surrounded by classmates, or a production, surrounded by other members of the cast.

Instructors all teach style under different circumstances. Within the ten-chapter organization, much flexibility is possible. Advanced or sophisticated groups can skim Chapters 1 and 2 for possible new questions, but the activities are not necessary, unless they wish to renew a sense of exploration or awareness of style in everyday life. Because so many actors are terrified of the subject, these chapters offers reassurance that style exists all around us, that none of us is totally ignorant, and that all of us do have style knowledge on which we can draw. The book is deliberately filled with more questions to ask and exercises to try than any group would wish to undertake, so that classes can pick and choose favorites without impeding their progress in any way.

Emphasis will also be influenced by the placement of the course within the curriculum. For example, my own class follows a voice course in which elevated speech and scansion are covered intensely, thereby allowing far more time to be spent on movement and attitude than on vocal issues in classical performance.

The chapters that deal with significant style issues that influence the full range of periods and genres are Chapter 3 ("Mastering style") and Chapter 8 ("Displaced style"), which offer vocal, physical, and psychological preparation as well as methods for rehearsing text. Those who are limited by time or desire an overview can isolate these two chapters for intensive work on what is demanded for classical performance generally, without isolating contexts.

Groups who wish to focus on one major historical period can combine the above chapters with Chapters 4 (Greek), 5 (Elizabethan), 6 (Restoration), the first part of 7 (Molière) or the second part of 7 (Georgian). This will also prove appropriate if the text is being used as a resource for the production of a single play. In this scheme, the group reviews general principles, then applies them in one clear context.

Those who are interested in the concept of style but not in those based in history can combine Chapters 3 and 8 with Chapter 9 ("The Isms") to explore modern styles alone. An entire term can easily be devoted to the journey from Romanticism through Postmodernism and beyond.

Other combinations are certainly possible. One class might elect to do just Greek and Elizabethan, for an intense focus on the heroic perspective. Another might do just Restoration and Molière, for exploration of wit and sharp comedy. If you are limited by time, but wish to offer actors a strong contrast, I would suggest units on Greek and Restoration (Chapters 4 and 6), because there are probably no two other styles that offer greater diversity and challenges for the performer. Inhabiting these two extraordinary, dissimilar worlds can offer a vivid experience in the huge range of stylistic acting.

Chapter 10 brings all the material into the actors' offstage life. It is an optional excursion. Those who have seen my other books will recognize my bias for the application of theatrical principles in daily life, but you are certainly under no constraint to share it. In our own program, the chapter is like frosting. Students find it stimulating, funny, and sometimes even moving, but time and focus constraints could limit it to a reading discussion assignment. The primary pragmatic issue this chapter deals with is the way style or lack of self-knowledge may be blocking his or her entry into the world of the play.

Ideal circumstances would allow a year to explore all the material here. Unfortunately, few of us teach under ideal circumstances. At the University of Oregon, we have only one ten-week quarter for this subject, but we do review all the material, with each actor performing a scene from two separate periods. Many suggestions and related documents regarding my own teaching situation are offered on the book's website (see below).

A single reader not affiliated with a course or a production will have no trouble exploring this material independently. For some of the interactive experiences, a partner would be helpful, but not essential.

For many actors, the text can serve as a reference in preparing for audition for a particular style play or as an important part of character analysis and personal rehearsal if cast in one. For the individual director, it can provide a brush-up on the style itself and some insights into shaping rehearsals.

I hope serious actors will keep this book easily available "on the shelf" and return to this material again and again over the years; if the initial exposure is a brief overview, it can at least alert them to what is ahead and frame future exploration. At various times in one's life (such as an upcoming audition for a Georgian comedy), this should be the "go to" resource for reviewing the conventions of that particular period. Style is a lifelong subject of study, for which this text can provide a basis.

NEW TO THIS EDITION

1. A website, www.routledge.com/textbooks/9780415485739, will offer considerable suggestions for teaching this material in class or for employing it in production preparation. Documents specific to teaching isolated skills (such as a sample scene and guidelines for mastering asides) have been added.
2. The site will also offer links to scenes and stills from films, supplementary research materials, and sources for further visualizing and experiencing productions of the styles examined.

3. Audio versions of the interviews with the five "guests" who appear in Chapters 4–7 can enhance the experience of the historical chapters.

4. The text has been divided into three distinct parts for greater clarification of intent, the first for finding style, the second for achieving it, and the third for exploring it.

5. The reader focus of *Style for Actors* has shifted from exclusively that of an American college classroom to a wider, more inclusively global or at least fully Western perspective, as has the selection of photos employed. The book also embraces the individual practitioner who may employ the text as a reference and guide.

6. Cultural references, particularly those relating to pop culture have been appropriately updated or made more universal, less time and culture bound.

7. References to films and DVDs wherein effective period style work is modeled have expanded beyond those to theatre works only, as has a general emphasis on technology as a resource.

8. New exercises (including a warm-up specific to Molière's plays and one for Georgian theatre) are included in chapters.

9. Group exercises have been numbered for easier reference and have been shifted, for the most part, to appendices to enhance the flow of the text, and to provide a clearer distinction between ideas and the exploration of these ideas in communal settings.

10. The book has been streamlined to approximately 80 percent of its original length, making it a considerably less daunting read. No relevant content has been omitted, but rather the text has been bled of digression, redundant explanation, and examples no longer meaningful to actors of the twenty-first century. The result is a clean, sharp, consistently focused reading experience.

ACKNOWLEDGMENTS

I am forever grateful to my close friend and sometime co-author Rocco Dal Vera for realizing that *Style for Actors* belonged at Routledge rather than its former publishing house and for pursuing that so proactively and persuasively. His support has been immeasurable. My thanks as well to publisher Talia Rogers for responding instantly and enthusiastically to the idea of a transfer and to an exciting, new, revised edition and for following through in a truly hands on and imaginative way. I am immeasurably grateful to Catherine Foley for excellent, insightful work as the development editor. Ben Piggott took over when illness forced Catherine's withdrawal from the project and was effective in the acquisition and arrangement of illustrations. Helpful comments were provided by the following reviewers: Dawn Arnold, Moving Dock Theatre Co., Chicago; Dennis Meher, Texas-Arlington; Charles Ney, TSU; Ed Hooks, San Francisco (actor training); Roberta Rude, University of South Dakota; Jane Boston, RADA, UK; Caroline Hadley, UWE, UK; Martin Johnson, Swansea College, UK.

PART ONE

FINDING STYLE

MANY OF US ARE confused by the whole idea of "style," since the term is used in so many artistic forms and activities. We also sometimes fail to recognize a style because we are so accustomed to it or alternatively to explore a style because we have decided it is so remote from our experience. This section is about recognizing and owning instances where we stylize our behavior to suit a circumstance. Many actors are terrified of moving outside contemporary realism, but fantasize doing so. These chapters offer reassurance that style exists all around us, that none of us is totally ignorant, and that in fact all of us have style knowledge on which we can draw.

The text begins with two chapters about style in daily life: sensing it, analyzing it, and using it to understand our own experiences. We all know far more than we think we do and travel outside our realistic behavior more often than we may have noticed.

The first chapter is about recognizing what you already do and know. The second presents ten categories for examining and entering a world—in the theatre or outside it. These categories are carried forward through the remainder of the book. They provide structure for all inquiries, since the answers to the same basic questions, as they vary from times, cultures, and genres, can illuminate not only the answers, but the questions themselves.

The third chapter analyzes the differences between a limited contemporary actor and one who comfortably performs the classics, to determine what characteristics all good style actors share. This chapter deals with significant style issues that influence *all* periods and genres.

1. RECOGNIZING STYLE: The eyes of the beholder
2. ANALYZING STYLE: Survival questions
3. MASTERING STYLE: The classical actor

1 RECOGNIZING STYLE
The eyes of the beholder

STYLE IS SOMETHING we all want and fear. We want to have "real style," but to be more than just "stylish." We want to be a master of style, never slave to it. We want style, without mistaking style for substance.

Since our feelings are ambivalent towards it in our own lives, most of us are tentative in our early efforts at style in the theatre. To understand style acting, we must recognize it in living, where the word is used synonymously with: form—manner—method—way—fashion—vogue—mode—chic—craze—fad—rage—practice—habit—air—distinction—typical presentation—characteristic behavior—elegance—wording—means of expressing—and execution.

Style is the way something is done, rather than the core act itself. In writing classes, separate grades may be given for *style* and *content*. A beautifully written essay may say nothing, or an awkwardly expressed one may have profound insights. Style is also perceived in terms of expectations. Contemporary realistic theatre, where each actor is cast close to age and type, is standard. It is our dominant style. Any time a show moves away, it is called "stylized" or is described as done in "The 'fill-in-the-blank' style". You stylize an event by boldly removing it from everyday, expected behavior. The more stylized a production, the more conventions or rules of make-believe the audience must accept, in order to appreciate it.

For an actor, "style work" may refer to any journey outside of mastered, known territory into new ground. This often involves changing yourself enough to believably enter another world, formerly unfamiliar to you or to most audiences. The same happens outside the theatre, where people who are thought of as having real style are those who move with relative ease between worlds.

DEFINING STYLE

STYLE IS A WAY OF UNDERSTANDING THE WORLD AND THEN ENTERING IT BASED ON WHAT YOU SEE

If you see the world as a vicious concrete jungle, you might wear leather and studs and often use the "f" word. If you see the world as an enchanted romantic garden, you might wear flowing chiffon and improvise poetry. If you change your mind in the middle of the day (stuck in chiffon, spouting the "f" word), you have trouble reconciling feelings with presentation. Style is the external manifestation of some inner drive. It is a set of choices in action, a relationship between what you feel and what you present in the world. The world may be a club, a country, a period, or a play. It may be all of the above.

A film scholar noted difficulties in mounting serious plays about infidelity in France, because the French tend to view the subject humorously or ironically. A belief shared by enough people is perceived as the dominant style. If you see a character in a French film being told about a neighbor's affair, what do you expect that character to do? Shrug? Smile? Wink? Briefly philosophize? Probably. Rage? Weep? Register shock? Get a gun? Probably not.

Too often in the theatre, outward manifestation of inward belief is picked up without the belief itself. When you attend a bad production of a period style play, you may see a series of poses, without a sense of anything going on behind them, as if a director had said "You should all shrug a lot and then smile because that's what French people do" and had neglected to explore the various *motives* in the culture that might encourage the act. Without belief, the whole venture looks hollow. There are likely to be shrugs in all the wrong places.

STYLE IS WHAT IS SHARED BY CHARACTERS IN A PLAY (OR PEOPLE IN A GROUP), WHILE CHARACTERIZATION IS WHAT MAKES THEM DISTINCT FROM EACH OTHER

All characters in a play share qualities, a collective characterization that ties them together. In some musicals, they *all* wear sequins and tap shoes (even to the office), and when someone says "I've got an idea!!!," they *all* lean way in to him and shout "What??!!" simultaneously. Yet, the sweet hoofer from Kansas in the chorus is clearly different from the temperamental, vamping star, even in this "stylized" world. They share style, but as distinct entities within it.

The balance between interesting, idiosyncratic, even quirky character work and consistent, detailed style work is what makes an exciting production. We want all the humans in the play so clearly defined that we won't confuse them, but we also want them to share enough to tie the play together. Offstage, most of us wish to "fit" into our communities comfortably, while still distinguishing ourselves as unique and special. We like to be part of the neighborhood without being mistaken for our neighbors.

Many plays and films are about group style wars. In *Romeo and Juliet*, two families, who seem very similar to most of *us*, war over their differences, which seem so obvious to *them* that nobody in the play ever bothers to say what they are. In most productions, it looks as if the Montagues don't like the fact that the Capulets wear red, and the Capulets don't like that the Montagues wear blue, and this ultimately leads to the death of the hero and heroine, who are color blind.

STYLE IS WHAT WORKS IN A GROUP

You encounter varying groups on an ordinary day. With each you try to determine what will get you by. When you move someplace new, you try to grasp the style of your school, city, department, job. You use groups to help you figure out who you are, joining some, avoiding others.

We choose some groups (religious, political, social, academic) and are thrust by fate (race, economics, family) into others. People who are nothing but their groups are a bore. Is there anyone more tedious than the person who seems to be *only* gay, Jewish, black, Capricorn, square dancer or stamp collector? Someone who talks of nothing else and presses her group into every conversation is a pain. We want groups to define us, not submerge us.

Yet membership is a social necessity, a tool for survival. Style is an ongoing struggle, rather than an accomplishment, as we keeping trying to fit in. If you get pulled over to the side of the road deep in Louisiana, and two police officers saunter over to you, you turn into as close to a Good Ole Boy as you can get away with in order to minimize your fine and avoid the county jail. You may start using the word "sir" for the first time in years. Because the stakes are high, you may amaze yourself at how *deeply* Southern you can be. In tense situations, stylistic maneuvers can tip the scales of justice.

STYLE INVOLVES EFFECTIVE STRATEGIC CHOICES. IT IS A LATITUDE, WITH SOME LIMITS, BUT MUCH CREATIVE SPACE

You return and repeat what succeeds, so a great opening line, an outfit that gets compliments, a tone of voice or way of moving that gets results will all be used again. If choices serve you well, they become habit and hard to change, even if they stop working. People can get *stuck* in style choices that served them in another era, but no longer wear so well. They have failed to stay alert for what works here and now. Style is understanding both rewarded and punished behavior in any set of given circumstances. Your family probably had a style when you were little, based on desired and undesired actions. Your parents just *loved* it when you did or said some things. Others were not tolerated. There were (probably still are) degrees of reward and punishment.

This pattern continues with every other group outside the home. If you do *A*, you will be punished in this group's worst possible way, and *B* will get you honor. But as long as you come through on certain issues and don't push certain others, you're O.K. There is a *big space* left over, a comfort zone, free of tension. Actors often want to know *exactly* what to do to act Sophocles or Shakespeare, living in terror of moving outside of O.K., visualizing audiences laughing at how stupid they look and throwing things. O.K. is actually the fun space. They fail to realize that there is a giant playground, and there are many ways to win .

STYLE IS BEHAVIOR PERCEIVED BY THE INDIVIDUAL AS NATURAL, WHILE OTHERS (OF UNLIKE STYLE) ARE PERCEIVED AS ARTIFICIAL AND CONTRIVED

We all have an amazing capacity, no matter how difficult a style was to master, that once we've got it, we forget what it was like before. Suddenly this is the *only* way to act. Those who act otherwise are perverse, retarded or both.

As each person views his own behavior as normal, so does each era. Look at old photographs of yourself and you're often appalled at what you once thought attractive. Plays match how the people *feel* about themselves. It is only when the group's view of itself alters that the old behavior suddenly seems stylized. Elizabethan actors had no trouble shouting above the groundlings because they thought of themselves as huge and ready to conquer the rest of the globe. Since we tend to think of ourselves as small grains of sand on the beach of life, in need of therapy or at least a back rub, our perception of "normal" behavior is cautious, defensive, and even neurotic compared with theirs. When reality is the issue, you need to ask "Which one?" When normality is concerned, you need to ask "On whose terms?"

STYLE IS THE JOURNEY FROM TOURIST TO NATIVE. IT IS LIVING IN THE WORLD OF THE PLAY— NOT JUST VISITING IT

The actor enters the play like a tourist, gets her rehearsal passport, becomes an immigrant, buys, settles, acquires citizenship, prospers, and, if all goes well, by opening night, appears comfortably native.

Rehearsals for plays are psychic relocations. No one walks into the first read-through with mastery. The process is like moving into a new neighborhood as a child or country as an adult. Even directors and designers, who have determined some of the territory, are still finding out what this play is about and how its world comes to life. But the whole process goes more smoothly if you pack well, learn some language and customs, and get all your shots. The rehearsal is a journey; the performance the destination.

The following categories are lifted almost verbatim from a traveler's guide for visiting a foreign country. I have found them useful for a production, when a cast prepares to journey someplace in Shakespeare's world such as Navarre, Illyria, or the Forest of Arden.★

TRAVEL GUIDE TO SHAKESPEARIA

A BRIEF HISTORY—WHAT TO SEE—EXCURSIONS—SHOPPING—WINING AND DINING—RELAXING—HOW TO GET THERE AND WHEN TO GO—PLANNING YOUR BUDGET—BLUEPRINT FOR A PERFECT TRIP

Speaking the language

Articles, nouns, adjectives, adverbs, possessive pronouns, demonstrative pronouns, personal pronouns, verbs, negatives, questions, expressing agreement and disagreement

Guide to pronunciation

Spelling and sounds, elevated classical speech, scansion, historical rhymes

Basic expressions

Greetings, good-byes, questions, forms of address, dismissals, commands, oaths, parentheses, useful words

Arrival

Customs, baggage, changing money, directions, reservations, rentals, transportation

Accommodations

How much, how long, decisions, bills, tipping, registration, service, checking out

Eating out

Types of establishment, meal times, eating habits, asking and ordering, menus, appetizers, salads, cheese, fruit, desserts, bills, complaints, beverages, snacks

Traveling

Horse, carriage, foot, inquiries, tickets, entry, eating, sleeping, baggage, lost!, barge, boat, magic, other means of transport

---

★Settings for *Love's Labour's Lost*, *Twelfth Night*, and *As You Like It*.

Sightseeing

Attractions, admissions, who-what-when?, religious services

Relaxing

Entertainment, dancing, fights, bear baiting, hangings, madrigals, masques, versification, sports

Making friends

Introductions, follow-up, weather, invitations, dating

Shopping guide

Shops and services, bartering, ordering, delivery, paying, dissatisfied, bookshops, crockery and cutlery, chemists, toiletry, hair, clothing, size, fit, accessories, music, jewelers-watchmakers, laundry, provisions

Souvenirs

Weights and measures, currency, credit, monetary units, deposits and withdrawals

Posting

Notices, mails, edicts, seals, proclamations, information sources

Travel

Directions, documentation, road signs, accidents, breakdown, on the road, repairs

Doctor

Symptoms, illnesses, wounds, prescriptions, dosages, potions, alchemists, witches

Reference

Regions, times, months, seasons, holidays, temperatures, conversions, signs

The traveler's guide can serve any play. If you prepare with the same excitement you would give a trip, research comes easily. Is all this information at the library? No. You start there, but the more you find out about the historical Illyria, Navarre, or Arden, the less it seems to match Shakespeare's. So you move from investigation (research) to inference (making connections) to invention (making it up!). The information *is* available in your imagination. The big difference between traveling to Shakespearia, Sophoclia, or Molieria and traveling to England, Greece, or France is that the former are kingdoms of the mind. They are *based* in history, literature, and theory, but they will only *actualize* in production. Much creation must take place. And you will be one of the creators.

Ironically, what was easiest during childhood "let's pretend" is often hardest now. Transforming the acting space by sheer power of belief, and deciding to live there, test both imagination and concentration. The audience always knows which actors feel like aliens, which are not entirely foreign but still haven't gotten their papers, and which have decided they *belong*. These last actors own the stage.

The basis for the power involved is willingness to believe. Small children *believe* they are the fairytale, legend, or cartoon figures they play at play, so they are believable and fascinating. You *are* a prince, sage, monster, or even god if you are available to your own imagination and courage. The great period style plays allow a glorious return to Once Upon a Time.

STYLE IS BEING GOOD ENOUGH AT BEING GOOD TO GET AWAY WITH BEING BAD

By the time actors reach this stage, they are feeling confident, versatile, commanding, and maybe even cocky. When you understand what works in a culture, then you can begin to *play* with it. If you know how to charm, impress, inspire, intimidate, move, amuse and seduce, you can get away with almost anything.

I will never forget first seeing Peter O'Toole's entrance to the throne room (as King Henry) in the classic film *Becket*. He dashes across the room, whips off his crown, tosses it over one corner of the back of his throne, and then throws himself on the throne with one leg hanging over the arm of the chair, ready to hold court. Of *course* a young, cocky monarch would act this way! He clearly knows protocol well enough to tweak it. Only a man who understands pomp and majesty would recognize when to mock ceremony and create his own court. In performance, the long hours spent learning the customs of the period give you the confidence to expand, realizing that there are many ways to do it, some yet to be invented—by you.

STYLE IS KNOWING WHAT PLAY YOU'RE IN

Have you ever found an actor's work striking and skillful, but not quite right? As if the actor was imposing a world of his own? As if he was not in the same show as the script and the other actors? In the theatre, you need to know what play you're in, and in life you need to know what game you're in. Otherwise, survival is unlikely and success impossible. What works in the back alleys of a Detroit slum doesn't work at all in the salons of St Tropez. And what works in a Sam Shepard play is unlikely to cut it in a Noel Coward. In one play, an actor might rip off his clothes and flaunt his naked self to impress someone he desires. In another, this tactic would be disastrous, and anything less than a subtle, witty remark, delivered with great (fully clothed) panache, would send his "intended" exiting with laughter and disdain.

The same is true in life seductions. Figuring out the predominant style is what most characters in films do. Critics have called this phenomenon "fish out of water" films. The central character, thrust into a new world, has to figure out the right style to survive there.

And style is *always* a struggle. Nobody ever has it down perfectly. Those who seem to have it are struggling to get better at it and to survive the next challenge. It is an ongoing, dynamic process. Characters in brocade clothes uttering rhymed couplets do not have their lives all figured out, and neither need you and I. What we can do is understand how each of these people feels and experience their worlds from their perspectives.

SUMMARY QUESTIONS

The eight definitions below can be carried into any context. If you put each in the form of a question, you will get survival/success information immediately.

1. How do these people understand or perceive the world around them?

2. What do they all share? How much the same do they seem to be?

3. What works in this group? What do they reward and punish?

4. What is the most effective strategy for me here? Where's my free space?

5. What have they learned to think is natural? What to them seems contrived?

6. What is the most expedient way for me to move from tourist to native? How could I live here?

7. Who gets away with things? How do they manage to? What did they have to learn?

8. Do I really know what play (world) this is? Am I fully here?

SIGHT AND SOUND: First style impressions

The way you look and dress creates a first impression, followed by the way you speak. We make instant judgments. In the first sixty seconds, we predict someone's education, social standing, political views, organizational skills, trustworthiness, income, maturity, background, and health. Relationships with "acquaintances" or "associates" may never get deeper than this first hit with strangers.

Industries are devoted to how to look. Magazines offer advice, not on what to believe or feel, but on what to wear and how to present. We are a visual culture. Before a big occasion, we narrow what we're going to wear down to several choices, and what finally determines the winner? Often the person we want to *seem* to be, not who we are.

The language of style changes as rapidly as each season's look. One phenomenon of the past decade is language that modifies a more blunt description of something into a far more respectful phrase, bordering on euphemism. Consider the following phrases that soften the impact:

Employment opportunities—Help wanted

Functioning on a limited income—Poor

Dissolving a marriage—Divorce

Previously owned—Used

Administrative assistant, office specialist, support services agent—Secretary

Substance abuser—Junkie or drunk

Person of color—(Insert any specific color, except blonde)

Affordable—Cheap or a bargain

Alternative lifestyle—Possible weirdo

In a relationship—Having sex

Motorcoach—Bus

Fixer upper—Uninhabitable

User friendly—Easy to run

Some assembly required—Hard to put together

Sanitation engineers—Garbage collectors

Adult social service center—Massage parlor

Fabric care center—Laundry

Chronologically gifted—Old

Non-monogamous relationship—Dating others, playing the field or sleeping around

Physically challenged—Crippled

____ [insert atrocity of choice] survivor—____ [atrocity of choice] victim

Disadvantaged—Poor and/or retarded

Special—Disadvantaged

Weight problem—Fat

Over-leveraged—Broke

"Psychologists have actually started calling ugly people 'those with severe appearance deficits.' It's getting so bad that any day now I expect to hear a rape victim referred to as 'an unwilling sperm recipient'."
GEORGE CARLIN ON EUPHEMISMS

While clothes and words are chosen, sight judgments are also based on stance, sit, expressions, timing, walk, gestures, and use of space, sound judgments on vocal quality, timing, articulation, pronunciation, pitch, volume, and nonverbals, all signals not necessarily consciously selected.

RITUALS AND LIFESTYLES: Finding patterns

Since we think only of *others* as stylized, we often don't notice stylized events in our own lives—ceremonies, formalities, prescribed patterns, rites, and sacraments. When a visiting relative leaves your home and walks to the car, do you follow along, and does each member of the family line up to do a hug or handshake before the visitor gets in the car and takes off? Do you all stand and wave until the car is out of sight? Is anyone who *fails* to take part in this ritual chastised and cold-shouldered later? The *real* good-byes may have taken place earlier, but this ritual, especially if the visitor has come a long distance, may be considered essential. Many feel cheated if an important experience is not stylized into ritual.

If a stylized event has become important enough to become protocol, the ceremony is just the surface of something deep in the bones and hearts of the people performing it.

People go about the same fundamental acts, in different ways. The acts and people are not really different. The style is. This knowledge makes it easier to stop judging others for surface issues and to take the time to find out who they are. As an actor, it makes it easier to find the connections between you and characters you play, and then confidently "refine" yourself around the differences, without being intimidated by them. One of the best ways to achieve this is to imagine a wide range of choices surrounding a single, simple act. If you take a basic, well-known song and sing it in a variety of musical styles, you instantly comprehend how much the song, changes and how much it remains the same.

GROUPS AND INDIVIDUALS: Your own style

While style is associated with groups, it is embraced by individuals. You need to know what impressions your own style choices leave in the world to recognize when your style may be infringing on, rather than serving, the character you are playing:

1. Of which groups do others "think" you are a member, whether it is so or not?
2. When in your life so far have you altered your own style most radically to get out of a sticky situation?
3. In what contexts can you get away with being bad? How did you get this control?

4. How would you describe your own standard way of dressing? How would others describe it?

5. What single article of clothing would others most likely associate with you? What kinds of people wear this kind of clothing?

6. What do you work hardest at altering about yourself before you present yourself out in the world each day?

7. What is your distinct lingo? What is your "style of speak"?

8. When you want to avoid being blunt or crude, what are your favored euphemisms?

9. How much do you influence the way others speak, dress, or relate? How easily influenced are you and by whom?

10. When you have traveled, where have you felt most at home and most like an alien?

To find out how you present yourself, ask others. But ask to ensure candor. Ask them to think of you in abstractions. When you "abstract" someone, because you are removing yourself from literal, linear, blunt, potentially embarrassing interaction, you answer truthfully. Abstraction allows you to call it as you see it.

Pick an answer in each of the following categories that reflects how you are perceived in the world. Answers are not what you would *choose*, but what you *appear* to be. You may like warm, sunny, summer days but project chilly, rainy, autumn nights. Abstracting captures essence, which may be different from taste. Consider yourself as: (1) fabric, (2) animal, (3) bird, (4) beverage, (5) mode of transportation, (6) city, (7) tree-vegetation, (8) color, (9) play/film/TV show, (10) scent, (11) type of day, (12) decade or era, (13) song, (14) mythological/fantasy figure, (15) landmark or building, (16) snack, (17) spice/flavor, (18) musical instrument, (19) painting or photo, or (20) toy.

As new group styles are explored in subsequent chapters, ask yourself how your style fits into each one. Use questions in this section as a reminder. If a style gives you problems, you may be imposing your own on it. You may have not yet decided to completely enter the new world. Or you may have not yet unearthed those parts of your own style that fit.

Recognizing style is rewarding, touching, and often amusing. For a number of years, my wife and I have, by accident, eaten out at an elegant restaurant on Prom Night. We watch struggles with style as brave explorers venture into unfamiliar territory. Tuxes, evening gowns, corsages, borrowed or rented cars, an ambiguous and expensive menu, a formal atmosphere, starched collars, wobbly high heels, intimidating waiters, polite, studied conversation. Each year we've asked ourselves, "Were we ever really that young? Did either of us ever drop our napkin that many times?" The answer "Yes!" comes resounding back. And we wish we could let them know that they can survive this, master it, and even learn to enjoy it.

Some look like they've decided to be intimidated and have a terrible time on this supposed night of celebration. Others ignore the style changes and act like they're in the school cafeteria. Others are full of discovery, *appreciating* their own newness and awkwardness in unfamiliar territory and even being able to laugh at it, but also experiencing little victories of elegance and adulthood.

For some of these people, tonight is a nightmare, and they will never venture this far from jeans and fast food again. For others, it is an introduction to one more way to have fun. Style is an ongoing discovery. You are always striving to get better at being who you are in public. This last group recognizes that possibility for growth. They are making it a great adventure.

(Note: Group exercises exploring ideas in this chapter are located in Appendix A.)

2 ANALYZING STYLE
Survival questions

THE WORLD ENTERED

AN ASTRONAUT steps onto the moon and Dorothy into a Technicolor Oz. Neither knows exactly what to expect in this new world. An actor is cast in a Shakespearean romance or a rock musical fantasy. Both offer adventure beyond real life. So why do some adventurers survive and conquer, while others get squelched and eliminated? Some are better at figuring out what is going on in a world. And then acting. Categories in which great travelers and actors make survival decisions:

1. Time—tempo and history
2. Space—public and private
3. Place—surface and safety
4. Values—truths and beliefs
5. Structure—control and change
6. Beauty—models and expression
7. Sex—recreation and procreation
8. Recreation—doing and watching
9. Sight—look and image
10. Sound—speech and song

All style concepts fall into these categories. The first eight are what cause the last two. The last two, however, are the first by which style is judged.

You can achieve membership in almost any universe if you know how it works. If you travel to a new place you look for majority choices. Whenever something comes up, ask:

➤ 1. How IMPORTANT or insignificant is this to people in this play (world)?

➤ 2. How POLARIZED or uniform are they in their views?

TIME: Tempo and history

➤ In what point in history is the play set, written, performed? How do these interact? How far does the audience or play move out of its own time? Do we update the script so it is "relevant"? Do we play into its period charm? Do we pull the audience back into history or push the play forward?

David Ball on "Changing eras"

Playwrights—even great ones—do not write for the ages. They write for their specific audiences at their specific times . . . problems arise when a play is done for an audience other than the one it was written for.

For example, twentieth-century Americans often read *Hamlet* as a play about Elizabethan English . . . But Shakespeare set the play in Denmark, knowing his London audience of 1601 had specific thoughts and feelings about Danes. Modern Americans don't share those thoughts and feelings; they aren't even aware of them. Shakespeare's Londoners had reason to think Denmark a terrifying place, peopled by warlike, bloodthirsty savages. Londoners knew that a few centuries earlier Danes had sailed up the Thames and set fire to London Bridge (hence the nursery rhyme "London Bridge is Falling Down"). And even in the sixteenth century Danes frequently landed on England's shores to attack isolated villages—killing, raping, and plundering before disappearing back to sea. To Elizabethans Denmark meant destruction, primitive brutality and terror.

Into the midst of such a world Shakespeare puts Hamlet . . . a *man* of introspection and considered thought versus a *society* of impulsive, arbitrary brutality. This conflict partly explains Hamlet's "inability" to act . . . It may be coincidence that no one thought Hamlet incapable of action until a hundred years after the play was first staged—right about the same time that the English perception of Denmark as bloody and brutal started disappearing.

For every play from a time and place other than your own, *consider what the original audience thought and felt about the world portrayed in the play.* Sometimes this takes a lot of research, but the result will be worth the effort.

Figure 2.1

David Tennant as Hamlet
at the Courtyard Theatre
© Robbie Jack/
Corbis

Successful productions move in every direction. The play moves up, the audience
moves back, and they meet at an exquisite point in the imagination.

➤   How **rapidly** does it move for most people? How **conscious** are they
     of time passing? How do they **record** or note time? What is the dominant
     tempo/rhythm?

Time can be thought of in generations, seasons, and full moons, or stop-watch split
seconds, deadlines, and cost. Tempo may move from speed-of-light to barely
perceptible. Rhythm may insistently throb or softly undulate.

➤ Do people **focus** mainly on the moment, on whole lifetimes, the future, the past?

The ancient Greeks dwell on the past, the Restoration on the moment, and Elizabethans almost breathlessly on the future. Where you focus in time can change the way you live—always making plans, savoring what is, or rehashing what is over. The past may mean bygone eras or the last half hour, and may be looked at with longing or regret.

➤ What lengths of **attention span** do these people have? Is **age** revered or feared? What is the relationship between youth and maturity?

Time passes according to how engaged you are. If you build complex trains of thought, someone can talk forever and keep you enthralled. If you are illiterate, you *must* listen because you cannot write it down or look it up. If you're a ten-second commercial/sound-bite type, you have little patience for exposition.

In some worlds, youth is associated with stupidity, in others freshness and purity of insight. Which ages are honored, which ignored? What is considered the peak of life?

SPACE: Public and private

➤ How is it **defined** and viewed? Is it literal, spiritual, philosophical, or abstract? How large a **bubble** do people carry around? How do **personal** spaces alter? How flexible are they? To what degree is **privacy** respected? What are attitudes towards **invasion** and force? How is space **violated**?

In a classic proxemics study, Edwin Hall observed a South American ambassador back a US diplomat the entire length of a huge hall while they talked. The northerner wanted two to three feet between him and his companion. The southerner was more comfortable with six inches. The one sensed his personal space being invaded, the other felt a great chasm unless they were close.

Touching, grabbing, pushing, and embracing, all standard in some cultures, can cause war in others. Have you visited a home where no one ever closes the bathroom door and they open each other's mail? Assumptions about privacy disappear.

➤ How do these beliefs **translate** into audience proximity, movement patterns, gestural ranges, relationships to properties, entrances and exits?

How large do people think they are? Never mind their literal height, weight, or strength. How do they *view* themselves? In most classical plays, the individual regards herself as larger than we do. She needs more space and fills more, simply to exist in all her personal glory, exuberance, anguish, or spirit.

PLACE: Surface and safety

➤ Is the **setting** rural, metro, coastal, inland, protected, exposed, confined, open? Is it new or old? What **influence** does terrain, flora, fauna, weather have? Does it have a specific or generic **character**?

Location and proximity influence belief. Those existing in a sleek, modern environment think of the future differently than those whose history is around every corner. Isolation can invite inflexibility or transcendence. Linguists maintain that the rolling hills of Ireland influence both lilt of speech and shifts of mood, just as the plains of the US Midwest lead to flat sounds and relative stability.

➤ How aware are they of other places? How **provincial** in perspective? Are they **citizens** only of this spot or of the world? What is the **relationship to nature**? To what extent is the environment altered or accepted?

Is life largely just I and my friends, or does it involve global concerns and causes? Do we batter nature into obedience or pay her obeisance?

VALUES: Truth and belief

➤ What are the **beliefs** most widely **shared**? What ideals? What are the **traditions**, and how large is the commitment to them? How are **friendship**, **family**, **trust,** and **community** defined, and how are these **bonds broken**?

Can you recall the first time something *you* assumed true was contradicted by someone else? Worse yet, did they regard your "truth" as silly? Devastating—to be thought both wrong and insignificant.

All groups share core beliefs, which form habits, which become customs, which form the basic rituals of life. There are cultures where it is traditional for the host to offer his daughter for the night to a visitor, and those where the violation of the host's daughter would be the most loathsome act possible. Every traveling salesman had better know the territory. In some cultures, a son is expected to challenge his father in battle. In our own, a record number of children have no firsthand knowledge of what a father *is*.

➤ What is the predominant **mood**? Who are role models, heroes, **idols**? What are shared **fantasies** and ideal futures? How do they define **sin**, consequences, forgiveness, ethics, justice?

Are these people happy, melancholy, pensive, despondent, or volatile? Who is placed on pedestals? Whom do they envy and emulate? What do they dream? How close are their lives to their dreams? Are their heroes alive or from legend?

Even the most tolerant societies have sin. Thieves have codes of honor, as do drug barons. How are social errors handled? How do you redeem yourself? Is any act beyond the pale?

➤ What gets **attention**? What holds it?

Audiences now favor laconic, nonverbal heroes who are strong and only open their mouths for one-liners. Most classical drama favors orators, masters of rhetoric who elaborate and soar on any subject. Characters in Elizabethan drama speak in brilliant verse because that is the only way any one in their world will listen to them.

➤ Value placed on **money**? Uses for it? What is the place of **God** and the church in life? Are these two ever confused? Is money embraced, rejected, pursued, tolerated, or worshiped?

How much doctrine and power surrounds the god of choice? Mythologist Joseph Campbell called the computer an Unforgiving, Old Testament God. Some of us have a relationship with ours like that of Lot and God. Others feel that "If God had meant us to take this life seriously, She wouldn't have created it that way."

➤ What kind of **humor** dominates? What role has laughter in society?

Laughter is the great lubricant of life. Some groups have no lubricant. What do they think is funny? Is the humor wry, witty, elevated, broad, vulgar, social, personal, nurturing, vicious, satiric? Is laughter a primary means of dealing with pain? Does it get people *through* life or help them avoid it?

➤ How is **fear** defined? How and to what degree is **emotion** expressed? How suppressed?

Who are monsters, demons, and dragons in this world? What do they think is the worst thing that might happen to them? Invasion from a neighboring country, being alone, being ridiculed? Is fear met head on, avoided, dealt with collectively or privately?

STRUCTURE: Control and change

➤ Who **leads** and who follows? How easy is it to bring about **change or justice**? How absolute is **authority**? What is the voice of the individual?

Nets surround societies, some iron, others stretchable. In most period plays, the net is more rigid than in our own world. Poor farm boys do not grow up to be Emperor. A misplaced word can result in a misplaced appendage. Changing one's destiny is limited to a golden few.

We, on the other hand, know how to sue, appeal, file grievance, plea bargain, and pursue parole. We have options. Many still feel utterly powerless within the system.

➤ How is **daily life** ordered? How is **family** defined? How are **etiquette** and rules set? How much emphasis is on **education**?

What is a typical day? Do mates bond for life or for the season? To what extent is infidelity, separation, bigamy, or divorce tolerated?

Is knowledge seen as a means to freedom? Who goes to school, and what do they study? What is inexcusable ignorance?

➤ How are **groups** created and identified? Which are most powerful? What **professions** dominate and how is **work** viewed? How is **information** spread?

Many classical plays do not involve "work" as we think of it. Characters do not have a "job" and pursue a "career." What replaces this use of time and energy? Remember that being a homemaker in classical drama may mean managing a staff of a hundred people.

BEAUTY: Models and expression

➤ What is the **look, most aspired to**, in this group? Who are the contemporary **ideals** of perfection?

Each age favors a pattern in dress, hair, body, skin, and adornment, all reflecting how people want to look. How do those not meeting that standard feel about themselves? What height, weight, shape, features, and colors are in? How close or distant is your character from "the look."

➤ What part does **fitness** play in physical attractiveness? What is the relationship between beauty, health, and **comfort**?

In our era, high muscle tone, low body fat, and cardiovascular fitness are serious considerations for personal attractiveness. Some of this was true for men in the past, but only recently for women. If God did not bestow the ideal look on someone, to what lengths will he go to achieve it? People now are willing to endure *enormous* discomfort (no pain, no gain) for long-range attractiveness, but very *little* discomfort (painful girdles, shoes, stiff fabrics, starched collars, rollers, elaborate make-up) for temporary attractiveness.

> Which **colors, textures, silhouettes** are favored? How important is **fashion**? How fast does it **change**? To what degree is **nature** altered in order to create a thing of beauty?

What do these color choices say about us? Is *illusion* of nature pursued or is the look *flagrantly* artificial in persons, homes, and lawns? How is beauty expressed? Do people paint, sculpt, compose music, write poetry? Are these encouraged or enforced?

SEX: Recreation and procreation

> How significant is sex? Which **areas of anatomy** are revealed, concealed, emphasized? What are sexual **stereotypes**? How is **sexuality communicated**? How is **seduction** defined? Is the **emphasis** on the act or the chase? On pleasure or procreation? What is the standard **courtship ritual**?

Because we share the act with animals, groups find rules to *separate* us from them. Between an elaborate, lengthy mating dance and a curt "Your place or mine?," what constitutes accepted foreplay? Is sex a diversion, sacred trust, sin, inconvenience, or the reason for living? Do spouses have any freedom to choose each other? Is there tolerance for love at first sight?

> How much tolerance for **deviation**? Accepted attitudes towards **infidelity**, towards **promiscuity**? What **degree of suppression or expression** of sexuality occurs?

Is experimenting with sexual preference, partners, positions, and potions appropriate? In some Latin American cultures, men and women openly smolder and flaunt themselves, because family protection around unmarried women is so strong that breaking the barrier is nearly impossible. The unlikelihood of consummation allows displayed sexual energy.

RECREATION: Doing and watching

> What is **fun**? What would be an **ideal social occasion**? An enjoyable day? **Participation** level? Are they doers or watchers? **Intellectual** life? Thinkers or mindless hedonists?

A party is filled with style signals—formal/casual, planned/spontaneous, structured/open-ended, elaborate/simple, intimate/massive, pleasure/business?

Is an *idea* fun? Are theories part of enjoyment? Or do they avoid analysis at all cost?

➤ What are common **shared** hobbies and **pastimes**? Differences between **sexes**? **Consumption**? Favored and coveted meals, drink, drugs? **Importance** of recreation in life? Standard view of **indulgence**?

Food fads reflect perceptions of the good life. Research topples each age's image of a good, healthy meal.

SIGHT: Looks and image

➤ How do all the above manifest themselves in the way the world looks, in **shapes, angles, light, shadow, patterns of movement**? In clothing, furnishings, props, hairdos, and jewelry?

Shared beliefs support sight. We may notice that everyone in a culture extends his pinky while drinking tea and holds the cup gingerly between the first finger and thumb. But *why*? Is there a rewarded way of standing and sitting, and if so for what reason? Which facial expressions are desired? Which gestures? Is there a walk that reflects sense of self? Do behaviors change in public or private?

Movement and contact

How do people approach each other? Are there standard bows and curtsies? How do they touch? How do they feel about space, their own and others'? Are special skills needed to maneuver inside this world?

SOUND: Speech and song

➤ How does it come out verbally? To what degree are **listening** and **speaking** prized?

Patterns of speech emerge out of shared feelings. We now live in a visual, nonverbal era, when vocabularies, writing, and literacy scores are dropping. Consider not only *what* people say, but how often, with what variety, and what is the role of silence.

What vocal quality is most desired, rewarded, emulated, and for what reasons? Is there standardized pronunciation or great variance? Which part of pitch register is employed? Is the word choice vague or direct?

Music and dance

What is the role of music in life? How do people express themselves through song and dance? Which composers and instruments are popular, and what does that say about life?

KEYS TO THE WORLD

It helps to have keys to get in—quick reminders to help you feel part of a new reality. Evocative images (stimuli for the senses), social success and suicide (extremes of rewarded and punished behavior), masking (which faces are put on), production (historical information on theatre events), and contemporary parallels (connecting our world to this one) can all help.

IMAGES

Is there a painting, sculpture, building, novel, essay, fad, landmark, concerto, invention, philosophy, custom, or quotation that captures the essence of the era?

SOCIAL SUCCESS AND SUICIDE

What is the single most devastating thing one person could possibly say to another (the Ultimate Insult) and the highest validation (the Ultimate Compliment) anyone could bestow or receive?

MASKING

Each world has acceptable faces. Literal masks and veils are worn in ours only at Halloween or Mardi Gras. Usually, masking is symbolic, as in lyrics "put on a happy face" or "smile though your heart is breaking." In public, what is most likely to be hidden, revealed, affected, or cultivated? How complex is the preparation, and how easy is it to puncture the mask? Under what circumstances might it become transparent, translucent, or fully opaque? How much is the mask acknowledged? To what degree is the difference between mask and face no longer understood?

THE PRODUCTION

How is all this likely to emerge in performance? How much do we match cultures? Because usually only men appeared on-stage until the mid 1600s, will our production feature an all-male cast? Will the Greek play be performed in an amphitheatre? Knowing how it was done there and then helps feed judgment on how to do it here and now.

THE PERFECT AUDIENCE

How should we behave to create audience rapport comparable with that of the original actors? How and where do we sit, move, circulate, interrupt? Do we offer verbal criticism? How do we acknowledge work well done? How much are we like or unlike what is being portrayed before us?

Figure 2.2a

A masked celebrant at the Venice Carnival

Figure 2.2b

Olivia Darnley as Hero in *Much Ado About Nothing* at the Theatre Royal in Bath © Robbie Jack/ Corbis

CONTEMPORARY PARALLELS

What is going on in contemporary society that matches the new world? Any silly fad can be as valuable as a major belief, if it provides a bridge. Where does this world contradict ours? What must be left behind in order to cross over?

SUMMARY STYLE LIST

The complete list of the preceding investigation categories is on pages ii–iii. There are more questions than anyone would care to answer. Use it to find issues in the world you wish to enter. Here is the Berlitz version:

Time—Tempo/rhythm? Age? Point in history?

Space—Bubbles? Privacy? Invasion?

Place—Setting? Relationship to nature? Awareness of others?

Values—Mood? Ideals? Money? God? Emotion?

Structure—Government? Daily life? Education?

Beauty—Looks? Comfort? Artistic expression?

Sex—Expression? Seduction? Courtship?

Recreation—Occasions? Participation? Consumption?

Sight—Stillness? Movement? Ritual?

Sound—Language? Listening? Music?

Entering the World—Images? Success and suicide? Masking? Production? Perfect Audience?

FINDING THE WORLD

When you are dealing with a real play, investigation should start with the text itself. Do not confuse the world that the playwright is *creating* with the world in which she may have been *living*. When Shakespeare creates the Athenian forest in *A Midsummer Night's Dream* or the witches' lair in *Macbeth*, he is writing a different world than Elizabethan London. Each script should be approached for the reality it alone creates. Each is a world to be discovered.

Each of these playwrights shares a period. They were/are contemporaries: David Mamet and Wendy Wasserstein, Tennessee Williams and Arthur Miller, Noel Coward and Eugene O'Neill, George Bernard Shaw and Anton Chekhov. If you know their work, consider how each writer reflects the time in which they write. Then go deeper into the world of the writer and consider how it is not reflective of the lives most people were living during that era.

Style research moves from general to specific. We consider:

- the period itself;
- the world the playwright creates (which may be close to, or far from, that he lives in);
- the world for this particular script (which may be like or unlike others he has written);
- the life of your character (who may be typical or unusual among the majority of characters).

If you discover something about Electra, you must ask "Whose Electra?" She is godlike to Aeschylus, heroic to Sophocles, and vulnerable to Euripides.

Principles that help you get inside a character in a play will help you do the same in a new neighborhood, town, country, or planet. The living world is less *set* than that in a script, but both worlds share the need for investigation and the potential for great rewards for skilled detective work. By careful research, you earn the right to make things up. Much of the World of the Play is a world of play.

(Note: Group exercises exploring ideas in this chapter are located in Appendix B.)

3 | MASTERING STYLE
The classical actor

TESTS OF TIME

REAL ACTORS long to act in great classical drama. These plays, having passed the test of time themselves, now test the actors. Can they transform themselves? Can they transport the audience out of today and here to Long Ago and Far Away, Once Upon a Time, and Days of Yore? Can they become larger than life and still be real? Those who can are much admired. Great plays, surviving the test of time, also carry the POWER of time. There is actor magic in them.

The next four chapters are devoted to the periods when drama rose to unparalleled heights, with the following playwrights most likely to enter an actor's life:

Ancient Greece (500–400 BC): Aeschylus, Sophocles, Euripides (Chapter 4)
Elizabethan England (1550–1620): Shakespeare, Marlowe, Jonson, Ford, Webster (Chapter 5)
Restoration England (1660–1710): Wycherly, Congreve, Farquhar, Etheridge, Behn (Chapter 6)
Neo-Classic France (1660–1700): Molière, Racine, Corneille (Chapter 7)
Georgian England (1775–1800): Sheridan, Goldsmith, O'Keefe (Chapter 7)

Actors who excel in period-style works do the same in:

Displaced drama (1900–present): Hampton, Shaffer, Frye, Anouilh (Chapter 8)

Displaced plays, also called costume drama, share acting demands with scripts from earlier eras. The author writes from our time but looks back to recreate another.

The skills of transcending time and space are involved, but the language is less difficult because it was formed for contemporary ears.

PERIOD STYLE ACTORS

➤ What makes an actor classical? Some actors are less bound in time and space than others. Try the following without reading ahead in this chapter:

1. Choose five well-known actors, whom you have not seen perform Shakespeare or other great works, but whom you would imagine would be good at it. Choose actors whom you yourself would hire for a full season of classical repertory. Call this your A list.
2. Choose five actors whose work you respect, but whom you would not consider highly castable in the classics. These must be actors whom you consider good, but not right for the kinds of role involved. Call this your B list.
3. Both lists must be performers you admire. Eliminate anyone who, on further reflection, you don't think is all that good.
4. Now write a short phrase (no more than four words) explaining your A choices.
5. Do the same for your B choices.

Figure 3.1

An actor from the A list. Daniel Day-Lewis © Kurt Krieger/Corbis

Several thousand actors and students have taken the "quiz" above. In recent years, the following names consistently emerge:

THE A LIST

Christian Bale, Angela Bassett, Cate Blanchett, Orlando Bloom, Daniel Craig, Russell Crowe, Judi Dench, Johnny Depp, Robert Downey, Jr., Colin Firth, Anne Hathaway, Hugh Jackman, Angelina Jolie, Nicole Kidman, Keira Knightley, Jude Law, Daniel Day-Lewis, James McAvoy, Ian McKellen, Helen Mirren, Edward Norton, Clive Owen, Gwyneth Paltrow, Natalie Portman, Jonathan Rhys Meyers, Daniel Radcliffe, Patrick Stewart, Meryl Streep, Kate Winslett, Forest Whitaker, Catherine Zeta Jones

THE B LIST

Jennifer Aniston, Drew Barrymore, Sandra Bullock, Halle Berry, Matthew Broderick, Steve Carell, Jim Carrey, George Clooney, Tom Cruise, Matt Damon, Robert De Niro, Patrick Dempsey, Cameron Diaz, Clint Eastwood, Sally Field, Will

Figure 3.2

An actor from the B list. Jodie Foster © Alessandra Benedetti/ Corbis

Ferrell, Jodie Foster, Jamie Foxx, Kate Hudson, Tommy Lee Jones, Ashton Kutcher, Tobey Maguire, Ellen Page, Sarah Jessica Parker, Julia Roberts, Seth Rogen, Will Smith, Hilary Swank, Reese Witherspoon, Renée Zellweger

There are more British and Australian actors on the A list, more comics on the B list. More A list than B list actors have stage experience. But beyond first generalities, patterns emerge:

A list explanations tend to include these words:

poise—grace—class—power—sophistication—presence—versatility—voice—boldness—size—sensitivity—eloquence—depth—control—command—stature—intensity—focus—clarity—mystery—universality—majesty

B list reasons often involve the preposition too, followed by:

limited—rough—flat—low class—conventional—shallow—comedic—crude—small—light—ethnic—informal—slow—contemporary—insensitive—weak—subdued—simple—monotonous—internal—awkward

Are the As better actors than the Bs? Not necessarily. The genius of some actors is to capture the time and place they are *in* and reflect it *back* to their audience. Henry Fonda and Jimmy Stewart were important examples, suggesting, with every fiber of their being, small-town Americana, decent, simple, virtuous, pioneer spirit, homespun wisdom. This is an extraordinary gift. But their gift is also their shared limitation. The idea of Henry Fonda in tights and doublet, speaking a sonnet, or James Stewart in powdered wig and brocade, indulging in wicked gossip, is hard to fathom, except as satire.

Try isolating those qualities in yourself that are right and wrong for classical theatre:

1. Read the B list reasons to yourself, mentally casting aside each tendency as you say the word. Identify those that do not leave so easily.
2. Read the A list reasons, giving yourself permission to take on those qualities in yourself. Feel larger, stronger, wittier, and more of a force to be reckoned with. Which words do not fit so well?
3. Go back and deal with the resistant words. Recognize and explore what may be blocking you. Promise yourself to get comfortable with more classic characteristics and to exorcise those in the way.

Sometimes directors do not *want* actors to develop classical qualities. To make the play more "accessible," its world is altered, as when *The Taming of the Shrew* is set in the Wild West or *Lysistrata* is set in modern Iraq. There are many right ways to do the classics. However, actors must develop the capacity to go with the production concept, whatever it is. Often it is traditional and elevated. That is our concern here.

COMMON THREADS

Actors who are classic chameleons can take us back in history or forward into fantasy. Being taken *seriously* as knight, princess, witch, wench, god, or sorcerer involves sewing these threads into one classical world.

Time—moves less predictably, veering wildly between breathtaking speed and the careful consideration of an idea. Because it is set "ago," it rejects scientific inquiry in favor of miracles as a way to explain life.

Space—is larger. Your concept of self radiates and flashes. You fill a void when you enter. The invasion of another's space is more likely to be direct and sudden (as in sweeping someone into your arms and kissing them or boldly striking an opponent) with less hesitation and sneaking around. Space is there to be taken.

Place—is both grander and simpler. You may be in the palace, forest, temple, battlefield, or public square. You may be on an island or mountain top. A more mundane spot, such as a drawing room, is merely suggested. You are less likely to have something to lean on, sit on, or play with. You are far more likely to occasionally acknowledge the presence of the audience. The place will change more by your imagination than scenic devices.

Values—involve following one's own destiny, which is often also the destiny of others, so their acts have great consequences. History is important, and the divine rights of monarchs more revered. No one holds attention without speaking well. Life is to be lived fully and forcefully, even in sin and error, not acted safely and softly.

Structure—means order comes from stars and fates, not generator and battery. Who you are when you are born is vital to who you will be when you die. Rulers (in country and family) are less often questioned. You play by rules or you change them, often the latter.

Beauty—is more abstract, the *expression* of it even more rewarded than the *possession* of it. You create beauty in your speech and create yourself when you go into the world. You handle far more fabric and accoutrements and it helps have features strong enough to match the clothes.

Sex—does not hide or cower. At times it drops from consideration because issues at hand are so much more significant. At others, it is the meaning of life. In general, it is dealt with more frankly and enthusiastically, with less giggling or embarrassment.

Recreation—often involves public celebrations. Shyness is less tolerated. Life is a banquet. Capacity to overindulge is more tolerated, even honored. Each person is expected to contribute to the event, to make the party happen.

Sight and Sound—involve greater contrasts. Stillness and economy are interrupted with bursts of physical boldness. You are able to do absolutely nothing and pull listeners into your consciousness. You are also able to reach out to the back of the theatre and embrace everyone there in energy and power. Clear, crisp, clean speech gives maximum attention to consonants as *shapers* of sound. Listeners never have trouble understanding, yet speech does not seem affected. You are able to speak at length with complexity and authority.

Sight and Sound can be broken into more specific categories. What follows are the notes most observed in rehearsal, the areas where young actors in classical plays are asked to make adjustments. This very technical detail can ultimately provide the path for emotional freedom:

> American actors seem to have a fear of words and of language as apart from emotions. I want to drop the intimidation factor. What American actors are frightened of is a sense of discipline and technique. But these things need not negate the emotional work. They don't end the mystery of acting, they preserve it.
>
> (Kenneth Branagh)

(For a classical warm-up, see Appendix C.)

Having stated that there are no rules, what follows will look like a list of rules. Think of them as *possibilities*. These are frequently requested and useful to have in your repertoire. They are stated here as absolutes, to avoid the tedium of further disclaimers. Remember, there are always exceptions. Bottom (in *A Midsummer Night's Dream*) is low class, Othello is ethnic, Iago is non–majestic. Select images to suit circumstances.

PHYSICAL LIVES: Dignity and simplicity

➤ How does an actor achieve a bearing that seems suited to greatness?

SITTING

1.   Furniture is intended for you to exhibit yourself, it is not plush and comfortable, but rather your personal pedestal. Sit on edges, *perching* as you might on a stool or leaning against a wall. Favor a straight back.

2.   Both descend and ascend with the *legs*, allowing the upper body to float erect as if you are riding on a horse from the waist up.

3.   Keep legs *uncrossed* if you are a woman prior to 1920 (unless you are playing a "brazen hussy or tart") or a man prior to the late 1800s. Men may make this move when ladies leave the room (so the gentlemen in *The Importance of Being Earnest* might cross their legs and light their cigars when alone together, but not when women are present). Not until skirts shorten is the move associated with modest or proper deportment.

4.   When seated, arrange yourself in an *asymmetrical* manner, with one foot angled slightly different than the other and one hand counterpointing rather than imitating the other. Enjoy the aesthetic picture you create as a seated work of art. Save symmetry for ritual (see Gestures).

5.   Visualize yourself sitting in a range of period clothes that demand *erect, steady bearing*. While flowing Greek robes seem as different as possible from tight, puffed Elizabethan doublets, both encourage similar postural choices. If you wiggle and shift, the Greek garment will fall off, and the Elizabethan one will cause you pain. Economy of movement allows you to save energy for where it matters.

6.   While we tend to sit down to speak, classical characters tend to *sit down to listen,* at the end of their speeches. The speech is often an extended public argument, so sitting symbolizes completion and readiness to hear from others, a final punctuation.

CONNECTING

1.   Instead of leaning in to make points, rise up to them, *lifting into the action*. Put the energy making you want to lean into your words and eyes instead. On-stage leaning reads as suppliant posture. You appear, no matter how strong your words, to be begging.

2.   Free yourself from the need to punctuate each crucial turn of phrase with a forward jerk of the head or "chicken neck." The effort going into head punctuation belongs in *real* punctuation, expressive vowels, and sharp consonants, instead of necks.

3.   When in repose, listening or evaluating, allow yourself *absolute stillness*, free of tiny, neurotic moves and shifts. When the need to gesture comes, find large, fully committed ones, whose energy radiates all the way to the ends of your fingertips and beyond.

4.   Your self-concept is closer to a god's. Let your *head float* high above your body like a helium balloon, tall, but with relaxed shoulders. If you have a chance to study the Alexander Technique, do so.

5.   Decide to be *taller than your scene partner,* even if there is no hope of ever achieving it. Decide to have a longer neck than anyone else on-stage, always rising to the occasion.

6.   You have less need to look at other actors, both when you speak and listen. Your *focus* is intense, but it is just as often on ideas and *images* as on the person with whom you are conversing. Your vision moves frequently beyond the moment, into possibility.

7.   Because speeches are longer, take them upstage. Relish this convention as both speaker and listener. Give up your contemporary sense of sharing in favor of acknowledging who needs focus.

8.   Once you connect with another actor, by eye contact, embrace, or simple touch, sustain it fully, instead of backing quickly off. Really *clasp or gaze*, without apology or second-guessing.

GESTURING

1.   Since your personal space is large, give yourself at least the *full extension* of your arms and legs in any direction as the minimal requirement for your comfort. Think of a large ball or bubble surrounding you, from which emanates your personal glow.

2.   Your arms cannot comfortably swing listlessly or drop to the side, because your clothing forbids it. The drape of fabric or droop of lace requires an *energized and ready wrist*. Arms frequently move up and out to make your meaning emerge from the bulk of your costume. Think of each gesture as a flash of light that illuminates what you have to say.

3.   In repose, think of allowing "*breath under the arms*," giving them a sense of relaxed readiness without closing in the torso.

4.   The audience automatically will fail to comprehend some words and events. Use the *space to clarify* what may not be understood through the line. Do not fear the literal (Hamlet can wipe off Ophelia's make-up when he speaks of women painting themselves) if it supports meaning. Locate the city, the buried dead, the gods, and any other important catalysts or forces through gesture. Think of the scene as a series of images where visual clarity can compensate for archaic language.

5.   Save *symmetrical gestures for moments of ceremony*, worship and ritual. Recognize that one side of the human body rarely falls into mimicry of the other, except when we are formalizing experience, which does occur frequently in classical drama.

Relish the perfect balance with which you are bringing the world temporarily into a state of complete order.

6. Allow big gestures to *unfold naturally*. Slowly return to neutral, instead of the impulse to quickly retreat from something so bold. Resist the temptation to take the shoulder into the move. The gesture may burst into being, but then let it die naturally.

Take a moment to review each of the summary words below, while practicing the action. It may help to do the exact opposite of classical first and then to transform like a butterfly from a cocoon:

perching	focus
descent/ascent	clasp
asymmetry	full extension
lifting	energized arms
punctuation	breath under arms
stillness	clarify in space
head float	ceremony
taller than others	unfolding gestures

MOVING

1. When crossing into another person's bubble, use clean, *strong invasions*. Either leave someone alone or go in for assault (romantic, sexual, violent, or sporting) with full commitment.

2. When you walk, let your *torso remain relatively motionless,* with the hips taking the challenge, not swaying right and left but in a strong rotation forward. Remember that you probably have no pockets, and your pants (if that's what you're wearing) do not rest on your on hips.

3. Imagining being drawn by *two pulleys*, one attached to the top of your head and the other to your chest, both in perfect synchronicity, works for many actors. "Lead with your nipples."

4. Think in terms of *gliding* rather than clomping. A singular accomplishment of the classical performer is to move quickly and gracefully around the stage (even in boots or heels) without noise, lifting the upper torso and regarding the floor as an ice arena. Sound of movement should not interfere with line readings.

5. *Display yourself,* parade, and pose for others on-stage with you. Sometimes take the *longest* route possible around furniture and use the distance to enhance your points. Drop twentieth-century presentation as apology and (often false) humility in favor of regarding yourself as a work of art.

6.   You cannot usually back up easily, because a long train, an awkward weapon, or some other impediment may be in your way. So how do you *move upstage? In curves*, figure eights, and figure Ss, all the graceful alternatives. And avoid tripping over your own clothes.

7.   *Match walk to speech.* Mesh tempo/rhythms. Aim to complete a move on the last syllable, perhaps even the last consonant of your line. Alterations from this pattern should be deliberate.

8.   Check the *relationship of the head to the rest of your body* periodically to let the head float easily high above. If this relationship is off, most connections below will be off too.

9.   *Do less and allow more*, so your movements are not hard work but inevitable. When you are trying to relax one body part, it is very easy to tense up the parts adjacent to it. *Relax all around* any area you are trying to release.

Repeat the process of the preceding section, this time drifting through space, weaving in and out of other actors' spaces, until it is time to touch or connect with them. If you are working alone, employ an imaginary partner. Let the key phrases motivate your own discovery:

> float
> strong invasion
> rotation walk
> two pulleys
> gliding
> display yourself
> move back
> curves
> head/body
> release adjacent parts

VOCAL LIVES: Crispness and clarity

Classical speech—sometimes called elevated, standard, stage, or heightened speech—is a cultured sound, free of distracting regional, ethnic, and faddish speech patterns. It means dropping sloppy diction and speaking with great clarity and dignity, so that you sound, without being affected, as if you could comfortably wear a crown.

VOWELS

1.   *Avoid flat or double vowels,* which take a long time and are shot through the nasal resonators. The "a" is the most distracting, with the word "flat" coming out

"flaaaaat". Don't allow vocalized breath to come through the nose as the sound is made. Flat a's tend to pop up in words such as pan, back, rat, hand, can, ant, example, sample, damp, tramp.

2.   Selectively sigh or *aspirate on a vowel for a lyrical or emotional passage*. Notice how, if you really mean something from the heart, you tend to elongate the vowel ("I *love* you," "I *mean* it," I'm *serious*"), but it only has impact if *other* vowels are not stretched as well, so that the contrast works. As you elongate the word, exhale slightly. Find key words and images to color and intensify with breath, widely used in life, but all too often edited in performance.

3.   *Honor each sound*. Tape yourself to identify where you tend to swallow or simply fail to say something. Pay particular attention to the pronunciation of connective words: "tuh" for "to" (alone and in other words such as "together" and "tonight"), or "fer" for "for," and "n" for "and." Do not compensate by punching up connectives, as in saying "ay" for "a" or "thee" for "the." This last change is only made prior to a word beginning with a vowel. Watch short verbs ("kin" for "can" and "git" for "get") and modifiers ("jist" for "just") as well. Fully pronounce connective words (to, for, and, the, of, by, with, has, should), but with secondary, light stress.

4.   Watch for *diphthong substitutions*. The word "now" is pronounced in a number of regions so that is seems to have at least three vowels ("a-ah'oh") in the middle. Watch for diphthongs that have become trithongs. The reason for the classic drill "How now brown cow" is the dropped jaw that allows this sound to emerge in an easy, unextended fashion. Danger words: now, sound, mouth, vowel, round, town, extend.

6.   Look for *vowel substitutions*: the replacing of one for another ("ou" for "oo" as in "pore" instead of "poor" and also in the words root, roof, route, or "i" for "e" as in "git" for "get," and these exchanges: pin–pen, min–men, linth–length, strinth–strength).

7.   Find the *liquid "u"* (ew), as in Duke, tutor, tuba, tune, tuna, stupid, Tuesday, astute, pulchritude.

8.   In words with optional pronunciations, *choose the more euphonic* or the one that is more pleasing to the ear. One standard is to pronounce the word "either" as EYE-THER rather than EE-THER, the former sound striking most ears as more musical and universal.

Again, take a moment to review each of these vowel guidelines, perhaps going way in the non-classical direction and then emerging into class act:

> flat vowels
> aspiration
> honoring each sound

diphthong substitutions
vowel substitutions
relaxed jaw
liquid U
euphonic choices

CONSONANTS

1.   Clean and sharpen consonants. Think of a *consonant as a weapon*, extraordinarily swift, highly muscular, and, like a natural athlete, effortless in attack. Avoid hard, bludgeoning consonants, which are like sledge hammers, in favor of clean ones like *darts*.

2.   *Honor terminal consonants*. Many of us do not speak the last consonant in a word. Classical characters use this final sound to twist or cap off their points.

3.   Pronounce the H in where—whine—white—which—when—what. The *"wh"* *is sounded as "hw."*

4.   *Do not swallow syllables*, reducing two of them to one in words such as jewel, gruel, cruel, duel.

5.   *Avoid a sound like "chew"* when connecting can't you—don't you—did you— what you—might you—remind you. End the first word with a tiny break before starting the second.

6.   *Multiple consonants need more weight* to keep from getting lost in a word such as "would'st". The toughest are dst, ths, sts, pts, fts, pths, lpd, lps, pnd, mpt, cts in words such as swept, slept, leapt, hand, last, first, soft, lisp, eighths, mists, frosts, accepts, lifts, depths, helped, yelps, and facts.

7.   *Do not drop middle consonants* in words such as recognize, realize, definitely, traveler, vegetable, accidentally, naturally, history, memorable, different, family, interesting, several, sentinel, little, endless.

8.   *Do not substitute voiced for unvoiced consonants* in words such as little, better, accept, access, dirty, and oaths. Watch d–t inversion in particular.

9.   *Do not work the jaw too much*, as this is useless effort and looks labored. Let the tip of the tongue, the lips, and the teeth do all the work in forming clean consonants.

10.   *Do not labor the upper mouth* to achieve crispness. Watch actors with superb diction. Notice that there is little visible movement at the top of the mouth. Practice looking in the mirror, then identifying just those organs involved in shaping the sound.

Stay with the same process as the previous exercise, drawing in these categories:

consonant as weapon
terminals
WHs
swallowed syllables
chew
multiples
middles
voiced-unvoiced
overworked jaw
labored upper mouth

SOUND

1. Expand back and move below, past the nasal resonators and head voice, which produce a thin, strident sound. *Explore the full range of resonating space and surfaces* available to you, not to cultivate a "pretty" sound but to find a varied textured one.

2. *Allow a full use of pitch,* top to bottom. Never be afraid of experimenting with your lowest and highest notes.

3. *Identify regionalisms* in your own speech that may distract from an audience's sense of the universal. Seek critical ears, ideally from listeners born outside your region. Do not aim to get rid of how you speak, but to cleanse it when needed.

4. *Include nonverbals.* Because great classical writing is so clean, the temptation is to think that characters do not grunt, groan, sigh, growl, hiss, moan, squeal, guffaw, and even belch. The writing is short on stage directions and embellishments. Fill it out. A gasp of surprise, a slight intake of breath in delight, or a sputter of exasperation can help add great life.

5. Experiment with *singing the lines* just a little more. Poetic verse is closer to music than contemporary, conversational prose. It has a definite rhythm, and the words ask for dips and glides.

6. *Root sound for power without stridency.* When you need to let it rip with anger or righteousness, don't let sound go up in pitch. It will seem more shrewish or whiny than strong. Let the sound emanate from deep within the torso at such moments.

7. Compete with your partners for *the fullest, richest sound and greatest variety.* This is a friendly match, full of appreciation for others' tone, but determined that no voice will be stronger and more versatile than your own.

PHRASING

1. Classic playwrights tend to build points, using *lists of three*, sometimes more. In a line such as "I hate, loathe, and despise you," each verb is more powerful and

deserves more punch than the one before it. Each list works towards the strongest item on it. Relish this build.

2. Characters often make a point so strongly that they are clearly not open to negotiation. *Practice the finality* of delivering each line as if it were a curtain line.

3. Except for rapid-fire exchanges of one-liners (stichomythia), the speeches tend to be longer, *much* longer than most of us are used to. Single sentences of ten or eleven lines are not uncommon. *Avoid the temptation to chop up the thought* in order to make it clearer. You risk your listener forgetting the subject of your sentence by the time you get to the verb! Work instead on developing enough control to speak longer on a single breath and to think faster, as the characters often do.

4. *Pick out target words*, the zingers that need greater stress, the ones that "get" your partner because they are so gorgeous, insulting, powerful, loving, or all of the above. While all sounds should be sounded, all words do not have equal value.

5. *Use punctuation as a speaking tool.* In the long, convoluted sentences of classical drama, view punctuation as a traffic signal that is vital for clarity.

6. Audiences are going to find some imagery obscure and difficult, but you can *clarify it by using onomatopoeia.* The writing is often poetic, metaphoric, and begging to be spoken for sensual as well as intellectual meaning. Let the evocative words transcend the language. Imagine that the audience either does not speak English or may not know the meaning of the following words. Strive to speak each so that it will be comprehended. Experiment with deliberate technical choices to help make the words sound like their meanings. Try the words by themselves, then in sentences so they have a context:

ABANDON	BUOYANT	DELICIOUS
ABNORMAL	BURLESQUE	DENSE
ABORTIVE	BURY	DILATE
ABSURDITY		DIRTY
ACQUIESCE	CAMOUFLAGE	DOWN
AFFECTATION	CANDLE	DRAMATIC
ANGULARITY	CARICATURE	DRUNK
ATTRACTIVE	CASTRATE	DURABLE
AVENGE	CAUSTIC	
AWE	CARVE	EAT
	COARSE	EGO
BASE	COLD	ELEGANT
BEGINNING	CONTEMPT	EMPTY
BOOK	CURE	ENDLESS
BOSOM		ENVY
BREEZE	DANGER	ESCAPE
BRITTLE	DEAD	EVIL

EXAGGERATE	INSINUATE	MOPE
EXUDE	INTANGIBLE	MULTITUDE
FADE	JAB	NAKED
FAIRY	JEST	NAUSEOUS
FAMILIAR	JITTERS	NERD
FAR	JOY	NIMBLE
FASTIDIOUS	JUBILANT	NONCHALANT
FATAL	JUICY	NOURISH
FEASIBLE	JUMP	NUDE
FEAST	JUNK	NUISANCE
FIRE	JUSTICE	NUMB
FREEDOM	JUVENILE	NYMPH
GALLANT	KAPUT	OBLIVION
GAUDY	KEEN	OBSCENE
GIGGLE	KICK	OBSESSED
GLOOM	KIDDING	OILY
GLUE	KILL	OLD
GORGEOUS	KIND	OPAQUE
GRASP	KINKY	OPPOSITION
GREAT	KISS	ORDERLY
GRIND	KNICKKNACK	OSTENTATION
	KNOWLEDGE	OVERWHELM
HAIL		
HALT	LANGUID	
HATE	LASCIVIOUS	PAGAN
HEAL	LAVISH	PAIN
HEROIC	LEAP	PALE
HINT	LOATHSOME	PALPITATE
HOWL	LONG	PARALYSIS
HOVER	LOST	PARCHED
HUSH	LOVELY	PATHETIC
HYSTERICAL	LUBRICATE	PECK
		PULVERIZE
ICE	MAGNIFY	PUNGENT
ILLICIT	MANIPULATE	
IMMACULATE	MARVELOUS	RACY
IMPOTENT	MEAN	RADIANT
INANE	MEEK	RAGGED
INCREDIBLE	MELLOW	RECKLESS
INDIFFERENT	MIST	RECOIL
INHALE	MOLD	RELAX

REPUGNANT	UGLY	WHEEZE
REVEL	ULCER	WIGGLE
RIPE	UNCERTAIN	WIND
ROTUND	UNDO	WONDER
	UNIQUE	WORM
	USELESS	
SAD	UNTENABLE	YAWN
SAUCY	UPROAR	YELL
SCANDAL	USED	YES
SCORN	USURP	YIELD
SECRET		YOUTH
SENSUOUS		YELLOW
SERENE	VACILLATE	
SHARP	VAMPIRE	YEAST
SMOOTH	VAST	YESTERDAY
SUPERB	VEHEMENT	YOKE
	VELVET	YONDER
	VENOMOUS	
TALENT	VOLUPTUOUS	ZANY
TARNISH	VIGOR	ZEALOUS
TENDER	VIRGIN	ZENITH
TEXTURE	VISION	ZERO
TIDY		ZEST
TOIL		ZIGZAG
TORRID	WALLOW	ZIPPER
TOUCH	WANTON	ZODIAC
TUB	WAVE	ZOO
TRUTH	WEAK	ZWIEBACK
	WEIRD	

VERSE: Language structured and heightened

All plays written up to the time of Shakespeare were in verse. Some continue to be. Many classical repertory companies and training programs require verse speaking as part of the audition process for acceptance. Verse is higher, fuller, and more rhythmic than ordinary speech. But, for the uninitiated, it is shrouded in mystery and intimidation.

So how is verse different? First it looks different on the page. Where most of what is written (prose) goes all the way to the end of the line, verse only goes a limited number of syllables and then stops. Where prose has capital letters only at the start of a sentence, verse has them at the start of the new line, regardless of where it comes in the sentence. Here is a verse speech:

If music be the food of love, play on;
Give me excess of it, that, surfeiting,
The appetite may sicken, and so die.
That strain again! It had a dying fall;
O, it came o'er my ear like the sweet sound
That breathes upon a bank of violets,
Stealing and giving odour! Enough, no more!
'Tis not so sweet now as it was before.
O spirit of love, how quick and fresh art thou,
That, notwithstanding thy capacity
Receiveth as the sea, nought enters there,
Of what validity and pitch soe'er,
But falls into abatement and low price
Even in a minute! So full of shapes is fancy
That it alone is high fantastical.

And here is the way it might look if it were prose:

If music be the food of love, play on; Give me excess of it, that, surfeiting, the appetite may sicken, and so die. That strain again! It had a dying fall; o, it came o'er my ear like the sweet sound that breathes upon a bank of violets, stealing and giving odour! Enough, no more! 'Tis not so sweet now as it was before. O spirit of love, how quick and fresh art thou that, notwithstanding thy capacity, receiveth as the sea, nought enters there, of what validity and pitch soe'er, but falls into abatement and low price even in a minute! So full of shapes is fancy that it alone is high fantastical.

There are many verse forms, but most dialogue in English verse drama is either blank (unrhymed) or rhymed iambic pentameter. The word iambic tells you the basic unit or foot is an iamb—an unstressed followed by a stressed syllable. Each foot has the rhythm "da Dum". The word pentameter tells you there are five iambs in one line. So the beat is approximately "da Dum da Dum da Dum da Dum da Dum."

The speech above is one of the most famous opening speeches (from *Twelfth Night*) in Shakespeare. The Duke Orsino is trying to get rid of the curse of being in love. Love is making him miserable, and the woman he thinks he loves is not responding. In the opening line, he imagines he might be able to feed the love he feels with music, hoping it will be stuffed, satisfied and fade away:

If music be the food of love, play on.

Showing unstressed and stressed syllables, the line might look like this:

if MUsic BE the FOOD of LOVE play ON.

This is a perfect iambic line (and many are imperfect), but the principles are simple. What you have read so far is about it. So what is all the fuss about? Verse is only frightening because it is new until you are no longer "verse virgin."

So why do authors bother to write in verse, which is obviously more difficult than prose? For some of the same reasons that songs are written to express what cannot be adequately shared in mere words. Verse is somewhere *between* song and regular speech, not so musical or fanciful as the one, and not so ordinary as the other. For the actor, verse offers the chance to play with both subtlety and grandeur, often at the same time.

The extravagance of the imagery encourages you to do extravagant things, which are also true, to be both big and honest. There is no definitive way to scan or speak a verse speech. Possible inflections and personal interpretations are many. Verse increases sensibility to words, rhythms, meanings, which come only from sound, to unexplainable meanings, deeper than the conscious mind can fathom. It tends to stretch an actor towards greatness.

Since Shakespeare's generation invented the prose drama, which now virtually dominates theatre, his audiences may have found prose lines as strange as you may find verse on first contact. He tended to mix the two in a script. Sometimes an entire conversation has one person talking verse and the other refusing to join, always answering in prose. After two thousand years of nothing but verse, the first prose lines must have been startling, but they immediately became comfortably familiar, and so can verse for you.

(See Appendix C for a complete listing of all terms associated with verse or for suggestions for mastering it.)

Some plays allow verse and prose to alternate. Shakespeare uses verse about 72 percent and prose 28 percent of the time. Hamlet himself speaks about 60 percent verse and 40 percent prose. Why would one switch? Verse is more likely to be spoken:

- by a character of high rank;
- to a parent, ruler, or stranger;
- in public and on formal, ceremonial occasions;
- when speaking of love, truth, honor, or the meaning of life, of the higher subjects.

Prose is more likely to be spoken:

- by a rustic, comic, humble character;
- by someone who feels momentarily rustic, comic, or humble;
- in broader, earthier circumstances;
- when dealing with more mundane or bawdy subjects.

In moments of high intensity, we fall into rhythms not unlike verse: (anger) "If YOU don't CUT that OUT I'll PUNCH you OUT" or "Get IN the HOUSE this MINute OR no SUPPER!" Recall recent circumstances where you were in emotional states and note the patterns you fell into.

Should you pound out the stressed syllables relentlessly? No, that would be stultifying. Verse is like a pulse, just under the surface but always present, like the beating of the human heart. It is there all the time and can be brought forward as in moments like those above. In rehearsal, it is useful to work in the extremes, sometimes beating out the rhythm too forcefully, other times ignoring it to go for meaning, almost forgetting that the speech is not prose. Gradually move towards bringing these wide swings of the pendulum together, so the speech is both rhythmic and natural.

Here are some of the most beloved verse passages to work on for scansion and balance:

> As an unperfect actor on the stage,
> Who with his fear is put beside his part,
> Or some fierce thing replete with too much rage,
> Whose strength's abundance weakens his own heart,
> So I, for fear of trust, forget to say
> The perfect ceremony of love's rite,
> And in mine own love's strength seem to decay,
> O'ercharged with burden of mine own love's might.
> O let my books be then the eloquence
> And dumb presagers of my speaking breast,
> Who plead for love, and look for recompense
> More than that tongue that more hath more expressed.
> O learn to read what silent love hath writ;
> To hear with eyes belongs to love's fine wit.
>
> (Sonnet XXIII)

> For within the hollow crown
> That rounds the mortal temples of a king
> Keeps death his court, and there the antic sits,
> Scoffing his state and grinning at his pomp,
> Allowing him a breath, a little scene,

To monarchise, be feared, and kill with looks,
Infusing him with self and vain conceit,
As if this flesh which walls about our life
Were brass impregnable; and humoured thus,
Comes at the last, and with a little pin
Bores through his castle wall, and farewell king!

(Richard, from *Richard II*)

R: If I profane with my unworthiest hand
  This holy shrine, the gentle fine is this:
  My lips, two blushing pilgrims ready stand
  To smooth that rough touch with a tender kiss.

J: Good pilgrim, you do wrong your hand too much,
  Which mannerly devotion shows in this:
  For saints have hands that pilgrim's hands do touch,
  And palm to palm is holy palmer's kiss.

R: Have not saints lips, and holy palmers too?

J: Aye, pilgrim, lips that they must use in prayer.

R: O, then dear saint, let lips do what hands do;
  They pray, grant thou, let faith turn to despair.

J: Saints do not move, though grant for prayer's sake.

R: Then move not, while my prayer's effect I take.

(Romeo and Juliet, from *Romeo and Juliet*)

These are perfect exercise passages for experimenting with verse.

The ironic element of learning to speak verse is that it seems so overwhelming, and then, one day, you get it, and it seems so easy. Instead of a monumental mountain to be climbed, it is hiking boots, compass, and map. It is a vehicle for *you* to drive that will greatly facilitate reaching your destination. It is so packed with information, so powerful, and so potent, that once you trust it, you have to make less effort than with prose. Verse gives you a guide for phrasing, frequently telling you how to pronounce names, which word or syllable to point up, and where the emphasis needs to be. It shows you that shifts in relationships have taken place and offers both interpretive hints and stage directions. It is easier to memorize because the rhythm helps you. It is also easier to retain, even after not working on it for a while. It gives you natural places to breathe. Well spoken, it is highly pleasing to listen to and aids you in keeping the audience's attention. It is concise and exact in its shape and ultimately it helps you think faster. As you get caught up in its builds and let it carry you, you feel greatly empowered.

> *"Dance is a measured pace as a verse is a measured speech"*
> FRANCIS BACON

SPIRITUAL LIVES: Heroic dimension

Theatre history is full of actors, not blessed with impressive stature or resonant pipes, who rose to greatness because *inside* was an extraordinary and hypnotic flame. Most classical characters think of themselves (and so we think of them that way too) as bigger, brighter, bolder, and more beautiful than mere mortals. They function in a larger emotional space, where laughter can be raucous and crazed, and where howling at the moon can be the only answer to the cruelty of the fates. The key is acceptance. Accept that you have potential for greatness and grandeur. Accept that you deserve nothing less. Here are some specific paths to believing:

1. *Variety of attack* is freeing. To reach the infinite variety within characters, explore more highs and lows, louds and softs, beauty and harshness, danger and gentleness, all. Allow *mercurial swings in strategy,* maneuver, and attitude. Fill the creative space.

2. *An unpredictable tempo* counterbalances the potential sameness in verse and archness in language. While stresses in verse dictate rhythmic patterns, they do not limit tempo. Let passion guide you through time and *timing.*

3. *Sudden reversals* are common. Characters tend to follow a line of thought or an objective, then suddenly drop it and move in another direction. They tend to go deeply into an emotion, wring it quickly dry, drop, and move to another. Accept this as part of the *nature of heroic perspective.*

4. *Do not play the ending.* Romeo and Juliet expect to win, to find a way out, to succeed, every time they plunge down one more corridor of hell. Watching their hopes crushed is profoundly moving. For the actors, this means no whining and no generalized playing of mood. It means more *positive expectation* and moment-to-moment playing.

5. *Accept archetypal reality* without judgment. You may represent Young Love, Insane Jealousy, Omnipotent Grandeur, or Silly Simp. By all means, work out detail, but don't fight symbolic function. It is thrilling to play a character who represents broad spectrums of humanity.

6. *Do not judge characters* from contemporary perspective and impose a reality that is not theirs. Ophelia (in *Hamlet*) is a weak and emotionally battered woman: to seek a contemporary strength in her is to judge her. Helena (in *All's Well That Ends Well*) falls in love with an arrogant, immature jerk. She is a bright and savvy woman. How can this be? Because he is the boy next door and a prince above her rank. This, in a fairy-tale reality, is reason enough. She is not lessened by her choices *inside* her particular world.

7. *Friendly competitions are ongoing,* as characters try to be wittier, sharper, more vibrant, pained, or pungent. They also acknowledge a point well made. They relish this competition. There is constant appreciation of others, while attempting to top them.

8.   Never forget the basic principles of *truth, focus, action, and objective* learned back in Acting 1. Far too many classical performances lack the basics, taking place in spaces that are neither hot nor cold, light nor dark, safe nor dangerous, public nor private. The characters are neither running late nor do they have all the time in the world. They are dying, or in perfect health, but nowhere in between. Make sure each question of *relationship, objectives, and influences* is dealt with, so you establish a reality on which you can build the grand elements.

9.   *Embrace the opportunity* to be evil, lurid, and violent. Go for it. Let go of any ounce of embarrassment or temptation to soften. Here is where you can *be* what you only *dream* about in real life.

10.   Learn to speak faster and clearer by learning to *think faster*. These people are quicker than many of us; their responses can often be lightning bolts. By thinking quickly, the words roll out with less effort.

11.   *Use the blue flame of anger* at least as often as the red one. When a fire is blazing, it is vivid and bright, but lacks the steady power of a pilot light or other focused fire. The most frightening anger can be that which is subtly directed, deadly, and non-negotiable.

12.   *Transform yourself into a better you.* You are only limited by your willingness. If you believe it, we will. In your imagination, make adjustment that with enough time, dedication, surgery, therapy, and prayer you could achieve.

13.   *Accidents are gifts.* If someone drops something, or a feather falls off a hat, instead of ignoring it, react as your character would. The fates are giving you the chance to respond fully, beyond the confines of the script. They are allowing you to heroically explore.

➤   Write out the terms below on a card or in your journal. Keep them, in rehearsal, where you can quickly look over the list. Meditate regularly on how you are doing and promise yourself to acknowledge each:

variety of attack	friendly competitions
swings in strategy	basic truth
unpredictable tempo	embracing evil
thinking faster	sudden reversals
blue flame	positive expectation
archetypal reality	a better you
accidents as gifts	

"When you play a king, the first important thing to remember is that when you walk into a room, everything around you, you own."
KEITH MICHELL

➤ Assume that you control your immediate universe. Enter and pass judgment on the mere mortals who surround you, even if only in your imagination. Communicate your power and mood in a single sentence. Some possible lines:

> "You have leave."
> "Let the games begin."
> "We are not amused."
> "All rise."
> "Off with his head."
> "Cease and desist."
> "Which of you has done this?"
> "You may approach."

SPECIAL SKILLS

While subsequent chapters deal with the peculiarities of each age, there are some common actor tasks, new to many of us.

1.   *Asides are common.* Right in the middle of a scene, one character turns to the audience to confide in them, ask them a question, give them a knowing look, or in some other way quickly connect with them before returning to the scene. These are most effective as sharp clicks. Keep your body facing the direction it was going and simply snap your head out to face the audience. This is especially true if the aside is very brief. If it is longer or more pronounced, try leaning sharply towards the audience. To punch it up one step more, dash quickly downstage to confide in us, then dash back to where you were and continue as if nothing has happened. Partners of actors doing asides need to look *away* at the moment of the aside to help the illusion. They need to find something to occupy them and to go into slow motion or freeze. Never watch the other actor do the aside. Help create the impression that, from your perspective, it never happened.

2.   *Audience address is often required* with perhaps only one character on-stage. Most work best as direct address rather than an attempt at deep introspective talking out loud to yourself. Because the plays move back and forth between overt acknowledgment of, and ignoring, the audience, think of the audience as your collective best friend and confidant. You have the most open, sharing, and honest relationship you have with anyone. No one ever lies in a soliloquy. Alone with the audience you speak the absolute truth (as you see it) and without embarrassment.

3.   *Rehearsal garments are fundamental* to get the feel of costumes to come. If they are not available, create them out of your closet or off your bed. Most characters handle a lot more cloth than we do. Capes, trains, lengthy sleeves, trailing ribbons, lace, petticoats—each age is different, but the garment is always challenging. *Wear* these

and do not let them wear you. Flip them out of the way. Command them. You have a lot of fabric because you deserve it. Dominate it. When wearing a floor-length gown or robe, expend as little effort to lift the hem as possible. Use just one hand and lift it only a few inches from the ground when you climb a staircase. You don't need to lift it at all when you descend a staircase. Recognize in each instance how little effort is needed to command the clothes.

4.　*There is frequent need to invent and ritualize contact*—forming a marriage bond or contractual agreement, showing signs of respect, exorcising demons, calling on the gods, pleading for help, handing someone the message from an oracle, maneuvers where we have no evidence to prove how they were done back then. Answers emerge in improvisation, trial and error. Let the character show you how he wants these rituals performed.

5.　*Cleaving is an essential skill.* Someone (usually male in these plays) grabs someone else (usually female), pulling her in for an embrace and possibly a kiss. This move is bold and involves enveloping your partner. A silly reminder of appropriate body positions is that you want Pee Pee (crotch to crotch) not Tee Pee (only your lips are really connecting, so you look like a tent on a reservation—in fact, you look like you have serious reservations about the whole thing) kisses. At the point in the play where this occurs, nothing short of audacious will work. Leave your modesty at home and cleave.

6.　*Characters are always pretending to be someone else,* and the actual disguise is so flimsy, you wonder why other characters wouldn't recognize them. This is a convention from eras with no films, photos, or close-ups to indelibly lock someone's image. Help it by seeing the character anew, investing the cape, hood, hat, or other piddling disguise with power.

7.　*The capacity to handle weapons believably* and to fight well is important to the classical actor. It is important to start early and work actively outside rehearsal. Just achieving enough finesse to make sure the sword at your side does not stick into you or someone else requires time. Combat scenes are rehearsed twenty times as much as any stretch of dialogue. Basic principles:

- Often, a fight is a scene about two people trying to kill each other. Remember, it is a scene at heart, with objectives and evaluations.
- The pauses where nothing happens are often the most interesting, besides giving you a break.
- There are only five basic cuts (attack moves) and parries (defense) moves in most swordfights, which are then repeated in limitless combinations. They are not difficult to learn, and fights are then less complex than they seem at first glance.
- Even the blows themselves break down into three distinct parts: the wind-up (size and speed show the audience how strong the blow is), hit (with a split

second pause after) and reaction or follow-through (which shows how hard the blow struck or took).

- Each stage is helped by nonverbal orchestration (grunts, howls, blades clashing, gasps, observer reactions, etc.), and the blow is the least important part. The clear signals are sent by parts wind-up and reaction. Do not be intimidated from the great fun of getting to die and kill without consequences. This skill is highly learnable.

SHARPENING CLASSICAL AWARENESS

Many actors who do the classics well also have some experience or aptitude in musical theatre. Our most popular stylized entertainment is The Musical. It is the journey outside realism most of us already know. Between musical theatre and high-brow classical drama, there are important connections. Both sets of plays often:

1. combine the intimate and the spectacular;

2. blend the oratorical and the naturalistic;

3. move back and forth between representation and presentation;

4. involve characters alone on-stage, pouring their hearts out in soliloquy or song;

5. have large casts representing entire cultures;

6. involve public scenes full of ritual and ceremony;

7. embrace the shared mythology of the audience;

8. involve characters who are archetypal and often heroic;

9. are often set in an exotic locale and/or a remote time period;

10. catch characters at their brightest and most intense, with minimum vacillation, indecision, or exposition;

11. are likely to have a "finale" full of pomp and spectacle;

12. require pouring out intense, heartfelt emotion without embarrassment or hesitation, for the actor to play both *big* and *honest*.

Once you learn to accept the reality of jumping up and breaking into song as a "normal" part of life, you have no trouble with the strangest conventions in the classics. If you can imagine a world where everyone in the laundromat breaks into synchronized song and dance on the washers and driers, you can probably imagine anything else. If styles coming up seem weird, remember that, to the uninitiated, *nothing* would seem weirder than the musical.

MOVING INTO SCRIPTS

Whether you are working alone on a monolog or with a scene partner, here are some guides for approaching text.

1.   Start working by completing everything you *do* know already. Study the script and put together a basic character analysis, based on evidence you find there. Do everything you did the first time you seriously worked on *any* scene.

2.   Don't worry for the moment about unfamiliar customs or staging conventions. These are worth researching, but the temptation is to jump too quickly to the unfamiliar.

3.   Get all the evidence you can from the script itself and start committing it to memory.

4.   Approach the character as human to human, as someone you want for a friend, hopefully a friend for life.

5.   Are there other, non-speaking or barely speaking, characters—guards, attendants, messengers—in the scene? How do you get it down to two or thee actors? If these imaginary others must be addressed, consider placing them out in the audience. This convention works fairly well and beats talking to empty spaces on-stage.

6.   Cut scenes down to no more than ten minutes, monologs to under three, just enough to have a good work-out. You do not need to an epic excerpt to learn to act with epic scope. Keep it manageable.

7.   If you are working in a class setting, the very first time you present the scene, try to take a curtain call in the appropriate style of the scene itself. Invent a bow if you do not have the actual information.

8.   If possible, present scenes at least twice, the second being a showcase where other classmates and guests try to actively interact with you. Because so many of these plays are presentational, the relationship of an actor to an audience is valuable to explore.

9.   Give yourself images and memories of the senses as you rehearse. Find paintings, sculptures, music, scents, foods, as many ways of stimulating your own senses as possible. Seek out and record a piece of music that could introduce your scene and in some cases underscore it.

10.   Remember that these plays are great because they are not easy. They provide a tremendous mountain for you to climb and an amazing view once there. But be kind to yourself and realize that this is big league material and it will take time. Shoot for perfection, but settle for excellence, and give yourself grace.

11.   Critiques are times to encourage each actor to trust his intuition. It is perfectly acceptable to say that an actor choice strikes you as too contemporary but you are

not sure why. Maybe others can help you with the why. I recommend dividing the critique session into two distinct parts, where what is working about the scene is identified first, so the actors have a sense of what they can now build on. Second, hit what is not working, but state this in terms of highly possible accomplishments. I like to call the critique parts as follows:

Greek scenes—laurels & javelins;
Elizabethan scenes—roses & thorns;
Restoration and Molière scenes—kisses & hisses;
Georgian scenes—cheers & jeers.

(Note: Group exercises exploring ideas in this chapter are located in Appendix C.)

ACHIEVING STYLE

THE NEXT four chapters will take the issues of time, space, place, values, structure, beauty, sex, recreation, sight, and sound into the periods in history whose plays are most produced in Western theatre today—the eras you are likely to get to enter if you become a classical actor. Because those plays acknowledged as great are often hundreds to thousands of years old and create worlds quite unlike our own, an actor wishing to experience this greatness will want the capacity to enter the worlds. This section is about understanding enough to do so. While there is a huge global menu of stylized performance, these chapters do not encompass that full range, but rather take a more pragmatic approach. We focus on classical challenges likely to face the western actor, examining the periods and playwrights most likely to be represented in classical repertory seasons, professional revivals and in programs of universities committed to classical production.

The four chapters address the beliefs, conventions, and acting guidelines for Greek, Elizabethan, Restoration, Molière (neoclassic), and Georgian (eighteenth century) plays.

In each chapter, a lively interview with an "expert" of the period is used to convey basic information. The following conventions will shape the interviews. The subject:

- knows all about our era, as well as his own;
- cannot tell us anything not available to us in our own library or through research; cannot reveal secrets hidden in history;
- chooses not to reveal personal details;

- has not informed his peers about electing to do this interview, so is participating on the sly;
- is a citizen of the world created by *writers* of the era, not necessarily of the *real* era;
- has indicated a possible need to be called back at any time and may therefore need to terminate the interview quite suddenly.

4. GREEK PERIOD STYLE: Three generations of tragic vision
5. ELIZABETHAN PERIOD STYLE: Theatre of earth and stars
6. RESTORATION PERIOD STYLE: Decadence as one of the fine arts
7. RELATIVES OF RESTORATION PERIOD STYLE: Morals and manners

GREEK PERIOD STYLE

4 THREE GENERATIONS OF TRAGIC VISION

THE WORLD ENTERED

POWERFUL DIFFERENCES exist between the civilized world of the plays' first audience and the primitive world of the plays themselves. The scripts are written in the classical period, but are about the Bronze Age, seven or more centuries earlier. The original audience is a patriarchal Athenian democracy. The plays dip into history and myth, sometimes back to a matriarchal Mycenaean monarchy. Almost all surviving production evidence is from the Hellenistic age, a good century or more *after* the playwrights created the plays.

Are you confused? When you read and study about ancient Greece, you should always stop and ask *which* ancient Greece this is. Imagine that centuries from now, scripts from the 1940s and 1950s are discovered and considered great. Imagine that all these plays are not about their own era, but one much earlier, say the time of Robin Hood, and they are about Robin, Richard the Lionhearted, Prince John, and the Crusades. Adding to the confusion, the only surviving production information is from the years 2040–60.

You could get depressed about how little we know of ancient Greeks in performance, or you could revel in the fact that, because we know so little about how to limit our imaginations, we have freedom to create. Why not choose the latter? Between the first major drama festival in 534 BC and the defeat of Athens in 404 BC, the theatre virtually soars to greatness, along with every other form of artistic expression and investigation. Only 3 percent of all drama written in that century is left, thirty-three tragedies, eleven comedies, and one satyr play. Three playwrights stand as the first giants of Western drama (see Table 4.1). Each presents the actor with a separate set of exciting challenges.

Table 4.1

Poet	Aeschylus	Sophocles	Euripedes
dates	525–456 BC	496–406 BC	484–406 BC
plays	90	123	92
extant	7	7	18
festival victories	13	24	4

Aeschylus, who lived long enough to remember tyranny but die in a democracy, is particularly remembered for introducing the second actor, reducing the chorus from fifty to twelve members, inventing the trilogy, making the dramatic part of the performance as important as the choral, writing the most magnificent choral odes, and developing wildly effective satyr plays

Sophocles is known for introducing the third actor, and later the fourth (in *Oedipus at Colonus*), increasing and standardizing the chorus at fifteen members, discovering serenity in tragic vision, adding subtlety and suppleness to drama, discovering the power possible in quiet moments and internal conflict, achieving the most poignant and moving of climaxes, developing the arts of plot and characterization, developing scenes into full acts with choral divisions, and providing the model for Aristotle's definitions of classic drama.

Euripides, the youngest, is known for increasing the number of characters and roles (but not actors), showing that drama can focus on the individual and on specific social questions, developing interest in abnormal psychology and its origins, disconnecting the chorus from the main action, combining realism and pathos in one event, breaking traditions, embracing controversy, innovation, courage, and independence.

Imagine being the first to accomplish any of their feats. Most of us would be thrilled to be remembered for any one of them. Together they give us visions of grandeur, serenity, and honesty, respectively. Half their surviving scripts are about one family—the House of Atreus. As you read the plays, remember that Clytemnestra and Helen of Troy are sisters-in-law. No dynastic soap opera ever produced a family so fascinating or two women more capable of unsettling their world and changing the course of humanity.

THE INTERVIEW

How would a poet and seer of the time respond to our basic questions? The subject of our interview knows sympathetic magic, drama festivals, and how to summon an oracle. The subject also claims to be related to a god and to have survived a visit to the underworld.

Time: pre-Homeric mythology to fifth century BC

Mycenaean: 1700–1100 BC; Archaic: 800–480 BC; Hellenic/classical: 480–323 BC; Hellensitic: 323–146 BC.

We live in the wide shadow of our past.

At what point in history are the plays set, written, performed? How do these interact?
"We act our own history, known and imagined. When you act the stories of your George Washingtons and Christopher Columbuses, and then go farther back for your Christs, and further still for your Adams and Eves, you come close to what we feel."

How far does the audience or play move out of its own time?
"A strong production is freed of time. Look less to your archeologists and more to the plays themselves for help. Answers lie in the poets' words."

How rapidly does it move for most people? How conscious are they of it passing?
"We have time for a good, thoughtful argument—always. We are deliberate and careful. We are less conscious than you of minutes, hours, and days, more so of harvests passed, festivals held, or famines survived."

How do you record time? How long does the action last?
"Time is periods of war and peace. The place of the sun, movement of stars, size of moon, and length of shadow are guides. Our plays are short by your terms, running perhaps an hour and a half (we present four or five in one day). Most honor the unities (time, place and action) with one location and cycle of the sun."

Do people focus on the moment or the lifetime, on the future or the past?
"Resolving the past is our task. Our plays begin near the end. The event—prophesy, curse, war, or betrayal—has occurred. Now it is revealed and understood. The future at the end of our tragedies is uncertain, bleak, close to unbearable."

> *"The life so short, the craft so long to learn."*
> HIPPOCRATES

What is your attention span?
"We can listen long. Rhetoric is our invention. Many are illiterate, so must hear and remember. When we deliver a message, we commit the words to memory and repeat it to the recipient without change."

Is age revered or feared?
"If lived honorably, life is rich in old age, with winter years full of respect and reward. Sophocles, our most honored poet, created his masterpiece at age ninety. Thespis was called Dangerous One when he created this creature called actor, but at the end of

his life, he was City Dionysia Victor, a poet's highest achievement. Honor comes when you are ready."

Space

I am the universe and my sphere is cosmic.

How is it defined and viewed? Is space literal or abstract?
"Space is soul, mind, body, and senses. Gods rule the sky and underworld. Man can be transported and transformed."

"When you produce the greatest effect upon the audience . . . are you in your right mind? Are you not carried out of yourself?"
SOCRATES

"We see all twice. We see stars but also a bear, lion, swan, giant, or bull *in* the stars. We see a sunset but also a chariot driven across the sky. We see rising waves *and* dancing sea nymphs, rustling trees *and* dryads dancing in them, bubbling brooks *and* naiads leaping across them. We see life through the gods. When thunder explodes, Zeus is angry, a volcano erupts as the smoke of Hephaistos' smithy, a tree or flower grows, to honor the god who seeded it."

"Be what you would seem."
PLATO

How large is one's personal bubble? What is privacy?
"We carry a large circle. We honor circles of others. We are not cold, but prize power and majesty. We are not small or uncertain. Within the home is strong privacy of quarters. We do not knock upon a chamber door—we scratch. All brutal acts occur offstage.

Yet, our plays are in public places with the chorus, ever visible and acts accountable. A life must bear scrutiny."

What are attitudes towards invasion and force?
"War hovers always. Justice deals with violation within city walls but not at its gates. A man prepares himself to be a powerful soldier, but speaker too. Words try mightily to prevent blows."

Place

The jury is always present.

Is the setting rural, urban, remote, coastal, inland, protected, exposed, confined, open?
"All, except confined. We are just outside the palace, shrine, city gates, temple, or sacred place in Greece, Asia Minor, Crete, Cyprus, Phoenicia, Egypt, or on another island. Someone arrives here always from a great journey.

We live outside. Our buildings are part of the surroundings, with columns beckoning the eye beyond. Your modern churches enclose the faithful to create sanctuary. Our altars are in the open air."

What is the influence of geography and relationship to nature?
"Seas surround hills, hot and dry, with abundant fig and olive trees. Thyme and sage scent the hillsides. The sound of cicadas fills a night more clear and cloudless than yours. We worship nature. We try to persuade her by offerings, by supplication, by a libation of wine, honey, or oil. We then accept the course she takes."

> *"Man is but a shadow of a dream. Yet if the gods bestow upon him but a gleam of their own radiance, bright flame surrounds him and his life is sweet."*
> PINDAR

Are you aware of other places? Are you citizens of the world?
"You use 'idiot' to mean low in intelligence. For us, 'idiot' means leading only a private life, with no service to the community. We are tied to our city-state, but we are members of the family of man. We also have slaves."

Values

Life of balance, death with honor.

> *"This ground is holy: here the brave are resting."*
> SIMONIDES

What are the beliefs most widely shared?
"Self-knowledge, harmony, and wisdom. Nothing in excess, until the time demands it. Then only unbridled fire will serve! Justice. Death before dishonor."

Truth is not to be hidden—no matter how painful. The play begins with something very wrong, not yet understood. The veil of appearance is then lifted. Truth in full agony and beauty is revealed. Truth is sought like joy. Suffering is the path to wisdom.

Our words have changed with time. Here are five of the most important to help you understand us. What have you done to them?

1. Justice (*dike*)—path or expected events (no moral judgment);
2. Virtue (*arete*)—efficiency or skill (no assumption of right or wrong);
3. God (*theos*)—a force free of death (not always a persona; whereas Christians say "God is Love," we say "Love is as god");
4. Irrational—freed of rational thought (not always undesirable);
5. Ecstasy—a state beside oneself, filled with emotion too powerful for the body to contain (not the same as happiness).

How do you believe the world began?

"Earth (Gaia) mates with sky (Uranus). So jealous is he of their offspring, that he tries to stuff all back into her womb. Her youngest son (Kronos) helps her by cutting off his father's genitals and throwing them into the sea. Three drops of genital blood fall upon Gaia, causing the birth of the Furies, while the genitals float away and form Aphrodite! Far from learning compassion from his own experience, son Kronos takes his own sister Rhea as wife and swallows all *their* children. But the sixth child, Zeus, escapes, returns as a man, disguises himself as a cupbearer, feeds his father a dreadful potion, and makes him throw up all Zeus's older brothers and sisters. These form the ruling gods. Sex and violence are at core of the creation."

What are the traditions? How are bonds made and broken?

"Ritual, festival, and debate—chances to act out and reaffirm belief—are our traditions. Community comes before family, then friendship. Word is honor. Break it and you welcome death and destruction. Swear by the dark river Styx, which must be crossed in the underworld, as the most sacred of oaths. Fail to honor a god for sparing your life, a good wind, or granting wisdom, and the god will avenge. Vengeance most feared is to the mind."

> *"Whom Zeus would destroy, he first makes mad."*
> SOPHOCLES

Figure 4.1

Aphrodite, goddess of love, and her son Eros
© Jupiter Images

What is the predominant mood?
"Passionately reflective."

Who are idolized?
"First the gods, second heroes of myth (Theseus, Jason, Ajax, Perseus, Herakles), third achievers. Most beloved of goddesses is Demeter, whose Eleusinian mysteries are the most sacred and secret. But our largest *cults* are for the youngest and most handsome—Apollo the light and Dionysus the dark. Our greatest hero, Herakles [Hercules] is, though mortal, accepted on Olympus. In addition to his standard heroic endeavors, he honors King Thespius one night, by sleeping with all fifty of the king's daughters!"

What are sin and justice?
"We do not turn the other cheek. We believe in full, public reckoning and the power of a curse. Betrayal of state is death. A curse, if not avenged, descends from parent to child until atonement. When young Teiresias by chance views Athena, virgin goddess, bathing, she strikes him blind. This is merciful. The price for looking at a god is death. Because he meant no harm, she grants him the gift of prophecy. Still, one look means no eyes. None fails to pay the price."

What gets attention? What holds it?
"Magnificence in mind and body. Those who excel are listened to. An actor will be listened to, provided he has a rib-cage as vibrant as the box of a lyre."

Value placed on money? Uses for it?
"Wealth means responsibility. Rich men of course pay for the theatre. Drachmas should serve Dionysus."

What is the place of God and the church?
"The gods *connect* us to the unknown. Religion is practical, tangible, constant, not entwined in ethics, but tied to sex. Our gods are close. Unlike your Jehovah, they show us their vulnerability, vengefulness, and carnality. We prefer gods we can understand. Your Jehovah is too perfect. Our heaven is ruled by a beautiful, terrible divine family to whom we offer sacrifices and whom we mock behind their backs. We are the mortals and they the immortals. Immortal is not past vanity or deceit."

What are the requirements to be a god?
"You must have a god for your father. Your mother, if not a goddess, must be at least a nymph."

What kind of humor dominates?
"We laugh openly at stupidity and ineptitude, satirizing anyone who is prominent. None is above criticism and mockery. It helps them avoid hubris. We believe there

are separate times for laughter, tears, and stoicism. Our City Dionysia ends with a comedy, after a day of tragedy, like dessert after a full meal."

How is fear defined? How is emotion expressed?
"We fear defeat, slavery, disgrace, infamy. We believe in clear, unfettered emotion. We suppress petty jealousy. We ward off the evil eye with a necklet of blue beads or dose our selves with Lethe water to help reveal what we know inside. Spit quickly, if you look too far into the future. It is bad luck to price the unborn calf.

"We hold these animals sacred: peacock, eagle, tiger, stag, snake, boar, white bull, cat, mouse, swan, owl, tortoise, and dolphin. Sympathetic magic, a connection between a thing and its name or symbol, guides us. As some of you use a doll (pricking it with pins) to torture a person, we believe your name means as much as your limb. If I write your name, curse it, and bury it—consigning it to powers of the underworld—I may be killing you. So I speak your name and touch your objects with care.

"It may not be the end. Our dead are stretched out on a bier, feet to door, in case. The family cuts its hair short to the skull. Visitors cut locks of their own, tie them in black ribbons, and hang them by the door. This may be repeated at a burial place. A death is honored with feasting and funeral games, not quiet seclusion. If you lived with honor, a bard may sing your name, and children may be taught your deeds. If so, though you have crossed the River, who would say you do not still live?"

*"The tyrant drinks his cup of pride
And climbs beyond our sight,
Then, blazing like an evil star
Falls into endless night."*
SOPHOCLES

"Poetry is higher than history, for poetry expresses the universal, history merely the particular."
ARISTOTLE

Structure

The Gods are vengeful but known.

Who rules and who follows?
"In the Athens of my life, a council of five hundred and a main assembly of fifty members hear and make law. In our *plays*, there is a ruler (king, archon, despot, oligarch, or ephor) with power to order death. But even the most powerful must win the approval of the citizen/chorus to survive. There is no absolute authority.

We invent history (from *historia* or investigation) as the first to tell truth with reason and not to revise and glorify our past. I see that some in your age have reverted to the old ways. We value the historian, but *revere* the artist.

He who rules is called the Shepherd of the People because he stands between the wolf and the flock."

What is daily life like?
"Time is given each day to develop mind and body. Blood relations are strong and volatile. Marriage is arranged for life. Instead of your furry little creatures, every residence has a house snake for luck."

How are manners and etiquette set?
"We respect custom, our own and others'."

Who is educated and how?
"Privileged males learn mathematics, philosophy, literature, music, athletics, ethics, persuasion, and dance outside the home, women artistic skills, spinning, and weaving within. We look for learning everywhere. The playwright/poet is expected to be a *didaskolos* or teacher on being alive."

> *"The unexamined life is not worth living."*
> SOCRATES

What professions dominate and how is work viewed?
"The city-state is foremost. Profession of public servant dominates. Later, acting becomes a profession. Singers, seers, prophets, shamans, and priests are revered. Actors are exempt from military service and have diplomatic immunity, so may be asked to carry secret communications between heads of state as they tour."

Beauty

Nothing matches the human body in the sun.

What is the look most aspired to? Who are the contemporary ideals of male and female perfection?
"Strong, statuesque, and proud, with keen intelligence in the eyes—eyes that are stern, radiant, gracious, without sentiment. Power in the limbs. Cleanliness, smooth skin, vitality, hair that is curled. Mesomorphic, symmetrical physical dimensions, well-muscled, with the effortless stillness and grace of the natural athlete. Sappho, whom Plato calls 'the tenth muse,' laments being short and dark, while rejoicing in her blond 'golden flower'daughter, Cleis. Sappho praises other women for pale delicacy and grace. Golden hair is chosen for characters of great beauty. The Olympians are models—Aphrodite, Eros, and Apollo in particular.

"And yet, Dionysus, the newest and most dangerous god, is dark, with exotic eyes and lithe, sinuous limbs. He *defies* the ideal and is thought, by many, the most beautiful."

What part does fitness play in attractiveness?
"The body must be fit for an ordered self and beauty. Vibrant good health, unrestricted garments, and little artifice are most desired. Athletic prowess is beautiful. Unlike your Olympics, at ours the pentathlon (one man mastering five events) is the highest honor.

Figure 4.2a

Dionysus, courtesy of the
Museo Nationale Romano

Figure 4.2b

Apollo © Jupiter
Images

"We take physical beauty as seriously as any philosophical issue. I believe you take it seriously but pretend to find it unimportant."

Which colors and shapes are favored?
"Vibrant, solid–colored (indigo, scarlet, purple, green, black, and saffron) garments, many with bold trim in key, stripe, or other geometric pattern. In theatre, colors are symbols—green for mourning, red for procurement, white with purple border for royalty. A hat indicates a traveler. White is chosen for mourning as often as black. The body is draped simply with cotton or linen for grace of line.

"We love fragrances and scent as adornment. Jewelry, particularly that with a tinkling, musical sound, is much loved. Earrings, more than adornment, are for warding off evil spirits."

How is beauty expressed in daily life?
"The surfaces of pots, vases, urns, bowls, and cups tell of our lives and legends. For occasions, pots are commissioned. A host might invite you to his home to celebrate your triumph, have you drink deeply from a cup, which, when you study its interior, shows a god in a situation like yours. After the final toast of the evening, he may personally dry it and present it to you as a remembrance.

"Tapestries and sculpture, both statues (with special fondness for *kouros* (nude male youth) and *kore* (draped maiden) and reliefs, express our spirit. Music and dance are part of every ceremony. The drama has never received such support before or since. The poet's gift is worshiped."

Sex

The planting of seed is fundamental to life.

How significant a part life is sex?
"Sex is a chance to touch the god in us: it is part of life, renewal, as breathing, free of shame. It is more and less important to us than to you."

What is considered a turn-on and turn-offs?
"Excellence! Those with victor's laurels will be sought after. Strength, dexterity, and will are desired. Obesity, indecisiveness, and cowardice are not. The body is seen. Our athletes, some dancers, and all male children appear nude. Undergarments are uncommon. The torso is honored in sculpture, but never upstages force from the eyes.

"The best way to ensure being able to mate with anyone of your choice would be to be a god. But that is probably true in your world as well."

How is sexuality communicated and seduction defined?
"We do not tease. We honor desire. Sex is union. If spirits meet, bodies may. Sex with the gods shapes belief. Your Jehovah pleasured himself with only one human, the mortal Mary, correct? Ha! Our Zeus has had everyone! Sisters, aunts, cousins, nymphs, and legions of humans! He is insatiable and able to take on any seductive form, from white bull to cuckoo bird. He threatens to seduce his mother when she tries to stop his marriage to his sister. Is he irresponsible and immoral? He is Zeus! Until you have had sex with a god, do not dare to judge, mortal."

What is the courtship ritual? How much tolerance for deviation?
"Marriage is a business contract, with courtship left to nego- tiators. A male's first sexual experience is likely to be with another male. The bond formed may involve partnering with one's lover in battle as well, believed to increase chances for victory. When you marry, your former lover may become godfather to your children and protector to your wife. If you die, and he is not wed, he is the one most like to marry your widow.

When asked if he still had sex during his advanced years:
"Hush, man, most glad indeed am I rid of it all, as though I had escaped from a mad and savage master."
SOPHOCLES

"Orgy may be part of a celebration. A giant phallus, symbolizing renewal, appears at public gatherings. When Aphrodite and Dionysus, two of our more carnal gods, mate, they produce an ugly child with enormous genitals, named Priapus. Most of us have small statues of Priapus in front of our homes. Aphrodite's cult is made up of honored priestess–prostitutes, known as protectors of the city."

Recreation

Dionysus must have his due.

> *"Wine goes in and tongues let out. Gentlemen observe a mean, Tippling, with good songs between."*
> ANACREON

What would be an ideal social occasion?
"Dionysian Festival is the height, but more often we choose quieter pleasures, such as dining and discussing ideas with friends. We seek balance between Apollonian wisdom and Dionysian inspiration. Nine is the perfect number, small enough for talk, large enough for diversity. We invent the 'symposium,' but you have again changed the word. Ours are livelier and more ribald than yours."

Intellectual life?
"Even our wildest rites are based on inspiration. You desire surprising plots. We know our plots. We want irony, subtlety, new motives, and causes for old deeds."

Food?
"Thick red wine is watered down according to time of day and occasion. Sharing a cup is a ritual of trust, pouring wine on the ground a ritual of honor. We recline at meals, where fruits of trees (figs, raisins, currants, olives) are always served with flat bread. Honey, almond cakes, and chestnuts are treats. A humble meal is barley bread and goat cheese."

How important is recreation in life?
"Your saying 'All work and no play make John a dull boy' sums up Apollonian/ Dionysian balance or golden mean. Pleasure, rest, and celebration are vital to free work, study, and thought. Apollo brings peace and music. He likes tears no more than the sun likes rain. He understands your pain and will take it away. He will slay the darkness and help you stir men's hearts and minds, if you offer him song. His is a calming love. And Dionysus?"

(Suddenly the subject stops and looks away as if in a trance)
"Hermes waits to escort me to my world. There is a goat to be sacrificed and a friend in need of an oracle. I will leave you some writings. Read of Dionysus yourself if you dare. I pour you this libation *(taking a bowl of wine that seems to have just appeared)* to honor your search and assist your discovery *(splashes wine suddenly)*. What were your thoughts just now? Were you worried about stains on the carpet? The waste of fine wine? The propriety of this happening in your office? You need not concern yourself. The stain will disappear with me. The wish remains. May you more often drop small thoughts and let the god emerge inside you."

(The subject points outside the window. I look and see nothing. I turn around and the Greek is gone, leaving this story of Dionysus behind.)

— DIONYSUS —

The youngest god has long dark hair, wears garlands of ivy, and is the only god with a mortal mother. He is ecstasy and horror, vitality and savage destruction. He is the god of the theatre, whom we worship when we perform.

Dionysus is created when Zeus seduces Semele, a mortal woman of astonishing beauty. Semele is tricked by his jealous wife Hera into asking him to give her one wish and to swear on the river Styx not to refuse. She asks to *see* him, but no mortal can view a god without dying. He has no choice. As she bursts into flames, Zeus cuts open her womb and his own thigh, where he keeps Dionysus full term. Dionysus goes through so many trials that he is born three times.

When Hera recognizes him, she makes Dionysus mad. He journeys through the East with an army of satyrs and maenads. He teaches men to make wine. His grandmother Rhea cures him and initiates him into the secret of women's mysteries. He decides to teach women how to celebrate him. When Ariadne, the great love of his life, dies, he places her crown among the stars, now known as Corona Borealis.

Worship of Dionysus is pure release of inhibition, resulting in union with nature and the creative force. He offers wine and sex as paths to ecstasy. Kings oppose him because he threatens law and order. He is the only god to rescue and restore women, instead of diminishing or raping them. He prefers their company, having been raised, for a time, in one of many efforts to protect him, as a girl.

The grapevine is each year severely pruned, lies dormant, then sprouts new life. His festivals connect planting, harvesting, and wine-making. Tradition involves singing over the sacrifice of a goat, a disguise in which he was once murdered by Titans. The term *tragedy* emerges, meaning goat song.

Dionysus, in your own life, may be mystic, musician, or murderer. He is the most dark and dangerous rock star, the consummate bad boy. He uses disguise more than any, especially panther, leopard, and lynx—the most graceful and savage of cats. Remnants of his worship take hold at Halloween and Mardi Gras. Dionysus is the one your mother hates when he comes to the house to pick you up. And not without reason. Your ride away with him (on his motorcycle?) feeling free and wild. Does he lead you to impending doom or to inspiration? It depends on you.

END OF INTERVIEW

SIGHT

Human gods walk the proud earth.

How do all the above manifest themselves in looks, movement and gesture?
Productions in ancient Greece took place in the open air before up to thirty thousand people, on stone bleachers in a hollowed-out hillside, surrounding two-thirds of the stage. We cannot generally expect to recreate these circumstances. We can strive for the *feelings* that must have been present. Four possibilities that are true for costumes are:

1.　Some attempt to match the original production: ornate costumes with long robes under short mantles, an *onkos* (ornate headdress indicating sex, age, and status of character) and mask of cork or linen (*prosopon*). These will restrict sudden, sharp movements, require an upright head, and severely limit peripheral vision. You must face the object or person you wish to see with your entire head, and each step must be taken with great care. If you are a chorus member, your appearance may be closer to normal attire. "Modified original" productions are common, employing half masks, mask-like make-up, or some other softening of the full mask/onkos effect.

2.　An effort to look like original audiences: a *chiton* (inner garment), a rectangular garment open at the right side, caught at both shoulders, short or long, belted around the torso and waist. It starts looking much like a large sheet and is all done in draping. The *himation* (outer garment) is a rectangular wrap draped around the body, restricting the freedom of one arm. A stoic or philosopher will wear *only* the himation. A *chlamys*, or short, square cloak may be worn by younger men and warriors.

If you are a woman you may wear a Doric chiton (a rectangle of wool folded over at the top and draped, with front and back attached at the shoulder with fibula, and girded under the breasts or at the waist) or an Ionic chiton (a wider garment with no overfold, often with a crinkled effect, ibula or buttons joining it along the top of the arms, girded to create a sleeve-like appearance). You may also add himation or a diplax , much like the male chlamyus. Athenian women sew up the open side of their chiton and consider Spartan women, who do not, sluts.

Men's hair is short, with younger men clean-shaven and older with well-tended beards. Women pin hair up, often braided, and cover portions with band or coronet.

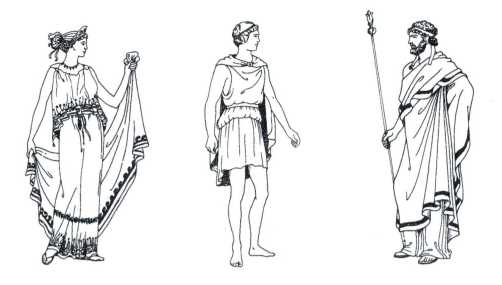

Both may have hair curled over the forehead and sides of the face. Feet, bare indoors, will wear a sandal or a leather boot/buskin outside.

3. You look as the characters probably did when they lived: In the Minoan–Mycenaean period involving the reigns of Agamemnon and Menelaus, women wear bell-shaped, tiered skirts, tight girdles at the waist, bared breasts, some headdress, and long curls down the back. Men wear a girdle, loincloth, a tunic with sleeves, greaves, and helmets with animal trims as tusks and tails, plus metal studs and leather fringe. Hair and beards are very long and crimped into serpentine tresses.

4. You look like the imagination of your designer: This is the most common choice. The look may move up to some future world, an invented fanciful antiquity, or attempt timelessness.

There are no featherweights in Greek drama, no airy, delicate, flighty, lightweight people, so the best costumes, regardless of details, will help actors achieved a tall, dignified, commanding, godlike presence.

MOVEMENT AND CONTACT

Hypnotic stillness alternates with strong, large gestures and full, forceful crosses. Because ritual is valued, symbolic and formal movements can be juxtaposed with those less studied. An erect torso with head upright, gestures with clearly defined beginnings, middles, and ends, are held for the duration of the thought. Loose wrists and elbows do not work. Arms do not move stiffly but rather free of distracting, weak, half movements. Imagine that all nonessential qualities (mannerisms, old habits, tiny movements) have been stripped away, so that only what is clean and necessary remains. These characters are archetypal, *simplified* to the point of purity and basic humanity, and then *amplified* by the enormity of their circumstances and the magnitude of their plight.

We have no evidence how ancient Greeks bowed, except for actions implied in the scripts.

1.   When supplicating, go all the way down to the ground and prostrate yourself. You may be extended anywhere, from a kneeling position with hands down on the floor, to fully lying face down before the honored one. You might kiss the garment of the person before you. If you fall to your knees, pull forward as you do so, with some of your energy pulling you up (not unlike sliding into the home plate) to avoid injury and to accomplish the move soundlessly.

2.   When kneeling, step forward as you bend, ending with the other knee on the ground and the one with which the move started now bent. Allow room between yourself and those to whom you are paying obeisance.

3.   Opening your palms to indicate the power of the person addressed is a universal act, as is taking the hands of this person with your palms up. You might proceed to place the hands of the honored one against your forehead.

4.   Invent codes with your scene partners or fellow cast members. Decide on a curse, a gesture of thanks, a calling upon the gods for help, a warding off of the evil eye, a silent signal forbidding someone to come closer, and other symbolic actions. This is opportunity for creating a world.

5.   Expressing grief is traditionally accomplished by covering the head and face and sometimes by raising a veil over the head.

6.   Men show friendship by grasping each other's forearms near the elbow; the commitment is further emphasized if you place the other hand on the friend's shoulder. This gesture (which evolves into our handshake) demonstrates that you do not have a weapon. You come open and unarmed into contact. Women are more likely to clasp hands.

7.   With the above exception, there need not be a significant difference between sexes. The directness and simplicity in the words should be supported by similar moves.

8.   The forehead can be used for a variety of moves. A clenched fist pressed to the brow is a gesture of homage to a god or person of great importance. Touching hand to brow and extending arm up in the air may be offered in salute, as may a fist across the chest. Touching two or more fingertips to the brow and lowering the head slightly indicates honor without extreme obeisance. A soldier may press a spear or other weapon to the brow by way of respect or to pass someone through an entrance.

9.   References to gods may involve extending arms towards the gods' home, up for Olympians, palms down for Poseidon, the Mother Earth, and the underworld. Address the gods, first focusing on their home and then spread out all around to acknowledge that the god may be anywhere.

SOUND

I speak for the ages.

How does this come out in speech and listening?
An aptitude for complicated lines of thought is to be cultivated. Experience with debate, forensics, and oratory helps, since these arts originate here. A moderate tempo often works. Awareness of rhythmic shifts *within* a dominant tempo is essential. The temptation is to give every image great weight and to fall into a ponderous delivery. The best arguers are full of surprises. The statues may be carved in marble, the *lines* are being invented as you speak.

> *"The proper method of delivery can change the speech. We must pay attention to it because we cannot do without it."*
> ARISTOTLE

Aristotle and others continually refer to the need for a well-trained voice. Sophocles's retirement from acting because of weakening of his voice is open acknowledgment that poets' and actors' arts are not the same. A full-rooted, resonant sound, with generous attention to the lower notes in your register, is crucial—an unsupported voice will not be listened to. The capacity to give consonants great weight is important, twisting, turning, darting, and spitting them without worry of affectation. Even through dignity, there is an animal connection to words. The dignity is that of the lion and the eagle.

Feel free to sing, chant, intone, declaim, and explore other ways to express words through sound, beyond simple speech. This is not just a scene; it is ritual and may shape destiny. The poets admire lean lines and spare sentences, supported by firm, direct delivery.

The tragedy is broken down into five parts:

1.   Prologue—exposition;
2.   Parados—processional entrances;
3.   Episodes—individual characters in action, five or six sections;
4.   Statismon—lyrical sections, involving singing and dancing, in which chorus comments on the action;
5.   Exodus—summary, frequently with a message, and choral exit.

Emotionally the play will move through:

1. agon—conflict
2. pathos—suffering
3. threnos—lamentation
4. epiphany—revelation of transcendent truth, spirit, godhead.

By their nature, each part can take a different vocal attack. Some passages demand highly poetic, lyrical speech. Others (the famous messenger speeches) need story-telling, tale-weaving, vivid description. Debate sections demand a lawyer's command of issues and language. Lamentation speeches need an operatic release. The quick one-line exchanges (called *stichomythia*) need sharp timing and crisp attack.

Ancient Greek does not translate easily. What is lucid in the original, takes many words to express in English. Verse lines seem, to Western ears, in a perpetual state of unresolved half-tones. Translations (see Chapter 8) vary language, structure, prose, and verse, so that the same play can be nearly unrecognizable. The originals have a pure simplicity and directness of language, but many flowery translations exist, so beware.

MUSIC AND DANCE

The Greeks believed that music could spur action, strengthen the spirit, undermine mental and spiritual balance, completely suspend willpower, and produce magic. Many scholars believe that performance was more like dance and song than realistic behavior, that all movement was ritualized, and speeches were chanted. Greeks knew harmony in three key modes: Dorian (strong and masculine), Phrygian (passionate), and Lydian (lascivious and effeminate). Popular instruments were:

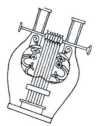

Lyre

The definitive Greek instrument has five to seven spun-silk strings, struck with a plectrum, sometimes using a turtle shell for sounding board, used to accompany poetic and choral passages. An oversized version, the Kithara or Phorminx, can be approximated by a Celtic harp or dulcimer. Hermes is said to have made the first lyre while still a small child, to lull his mother to sleep and go out to play wherever he wanted.

Aulos

A double- or single-reed wind instrument spanning three octaves, with a rich, low, resonant sound, used to accompany solo passages. Today an oboe, clarinet, or a bagpipe chanter can be used.

Percussion

Cymbals and drums establish rhythms and guide choral moves. A modern percussion section can punctuate movement and shifts of action.

What emerges is a sound of haunting simplicity. Imagine a delicate string, low reed, and simple drumbeat beneath speeches, offering subtle, evocative accompaniment, with descending notes in simple, monophonic patterns. Synthesizers can create a timeless, compelling, and not quite identifiable sound.

Dance is responsible for the very life of Zeus, god of gods, and it is so honored. (To prevent his father from eating him alive, the Curetes dance over baby Zeus in a wild, leaping, noisy, shouting, sword-and-shield beating display, so that father will not hear son crying.) Dance means any rhythmic movement, juggling, tumbling, ball tossing, time games, hand, foot, head, and eye movements. Evidence suggests Greek dance involved more hand and less foot movement, than ours. Dances may be ritual (sacrifice, prayer, exultation), funereal (slow, curvilinear dirges), processional (lines, chains, small clusters), war (vigorous attack and defense moves), and Dionysian (planned wild, disordered chaos suddenly emerging into surprising patterns).

KEYS TO THE WORLD

IMAGES

The names of gods fill the plays and serve as evocative models. Some may be more familiar to you in their Roman versions (see Table 4.2 below).

Table 4.2

Greek	Roman	Identity
Zeus	Jupiter	King of all the gods
Hera	Juno	Wife to Zeus, goddess of marriage and children
Poseidon	Neptune	King of the sea, god of horses
Demeter	Ceres	Goddess of planting, harvest, rebirth
Athena	Minerva	Goddess of wisdom and courage
Apollo	Apollo	God of healing, arts, the sun
Artemis	Diana	Goddess of the moon, hunting, chastity
Aphrodite	Venus	Goddess of love
Eros	Cupid	Her son
Ares	Mars	God of war
Persephone	Proserpina	Daughter of Demeter, queen of the underworld
Hades	Pluto	King of the underworld
Hephaistos	Vulcan	God of fire, crafts
Hermes	Mercury	Messenger of the gods, patron of travelers, transporter of souls
Dionysus	Bacchus	God of wine and inspiration
Kronos	Saturn	Father of Zeus, Hera, Demeter, Poseidon, Hades, ruler of first generation of gods

Try this invocation:

Greek warm-up

Aphrodite give me beauty and freedom.

Apollo give me harmony and clarity.

Ares give me courage and power.

Artemis give me vision and light.

Athena give me wisdom and strategy.

Demeter give me growth and renewal.

Eros give me love and magic.

Hades give me intuition and objectivity.

Hephaestus give me skill and creativity.

Hera give me nurturing and commitment.

Hermes give me swiftness and connection.

Hestia give me safety and identity.

Poseidon give me loyalty and feeling.

Zeus give me strength and will!

And Dionysus, to whom my art is dedicated.

Dionysus give me inspiration and passion!!!

Now all the gods fill me with fire.

Drive me to destiny and wonder.

Help me go beyond the real and into ecstasy.

Help me find the god in me.

Let me understand. Let me act.

Other images from the Greek world

Nothing in excess (not every day is a Dionysian rite)

A balanced life (humility balances pride, passion balances reason, mind balances body, human limitation balances ideal vision, rational balances irrational, law balances ecstasy)

Wisdom above all else and above all other knowledge, self-knowledge

The polis (city-state) as center of life

Any simple act may have infinite reverberations and catastrophe

Fertility of soil and fertility of woman mean survival

The Acropolis (cult sanctuary of Athena, place of the owl, the snake, the sacred spring, and the cave)

Temple of Hera—Battle of Lapith and the Centaurs—Exekeias' Dionysus cup—Euphronios' krater—the Kritios boy—The Bronze warriors

In every act ask: Is my honor in this? Was this well done?

Social success and suicide

You will know success by receipt of the Ultimate Compliment:

> "You are a balanced human. You bring honor to your people."

Balance is accomplished by reaching beyond personal vanity to service. To excel so as to reflect glory *back* on those whom you represent is the ideal. You could only top the accolade above by adding "and honor to my home as well."

Your failure in this world might come from receipt of the Ultimate Insult:

> "You are selfish and unworthy."

To be Greek is to serve and deserve to serve. Only petty creatures are too pre-occupied with themselves to do so. Some who are selfish can still give, but to be self-absorbed and inadequate to the task? Get the hemlock! A strong contender for worst insult would be "You have set yourself above your fate. You have become an offense to the gods." The recipient has succumbed to hubris and will pay.

To be successful, you must:

1. develop your mind, body, and skills to their fullest;
2. give to the city-state with a generous heart;
3. find ways and means of achieving excellence;
4. find the god in you to move with force on earth;
5. allow both your passion and your reason full expression.

Suicide may be committed by:

1. becoming full of yourself (hubris), offending a god and subjecting yourself to retribution (dike);
2. leading a private life with no concern for the general well-being;

3. allowing yourself excess in any of the appetites of life;
4. being disloyal;
5. being stupid.

MASKING

The play was written to be performed in a mask, so rehearse in one at least once. Spend time choosing it, studying it, putting it on for brief periods of time. Let the power of the god enter you, along with the power of actors who have taken on this character before. If you can spend time in the storage area of your theatre or in a shop that sells masks, try on several. Let the spirit of the mask enter yours while leaving it intact. Let the mask itself tell you how to respond. Wearing the mask will reveal how limited peripheral vision influences a stately bearing and a full body pivot in any direction and towards any listener. Speak to the mask, as "you" at first and then "I" when you feel part of it.

There are only seven surviving vase paintings *known* to show fifth century masks. They are all softer, more natural, and less tortured than our earlier impressions of ancient masks. The mouths are only slightly open. Their expressions have endlessly shifting meaning. Regard the mask as life giving, not taking, as offering revelation, not concealment.

Characters also mask themselves in Righteousness, choosing to think themselves correct and resisting negotiation. In modern therapy, a frequent goal is to give up the need to be right all the time. The Greeks do not give up.

THE PRODUCTION

Rehearsing in a large outdoor space and in full mask can help you grasp power and openness. Your actual set will probably be clean and simple, an exterior with sky beyond and a large open space for choral movements. It will probably attempt to capture timeless dignity and raw power.

What to us is the strangest ingredient in Greek tragedy made it most moving and involving for the original audience. The chorus is the ideal spectator for the event. They are supposed to comfort and guide the audience, expressing the attitudes of an average citizen of this community, introducing new characters and questioning them, chastising characters behaving inappropriately, offering comfort and sympathy to victims, explaining puzzling events, and clarifying motives. They may pray, lament, celebrate, contemplate, or share ironic observations. They have a group identify, but each member also has a single identity, not unlike a contemporary chorus for musicals. When the chorus appears, we should feel comforted and connected. They clarify.

"There is not function more noble than that of the god-touched Chorus, teaching the city in song."
ARISTOPHANES

The chorus declines in importance as the drama moves forward. Those of Aeschylus are involved and committed. Sophocles' are concerned but detached. Euripides' (with the stunning exception of The Bacchae) are ironic, remote, sometimes even in counterpoint to the event.

THE PERFECT AUDIENCE

The audience arrives full of anticipation for illumination of the human experience. You are not just going to have a wonderful time and experience spectacle and wonder, but you will gain insight into your life. If you are approximating the original audience, as part of a class or rehearsal exercise, indicate your displeasure by hissing. You will probably choose not to throw olive pits, much less stones, in spite of precedent. Applause may be indicated by clanging objects together or stomping your feet.

CONTEMPORARY PARALLELS

Some connections between then and now:

1. A preoccupation with the body and physical fitness and a belief in the relationship between fitness and other excellence—beauty associated with strength.
2. The nude or semi-nude male has never been more visible (for the Greeks in person and sculpture, for us in print and film) as symbol of beauty, at least equal to that of the female.
3. A desire for natural, unspoiled elements in food, clothing, and possessions, in keeping things simple.
4. A powerful desire for comfort in everything worn, touched, or reclined on.
5. The impulse to work hard and then party hard, to categorize life experiences.
6. An obsession with sports events bordering on the maniacal.
7. A belief in democracy, the rights of the individual, and the need to protect them.
8. A commitment to open debate as the means by which issues can be settled.
9. A feeling that each life phase has its own rewards and wonders, so that neither youth nor age is perfect.
10. A constant re-examination of authority, with all power figures ready targets for satire.

It is too easy to think of the Greeks as distant from us. The sky full of constellations named for them still watches over us. From the Olympics to mathematics, astronomy, engineering, architecture, medicine, money, law, literature, and scientific inquiry, they invented most of what we do. They believed in magic, but we have as many things as they that we cannot figure out.

PLAYS AND PLAYWRIGHTS

Here are those scripts most likely to be produced:

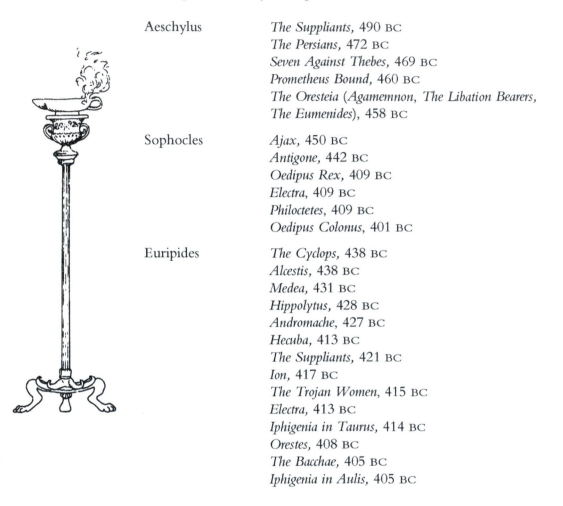

Aeschylus	*The Suppliants,* 490 BC
	The Persians, 472 BC
	Seven Against Thebes, 469 BC
	Prometheus Bound, 460 BC
	The Oresteia (Agamemnon, The Libation Bearers, The Eumenides), 458 BC
Sophocles	*Ajax,* 450 BC
	Antigone, 442 BC
	Oedipus Rex, 409 BC
	Electra, 409 BC
	Philoctetes, 409 BC
	Oedipus Colonus, 401 BC
Euripides	*The Cyclops,* 438 BC
	Alcestis, 438 BC
	Medea, 431 BC
	Hippolytus, 428 BC
	Andromache, 427 BC
	Hecuba, 413 BC
	The Suppliants, 421 BC
	Ion, 417 BC
	The Trojan Women, 415 BC
	Electra, 413 BC
	Iphigenia in Taurus, 414 BC
	Orestes, 408 BC
	The Bacchae, 405 BC
	Iphigenia in Aulis, 405 BC

SCENES

In some instances, lines assigned to the chorus may need to be cut or reassigned to the character closest to that point of view, in order to shape the following scenes with only two or three actors.

Agamemnon

CLYTEMNESTRA, AEGISTHUS, CHORUS
The unfaithful queen and her lover attempt to justify their murder of her husband to the representative of the people of their city.

Antigone

ISMENE, ANTIGONE

Defying her uncle's orders that her brother, who sought rebellion against Creon's government, not be given burial, Antigone meets secretly with her sister to ask for her help in a deed certain to bring about her execution.

CREON, HAEMON

Father and son face the disintegration of their relationship as they differ over love and loyalty.

The Bacchae

PENTHEUS, DIONYSUS

Failing to honor the god, the city's leader has him captured and refuses to recognize his divinity until it is too late.

Electra

CHRYSOTHEMIS, ELECTRA, CLYTEMNESTRA

One sister warns another against confronting their mother about the death of their father, but Electra, in her pain, approaches the queen at the altar of Agamemnon's grave (also can be performed as two separate two-character scenes).

Iphigenia in Aulis

CLYTEMNESTRA, IPHIGENIA, ACHILLES

Can the queen sacrifice her daughter to avoid war?

Iphigenia in Taurus

ORESTES, PYLADES, IPHIGENIA

On a remote island, separated for many years, brother and sister are unexpectedly reunited. She is now a priestess, he a fugitive.

The Libation Bearers

ORESTES, ELECTRA

Meeting at the tomb of their father, brother and sister lament the indignity of his death and plot vengeance on their mother for her part in it.

Medea

JASON, MEDEA

Medea avenges her betrayal and exile by her husband, poisoning his new wife and then slaughtering their two children. Jason encounters her and the bodies of their offspring.

The Trojan Women

HECUBA, HELEN, MENELAUS

Troy is defeated. All Hecuba's children and grandchildren are dead, except one daughter who is insane. The Greek king has come to Troy to claim his unfaithful wife who has been the cause of the war.

TALTHYBIUS, ANDROMACHE, HECUBA

The Greek captain is a caring man, but there is no easy way to separate the queen, her daughter-in-law, and her grandson, each destined for a separate horror.

(Note: Group exercises exploring ideas in this chapter are located in Appendix D.)

SOURCES FOR FURTHER STUDY

Adler, Mortimer J., *Aristotle for Everybody*, New York: Macmillan, 1978.

Anderson, M.J. (ed.), *Classical Drama and Its Influence*, New York: Barnes & Noble, 1965.

Bickerman, Elias Joseph, *Chronology of the Ancient World*, Ithaca: Cornell University Press, 1980.

Bieber, Margarete, *The History of the Greek and Roman Theatre*, Princeton: Princeton University Press, 1961.

Bolen, Jean Shinoda, *Goddesses in Everywoman*, New York: Harper & Row, 1985.

Bolen, Jean Shinoda, *Gods in Everyman*, New York: Harper & Row, 1990.

Brooke, Iris, *Costumes in Greek Classic Drama*, London: Methuen, 1962.

Earp, Frank Russell, *The Style of Sophocles*, New York: Russell & Russell, 1972.

Gagarin, Michael, *Aeschylean Drama*, Berkeley: University of California Press, 1976.

Goldhill, Simon, *How to Stage Greek Tragedy Today*, Chicago: University of Chicago Press, 2007.

Graves, Robert, *Greek Gods and Heroes*, New York: Dell, 1960.

Grube, George M.A., *The Drama of Euripides*. London: Methuen, 1973.

Guthrie, W.K., *The Greek Philosophers*, New York: Harper & Row, 1950.

Hamilton, Edith, *Mythology*, Boston, Little, Brown & Co, 1942.

Hope, Thomas, *Costume of the Greeks and Romans*, New York: Dover, 1962.

Johnson, Robert A., *Ecstasy*, San Francisco: Harper & Row, 1987.

Kirkwood, Gordon Macdonald, *A Study of Sophoclean Drama*, Ithaca: Cornell University Press, 1958.

Kitto, H.D.F., *The Greeks*, Chicago: Aldine, 1964.

Ley, Graham, A *Short Introduction to Greek Theatre*, Chicago: University of Chicago Press, 1991.

Oates, Whitney Jennings, *The Complete Greek Drama*, New York: Random House, 1938.

Pickard-Cambridge, A.W., *The Dramatic Festivals of Athens*, Oxford: Oxford University Press, 1953.

Taplin, Oliver, *Greek Tragedy in Action*, Berkeley: University of California Press, 1978.

Webster, T.B.L., *Greek Theatre Productions*, London: Methuen, 1970.

Webster, T.B.L., *The Tragedies of Euripides*, London: Methuen, 1967.

Wellesz, Egon (ed.), *Ancient and Oriental Music*, London: Oxford University Press, 1936.

Wiles, David, *Greek Theatre Performance*, Cambridge: Cambridge University Press, 2000.

Wood, Michael, "The Art of Greece," in *Art of the Western World*, New York: Summit, 1989.

DVDS

Electra, The Trojan Women, Iphigenia (Michael Cacoyannis)
Cacoyannis is considered the première interpreter of Greek tragedy on film. Any of the three would be a good first exposure to the style.

Oedipus Rex (Tyrone Guthrie)
A highly effective Stratford Festival production with masks, as austere, ritualistic, and formal as the original productions probably were.

Medea (Zoe Caldwell)
Dramatic, intense adaptation of Euripides' play by Robinson Jeffers, effective in its full-out attack and force.

Songs of Sappho (New York Greek Drama Company)
An attempt to authentically recreate performances of poetry accompanied by dance as they might have been done in the poet's own lifetime.

Troy (Wolfgang Peterson)
While the film is forgettable and even presumes to rewrite Greek mythology, the DVD features include an excellent delineation of all the Greek gods.

Gods and Goddesses and *In Search of History: The Greek Gods* (The History Channel)
Intelligent examination of each of the Olympian deities.

Greece: The Crucible of Civilization (Cassin Harrison)
A PBS documentary tracing the full history of the ancient Greek empire, intelligently narrated by Liam Neeson.

5 | Elizabethan period style
Theatre of earth and stars

THE WORLD ENTERED

OVER TWO thousand years pass before unquestioned greatness returns to the theatre. Plague, war, and famine have wiped out much of the world's population and, for a time, theatre itself. Then a mighty England emerges as ruler of the known globe. A queen of majesty and diplomacy guides this venture, and the English language explodes, increasing by a fourth, with over ten thousand new words added in less than a century. Never, before or since, has a language grown so astonishingly. The drama is where the new words soar.

The term Elizabethan is not limited to the birth through death of Elizabeth I, but can mean any time between the ages of Henry VIII and Charles I encompassing Elizabethan thought. By the time she takes on the crown, emphasis has shifted from power struggle to commerce. The feudal system is dead. Because her father broke with Rome and created his own church, Elizabeth, at her coronation, becomes both head of state *and* head of church. She has no higher allegiance than her own vision.

The English can now do no wrong. Some "impossible" recent events include Drake's voyage around the world, Raleigh's exploration of North America, and an astonishing naval victory over the Spanish, who have previously claimed title to the greatest naval fleet in the world. Elizabethans have already found "more things in heaven and earth" than ever previously dreamed of. They regard the world as *theirs*.

Though providing an important backdrop, the Elizabethan era is not what most of the plays are about. The playwrights opt for more exotic choices. Living in an extraordinary world, they often place their plays in worlds that exceed even their own. Understanding this style means entering the *imaginary* lives of the writers, beyond their day-to-day existence. It also means acceptance of miracles.

THE INTERVIEW

What follows is an interview with an expert, familiar with court, country, and city life, close friends with Ben Jonson and William Shakespeare, and a dabbler in the occult. Our expert has lived in the plays themselves (in kingdoms such as Shakespearea and Jonsonia) as well as in London. The interview was set up with the help of alchemy and witchcraft. The speaker lapsed occasionally into blank verse or rhymed couplets, claiming that any other form of expression would be inadequate. The subject felt informal this day, so addressed me consistently as "thou." I was never quite certain if this was because the expert liked me or felt the disdain for me that one might for a servant. Immediately after the conversation, said expert disappeared in smoke.

Time 1550–1625

> Love alters not with his brief hours and weeks,
> But bears it out even to the edge of doom.

In what point in history are the plays written, set, and performed?
"Written in the years above, our plays be *set* in times ancient, all the way forward, to times not yet lived. They be not about a moment in time but about *all* time. E'en the "history" plays alter fact to suit vision. And what vision! Our poets do play with time, so thou be'est ne'er certain how many days or years have gone by in our plays. Time will seem different in performance than it doth appear on paper."

How far does the audience or play move out of its own time?
"If moved far out of the Renaissance, they lose majesty. But lose power? Not a whit! Our plays fit every period known or imagined by man!"

How does time move?
"We stride forth in glory and every prospect doth exist on our horizon. We do take more time than thee to smell the rose. We note tolling of church and tower bells, but still watch sun and moon as truest guides. Whilst change be ever constant, so is our queen."

> *"Semper Eadem:*
> *Ever the same through*
> *all alteration."*
> MOTTO OF
> ELIZABETH I

How do you record or note time?
"A fortnight past, when our glorious queen did visit the estates of Lord Leicester, the clocks were stopped for the duration of her stay, since, quoth his lordship, 'Where

Virginia is, there time stands still.' She doth have such power o'er her lords and we, her subjects, have such power o'er the world! Time is oft' times Capitalized, spoken to, personified. Ay, marry, no other subject is addressed more often in our plays. Father Time is a powerful man with two strong daughters, Fate and Truth."

What is the dominant tempo/rhythm?
"Blank verse captures our lives, like unto the cantering of our horses, the beat of our tabors and the pulse of the human heart."

Where do people focus?
"Past exists merely as catalyst to future. We dwell not on deeds done, but thrust ahead. Yet, if ye wrong us, think not our memories are so short that we shall fail vengeance no matter how bloody or long it takes. We think of lifetimes and generations to come. Ye can always imagine the *next* scene at the end of our plays, be it wedding celebration, reunion feast or funeral procession."

What attention spans do your people have?
"We listen not unless thou speak'st boldly and beautifully, with pride in thy heart and vision in thy tongue. Those worthy of attention, receive it, by commanding it. If thou speak'st well, we will stay with thee. If not, see to thyself."

Is age revered or feared?
"Youth is a sadly brief and fleeting time, like unto to the lives of flowers. Childhood, as thou know'st it in thy time, doth not exist in ours. Children dress and act as we do, are expected to be interested in philosophy and to make worthy conversation at table. We tolerate not silliness. Our poets are as infatuated with the last days of boyhood as the first dawn of womanhood. Boys and women are seen as similar, the oncoming of beard and drop in voice regarded with some sadness."

Space

I stand amidst the spheres and I stand tall.

How is it defined?
"Britannia doth rule the world, and her cathedrals thrust toward heaven!"

"All places are distant from Heaven alike."
ROBERT BURTON

How large is personal and private space? How flexible?
"Huge! We fill the universe with self. The higher thy class, the larger thine own space. Yet, space alters oft' betimes. We embrace heartily and seize what we want, and then spheres burst. A man may seek to be alone when not fit company. When in public be expected to *take part* and save contemplation for anon."

What are attitudes towards invasion and physical force?
"Grant me a moment to gather my thoughts *(pause)*:

> No where is man more noble than in war,
> Provided that he fight for noble cause.
> 'Tis England's turn as lion now to roar.
> And vanquish any who oppose our laws!

Dids't serve? 'Twas extempore. Forgive me. The muse captured me. Space is invaded forthrightly—grabbing a woman and kissing her full, slapping a glove across an opponent's face, or thrusting a dagger into his body. Word or blade may confront ye at any time."

> *"Our swords shall play the orators for us."*
> CHRISTOPHER MARLOWE

"Yet, be forceful *and* eloquent in execution for invasion without grace is ill thought of."

How do these ideas affect the theatre space?
"Our theatre symbolizes the universe, from trap doors (hell) up to canopy (heaven) so all elements exist within the Globe. Our four famous theatres all exist within a few streets of one another in South London, *far* from palaces and cathedrals. Nearby is "Clink" prison (a term ye have stolen to mean *any* prison) and other jails. Thieves, prostitutes, vagabonds, and beggars do live here, so those who cross the bridge do journey to the wrong side of the Thames. In this dangerous darkness, magic rises and all manner of humankind cross paths."

Place

My home is the world and where I am I own.

Where are the plays set?
"Our scope is epic. Our settings may be throne room, hovel, peaceful garden, or raging tempest. Our plays sweep through the known world, both tamed and wild, and magical, imaginary lands, new minted in our minds. Scenery changes little; the *lines* make powerful suggestion and the rest, my friend, be acting! "

And space in daily life?
"Our population has grown from three to four million in under sixty years (more new people e'en than words), with massive movement to London and new debate 'tween country pleasures and with those o' the city. New inventions (the chimney! carpenters tools! glass!) allow smaller rooms, windows, light, more indoor time, and houses now are oft' built in the shape of an E. Can'st supposition why? The most important new space is the long gallery, a place of exercise, dancing, and music, with fireplaces and family portraits o'erlooking the garden. Home now is center of life, for better or worse:

Flowers and time to tend them endure as our pride and joy! Garden is as vital as gallery for walking our footpaths of knotted ribbon mazes."

What is your relationship to nature?
"Nature may give trial and torment or peace and safety. Natural order and goodness can be corrupted, but we believe in the Noble Savage."

"Charity and beating begins at home."
JOHN FLETCHER

How aware are you of other places?
"Though England be the sceptred isle, we are entranced with Italy and the Machiavellian mind. We do cling to simple superstition *and* yet yearn for reasons. Many are disturbed by the new theory of Copernicus, which says the earth is not center to the universe (with all spheres circling us), but that it doth forsooth revolve around the sun!! We explore land and sea as readily as mind and soul."

Values

One man in his time plays many parts.

What are the beliefs most widely shared? What ideals? Which truths assumed to be self-evident?
"I will teach thee to become an Elizabethan! A person worthy of Shakespeare and the stars. Stand up. No, taller, Bartonio! Is that not thy name? Well, I *choose* to call thee Bartonio. Up, man! Now this be what thou call'st a 'warm-up', a thing we do not require as *we* are always ready! Stand tall, sirrah. Speak these words and believe them!

> MY SPIRIT LIFTS ME HIGH ABOVE THE GROUND.
> I HAVE AN ANSWER READY FOR ANY MAN.
> I HAVE THE WIT TO JEST EVEN WITH SAINTS.
> I AM AS TRUE AS FLESH AND BLOOD MAY BE.
> I WAS NOT BORN TO SUE BUT TO COMMAND.
> THE HEAVENS BLAZED WITH LIGHT UPON MY BIRTH.
> I AM PART OF A GLORIOUS COSMIC ORDER.
> I STAND ASSURED AND FIRM UPON THE EARTH,
> AND AM CALLED UP BY AN UNFOLDING STAR.
> I WALK ONE TINY STEP BELOW THE ANGELS.
> I MOVE WITH CONFIDENCE TOWARDS GODLINESS.
> I AM THE BRIDGE BETWEEN ALL MATTER AND SPIRIT.
> I AM A COURTIER, ADVENTURER, POET, SWORDSMAN,
> A WIT, PHILOSOPHER, MUSICIAN AND A GENTLEMAN
>   (or LADY).
> I SING AND DANCE TO THE MUSIC OF THE SPHERES.

I KNOW THAT MUSIC BOTH HEALS AND TRANSFORMS.
I HUNGER FOR MY LIFE AND WILL DEVOUR IT.
UPON THIS GARDEN EARTH, I PLANT MY SEEDS.
MY THOUGHTS ARE GREAT AND SO WILL BE MY DEEDS!

"Well done! Now, dost answer thy question? Say these words aloud daily and someday, perchance, thou wilt be worthy to be called Elizabethan."

What is your dominant mood?
"Ours do swing like pendulum from dark to light, laughter to tears and back. We are open to emotion and welcome change. We do place comedy in e'en the most tragic plays, as the Porter, forsooth, in *Macbeth* and the gravedigger in *Hamlet*—welcoming irony, counterpoint, and antithesis. A sad lament will have a humorous turn of phrase. A joyous paean will be shadowed with dark, disturbing images. We do savor all the turns the heart can rightly urge, *save two*. Whining and sullenness we do not countenance. These must be supplanted with turns more lively. 'Tis better to be merry or weep than chide and pout."

Are there forces beyond your control?
"Four humours of the body (melancholy, phlegm, blood, and choler) dominate moods, and the position of the stars will change fortunes and feelings. Harmony is sought and Chaos avoided."

Who are your idols?
"Gloriana sets the tone for majesty. Her favorites (Essex, Raleigh, Leicester) are briefly imitated 'til out of favor. Exemplary lives find lasting admiration. Belike the most admired man of our era is Sir Philip Sydney, who did die generously at war and was regarded as th'epitome of chivalry at court."

"They are never alone that are accompanied with noble thoughts."
SIR PHILIP SIDNEY

What do you admire most?
"Verbal eloquence doth find honor above all other accomplishments. To have another man say 'Roundly replied!' is to have won the day!"

"Silence is the virtue of fools."
FRANCIS BACON

What do you hope for?
"Our capacity to dream of honor, glory, wealth, and advancement knows no bounds. Why should it when our lives exceed most men's dreams?"

How do you define sin?
"Sin is the corruption of God's creation. Man *is* corrupt and may attain salvation through living generously and faith. Sin is failing to battle for the seven virtues to win over the seven vices inside thyself."

And justice?

"The word of a gentleman is oft' accepted in court of law without oath, so rank indeed hath privilege. Yet, for thousands of years, a poor man would ne'er be heard. Now at least he may speak. Pray he speak well, if he is in the right. And that the gentleman will show him mercy."

What gets attention?

"Effectiveness of assertion!"

The value and uses of money?

"No character, in our plays, lacks sufficient means to survive. Money doth beget information, reward a service or a servant. 'Tis meet to have gold to travel painlessly or provide dowry. Greed is a sign of corruption. Our favorite money? 'Tis called a Sovereign."

> *"'Twas God, the word that spake it,*
> *He took the Bread and brake it;*
> *And what the word did make it,*
> *That I believe, and take it."*
> ELIZABETH I

What is the place of God and the church in life?

"We believe in God and pray each day. He is not to be questioned. His servants are. Pope and Church of England, Catholics and Protestants forever arguing doctrine! Enough!!"

What kind of humor dominates?

"Laughter is our defiance of war, plague, age, and oppression. Laughter bursts forth as raucous, hearty, joyous release. During our most solemn event, some detail will go wrong and provoke laughter. Later we may well recall that moment as the best! We do love puns and language tricks, but love what thou call'st a 'groaner' as much as more elevated and ironic turns of phrase. We take not ourselves too serious."

How is fear defined?

"The greatest fear is desperate silence. We wear our hearts, not on our sleeve alone, but in our words. Our greatest *shared* fear is Chaos, which can bring down the whole of creation. We fear God, the Devil, evil spirits, the wrath of our Monarch and lesser leaders. We fear disease, famine, and death. We no longer fear the Spanish.

> *"Whether I am doomed to live or die,*
> *I can do both like a prince."*
> JOHN WEBSTER

Fear, when the moment comes, gives a man the chance to prove his mettle."

Structure

Order exists. Humans must needs find it.

Who rules and who follows?
"Each species hath a natural leader. For us it 'tis Elizabeth, for the angels God, for animals the lion, birds the eagle, trees the oak, and down through the great chain of being, to plants and basest minerals. Each of us doth know where we stand 'twixt Elizabeth and scullery maid. The body human has three monarchs: liver, heart, and brain. The world is made up of four ruling elements: earth, water, air, and fire. Each class excels all others in some single way. E'en the lowly stone hath the glory t'exceed the rest in strength and durability. The chain looks thus, with each link:

1. God—perfection
2. Angels/ether—pure understanding
3. Stars—fortune
4. Elements—being
5. Man–feeling and understanding
6. Animals—sensation
7. Plants—growth
8. Metals—durability.

Man is in the middle, without perfection or durability, but central to the chain. His position is most difficult *and* most full of recompense. Our men be led by a woman, and we believe in the Divine Right of Kings:

Justice runs quick and brutal. Executions are widely viewed and worthily bethought as reminders of consequence! Nobles be beheaded, low-class felons hung."

> *"I have the body of a weak and feeble woman, but I have the heart and stomach of a king, and of a king of England too."*
> ELIZABETH I

What is the pattern of daily life and family?
"Our country's women live much freer than those of Europe. Visitors are shocked that they may kiss our wives and daughters in friendship and find it antic that 'tis not customary t'invite a man to dine without also inviting his wife. Women may go out (in groups) unescorted, yea, e'en to public ale houses. Widows assume full ownership and control of property. Some run businesses. Women exist as legal equal of men betimes, 'til they marry. At that time they become property."

How is etiquette set? How flexible?
"True spirit of courtesy exceeds how a man stands or holds his knife. We ask ourselves if the behavior was honorable, not if it broke some rule."

And education?

"For the first time, half our population is literate! School hours are long, with arduous copying major means for learning. Boarding schools are new, teaching Latin, English grammar, music, logic, rhetoric, geography, history, mythology, Hebrew, Greek, Italian, French, penmanship, reading aloud, and drawing. Queen Elizabeth is master of all of these, yea and Spanish and astronomy besides! Her work with tutor, Roger Ascham, did begin when she was three and she is superior to most men in learning."

> *"There is not such whetstone, to sharpen a good wit and encourage a will to learning as is praise."*
> ROGER ASCHAM

What professions dominate?

"'Tis an exacting office being lord or lady, with huge staff to lead and lands to tend. Work doth involve foreign service, collecting of debts, leasing of lands, and military obligations. Below nobility is merchant class, working class (artisans, shopkeepers, actors) and underclass (servants, laborers, shepherds, vagabonds). The Black Death moved us from farming to shearing sheep, where one man can the fill the space of twenty if he but tend flocks instead of crops."

Beauty

Where'er light shines is beauty to be found.

What is the look most aspired to?

"Fair is favored over dark. Some heroes fall in love with raven-haired beauties, but ask themselves 'Wherefore?'. Both sexes wish to deport selves tall. Long legs and necks are envied. Men must have strong, well-formed legs."

Who are the contemporary ideals?

"The Queen do be much envied for her slim waist, kept all these years. Hair most coveted is red or blonde curls. Ye should by now know why. 'Twill ne'er hang from a woman's head nor touch her face; but swept up and decorated. Wenches' faces strive for fair, pale, smooth skin, high forehead, widow's peak, red lips, and startling, lively eyes. Within the volume of fabric worn, graceful hands and feet gain much attention when they emerge. Perchance because we see so little, we cherish each glance. Men's hosed legs be the only full appendage exposed."

What part does fitness play in attractiveness?

"We live active, dancing and riding for hours on end, practicing with spirit to excel at both. In our parlance the word 'proper', by the by, as in 'he will make a proper man', doth note the physical attributes of the man, not his manners. Elizabeth exercises each morning by dancing six to seven of our most strenuous dances, The Galliard."

Which colors and shapes are favored?
"Splendor is beloved—gold, black, white, and silver—heavily bejeweled. Dark silks and velvets reflect and absorb light, like the lining of a jewel box. Brighter colors flash through slashed openings or from attached precious stones. 'Tis not meet to look less than thou art. The new looking glasses (of polished metal) are in high favor."

Is nature altered in order to create beauty?
"Belike the issue can best be summed up by this exchange 'tween Viola and Olivia in *Twelfth Night*. Olivia unveils herself and, quoth she, 'Tis not well done?' Viola doth reply 'Excellently done, if God did all.' Olivia, after a moment of recovery from this sly retort, and the inevitable laugh it doth provoke from the audience, assures her it is natural and, quoth she, 'will endure wind and weather.' Often, in truth, 'tis excellently well done, but 'twill not endure wind and weather."

How is taste defined and what artistic expression is favored?
"Fie on thy word 'taste', Bartonio. Nothing is deemed vulgar, crude, or unseemly, if it hath great accomplishment. By this hand, all should'st be able to write a sonnet, sing a madrigal, play a lute, declare a position, and ride a horse. Those with imagination move beyond these trifles. A pox on any who fool who would do less!"

Sex

> In life's great banquet, sex may be any course,
> In sooth, it may perchance replace the meal.

How significant a part of the collective consciousness is sex?
"Only a worthy quest will replace lewd bawdry in our lives. Mating is openly talked and joked about. E'en our young virgins do oft' engage in ribald repartee."

> *"True love is a durable*
> *fire,*
> *In the mind ever*
> *burning,*
> *Never sick, never old,*
> *never dead,*
> *From itself never*
> *turning."*
> SIR WALTER
> RALEIGH

What is considered a turn-on and turn-off?
"Men learn to swagger and display with grace and must be quick of wit and strong of body. A woman may be soft of demeanor, but sharp of mind, quick of tongue, lively of spirit, and graceful of movement. Both must appear modest *and* assertive. The shrinking violet hath no place in our garden."

What is the courtship/seduction ritual?
"Each man doth court the Queen at all times. Thus, the 'courting' of the mistress of any manor is accepted ritual. Serenading, music, poetry, flowers, tokens, missives, and passionate declarations abound. There is no tactic ye employ now, in a pinch, that we do not employ as a matter of course. Speak foreign languages to woo thy beloved, and perfumed sheets may keep her in thy bed, a massive, carved, oak, costly,

elaborately furnished, often canopied, embroidered masterwork. 'Tis passed on to future generations or friends, *not* to one's spouse. Yet, a patch of grass will do as well. A merry chase is good sport, and consummation devoutly to be wished."

How much tolerance is there for infidelity?
"Our plays talk of horns, meaning cuckolds. We jest about unfaithfulness and believe if a man does not 'serve' his woman well, she may leave him with horns on his head, growing longer at each of her indiscretions. Infidelity between a man and woman, each married to others, be not likely. Servants be more in danger than the lady or lord of the manor nearby. If thy mate do tire of thee, watch more for poison in thy cup or help falling down the stair, than for divorce court."

Is there any suppression of sexuality?
"We have such tolerance for excess and appetite that few would judge another as desiring too much. We call our brothels 'stews'."

Recreation

Each triumph doth deserve a celebration.

What is most people's idea of fun?
"At a stroke, merriment can transport an ordinary moment into nimble playfulness, word game, wit, delightful tune, or joke reverberating in the public square. 'Fun' (as thou call'st it, a tiny word for such bountiful pleasure) doth await 'round every corner, eager for discovery. Every person plays an instrument, singing rounds is common family pastime, and dancing so honored that Elizabeth hath promoted courtiers for no other deed save brilliant leaps and turns."

What would be an ideal social occasion?
"Rejoicing o'er a recent victory—our ships at sea, our wits at court, or our swains at wooing—is cause for celebration. A nuptial? 'Tis e'en greater cause! We celebrate many festivals you do not—The Vigil of St John the Baptist, Midsummer's Eve, Harvest, Lord of Misrule, Twelfth Night, Feast of the Virgin, Shrove Tuesday, St George's Day, Tournament Day, and May Day. And, Lord warrant us, we *create* occasion for more! The Puritans do hate it when we dance around the maypole. Fie on them."

"Best while you have it use your breath, There is no drinking after death."
JOHN FLETCHER

Are you doers or watchers?
"We devour life. The hunt (deer and hare) is sport of kings, alas, of outlaws and poachers as well. Hyde Park is still wild enough for Elizabeth to hunt therein. Though every boy over age seven must, by law, be taught how to shoot bow and arrow, 'tis now practiced for pure pleasure. Hitting of bullseye with arrow or tongue—we like it well. We love to watch blood shed—

cockfighting, baiting (divers dogs let loose on a chained bear, bull, or badger), or public executions (hangings, beheadings, and burnings). Thou might'st spot thirty heads o'er the bridge on the way to the theatre and amuse thyself attempting to identify them! Baitings cost a penny. Hangings are free."

"When the bad bleed, then is the tragedy good."
CYRIL TOURNER

"Elizabeth composes music and verse and plays the virginal. Sit and wait for *others* to entertain her? Fie! 'Twould not do for our good Bess! Since 'tis not thought seemly for nobility to sign their name and be credited, all do thus for pure joy, without thought of honor."

What are common, shared pastimes?
"Lord warrant us! Outdoors there be donkey and horse racing, cudgeling, wrestling, tennis, eating contests, sack and wheelbarrow races, lawn bowling, boxing, greased pig chases, and silly sports, such as grinning through a horse collar—with funniest grin winning.

Football is violent by your standards. We bother not with team number limits, lines, or penalized fouls. In fact, it sufficeth us to forego most rules altogether. Entire villages and districts may challenge each other. If the Spanish watched us play football, they would ne'er e'en have considered war. Falconry is high sport among the gentry, and pets are loved. Our queen has six lions, one lioness, one wolf, one tiger and e'en a porcupine. Tamer mortals have tamer creatures.

"Why what an ass thou! Dost thou not know a play cannot be without a clown?"
BEN JONSON

Inside, we play bells, board games, dice, and cards. Sewing (crewel, lace, tapestry, appliqué, quilting, braid, and embroidery) hath reached undreamed of heights. Yet list, the most loved pastime of all, I warrant thee, is going to the theatre! Nie unto twenty thousand, or one-tenth of the population, attending public performance and a like number private ones."

What is food and its function?
"Potatoes (from Raleigh's American expedition), figs, apricots, and currants newly visit our gardens. At 11 a.m. we devour hot food—beef, mutton, lamb, veal, hare, eel, salmon, duck, rabbit, pheasant, pigeon, rook, pig, turkey, quail, partridge, woodcock, capon, seagull, blackbird, lark, peacock, meat pies, sausages, breads, butter, cheese, boiled vegetables, fruits, and puddings served on pewter or silver service. Forks are still rare. Jupiter! Was not piercing the animal once, when we killed it, enough?! A vexation to keep stabbing it say I!"

And beverages?
"Wine and sack are now oft' imported, but ale houses exist on every corner, and beer is the true beverage of our people. By my troth, I have a great thirst. Methinks this

'interview' as you call it, sufficient reason for celebration. Invite thy friends and we shall feast! Let all who come ask away! We shall dine and dance and 'interview' 'til the lark beckons the dawn! We shall . . . Ah, no, I cannot. I hear my muse calling me. Forgive me friend. I must return to my time and seek my destiny. I will leave some jottings to assist thee in the rest, Bartonio! Myself must write a sonnet for my beloved and deliver it myself upon the moors. Fare thee well. Rest you merry. I go!" (*exit in smoke*)

END OF INTERVIEW

SIGHT

As we do march forth, all the world takes note.

Our most dazzling rock star could be eclipsed by a resplendent Elizabethan lord or lady making an entrance, both in personal adornment and sense of self. Only a few comedies are likely to be costumed in authentic Elizabethan garb, because the extravagant padding, called "bombast," makes actors resemble hockey players. Those elements most chosen in production, usually with modifications, are:

MEN

Head—Hair is collar length, with trimmed beard and moustache for mature men, and young bucks clean-shaven. Hats, worn inside, are flat and usually round, with notched brims. A stiff ruff frames the throat.

Torso—A white, oversized shirt, shirred at the neck and wrists, may be worn under a jerkin or sleeveless vest. A doublet may top a waistcoat. The final touch is the

codpiece, which begins innocently as a practical triangle to fill the crotch area between the tops of hose, tied to the waist, by points. Codpieces develop, however into ostentatious, extravagant works of art, often stuffed, sometimes slashed, bejeweled and bedecked.

Over garments—An overcoat is possible, longer for older characters, with a huge, often fur collar. Capes of various kinds, long, short, draped or stiff, may be employed. Usually, they are full circles and often hung over one shoulder. A soldier often wears one small piece of his armor to remind others of his profession.

Feet—Shoes are may be without heels and soft leather or velvet. Boots are loose enough to turn down or reach to the upper leg, held by straps to the doublet.

WOMEN

Head—Hair moves from middle part and heart-shaped cap, early in the time, to curled, ribbonned, plumed, and jeweled, at the end. Wigs are popular. Ruffs, the major distinguishing feature of the period, move from one inch to nine. Wrist ruffs often accompany.

Torso—A chemise with low bodice, a petticoat or kirtle stretched tightly over stays and hoops. A farthingale (hooped petticoat supporting the shape of the skirt), basquine (corset to shape the bodice), and a stomacher may be among the encumbrances. Corsets are called "bodies," later to become "bodice." Some are made of steel! An over-skirt–under-skirt combination is likely. The over-gown moves from bell shaped early in the period to the enormous farthingale look later. Sleeve treatment changes from wide openings pulled back at the elbows (angel wings) to puffed leg o'muttons.

Feet—Soft slippers are gradually replaced by heels to add stature.

Pieces of clothing may be tied together with laces called points. Earrings, brooches, chains, and rings are favored jewelry for both sexes, the male wearing one earring, often a pear-shaped pearl drop. All four fingers and thumbs may be ringed. Anyone might carry a flat fan, decorative money pouch, or a pomander (an orange or apple stuffed with clove) to keep "bad aires" away. These items may hang from the waist. Gloves are works of art, with gauntlet cuffs heavily embroidered, often bejeweled and fringed, in leather of many possible colors. They are also favored gifts.

Elizabethan productions that are not moved forward in time are likely to move back because the look is more graceful to present day audiences. Gothic, High Renaissance and Tudor are popular period choices.

MOVEMENT AND CONTACT

An enormous sense of self and bulk of fabric contribute to assertive, direct, and commanding moves. Anything inconsequential would be altogether lost across the room and fail to suit the spirit of the times. The following bow and curtsy are often used in production. They bridge the gap of several centuries.

Men's bows

Step forward on the left foot and lift the torso high as a signal of the bow about to take place. Keeping the left leg extended and relatively straight in front, "sit" on the bending right leg (which has formed a 45 degree angle), keeping the torso lifted until the sit is completed. Your eyes are on the person to whom you are bowing. At the last minute, the eyes dip down, and depending on the amount of obeisance being paid, the head, upper torso, or more may be bowed inward. Return the upper body eyes first, then move to a standing position. The temptation will be to incline upper body too early and too far and to stick your behind out behind you. For much of the bow, you appear in upper body, as if you are on horseback. The hand crossing the body may be used to remove and replace the hat during this maneuver. The other hand may guide the sword at your side, up and back, so that it does not scrape the floor. The free hand may also indulge in a salute or personal flourish of some kind.

Women's curtsy

Hold the upper body as above, the legs doing all of the work until the curtsy is nearly complete. The initial step forward is followed by the right leg moving close behind and beneath the left. The left will be bent in a kneeling position when the curtsy is completed, with the right supporting the body weight, either just beneath the left or with the right knee touching the floor. The arms may begin facing inward and move up and out like wings as the curtsy is completed, or may remain in, with palms also facing together. Hand moves may be personalized.

Bows and curtsies range from deep and close to the floor when honoring Herself, to slight (with only the smallest tilt of the head and eyes quickly gazing downward) in a perfunctory acknowledgment of an equal, or to someone of whom you are suspicious and with whom you wish to lose eye contact only momentarily.

Hand kissing

The woman offers her hand, palm facing downward, with a rounded but extended arm. The man takes it lightly in his own. He kneels very slightly with his eyes locked on hers. Then he lifts the hand to his lips and only looks down at the instant of hand–lip contact, then reversing the movement exactly. The temptation will be to lean too far in and dive for the hand, instead of lifting it to you, or to spend too much time looking at the hand, not enough into the eyes of the lady.

Reverence

Kissing one's own hand (or pretending to with an air kiss) and extending to another is a highly respectful tribute or greeting, always done at the start and end of a dance, but possible at countless other moments. The *top* of the palm is kissed, and flourishes may be added.

SOUND

This Mother tongue resounds second to none.

The authentic sound of the period is a guttural, full, earthy dialect, with great weight placed on consonants, including rolled, hard r's and intensely colored vowels, with pitch often changing on the vowel. It sounds like a thick Scottish brogue mixed with American Appalachian. It bears *no* resemblance to contemporary, upper-class British ("received" or "Oxfordian") speech. It is highly expressive. Words are both caressed and punched.

Want to sound like a real Elizabethan? Here are the basics to try with a speech. Remember to employ hard consonants and high energy.

1. Want rhymes with pant (water—hatter), aw for aa.
2. Take rhymes with tek (make—mek, table—teble); draw it out.
3. Head—haid, dead—daid, bread—braid.
4. I—uh-ee (my—muh-ee, die—duh-ee, fly—fluh-ee), not oi.
5. Mercy—maircy, with very hard r.
6. Fair—fat a and uh-ee sound, so faa-er.
7. Neither—nayther.
8. Day—long i and short a—daa-ee.
9. Lord—loord, word—woord, come—coom.
10. Down—uh-oo duh-oon, house—huh-oos.
11. Cup—coop, up—oop, cut—coot.
12. Love—luv.

> *"A player adds grace to the poet's labours: for what in the poet is but ditty, in him is both ditty and music."*
> JOHN WEBSTER

Take a speech you are working on, or one from Chapter 3 (pp. 44–7), transcribe it and read it aloud with the above sounds. Remember the force and relish when returning to standard speech and let it help you exorcise once and for all any attempt to sound high tone.

ELIZABETHAN LANGUAGE GUIDE

Here are examples from Shakespeare and his contemporaries:

(pp. 44–7)

Table 5.1

Forms of address	*Respect*		
	My lord (My lady)	Friend	Young gentleman (Fair lady)
	Reverend sir (madam)	Most worthy sir (madam)	Learned, honored . . .
	Gracious . . .	Lad or youth	Gentles

Table 5.1

Forms of address
continued . . .

Honor

Your grace	My liege	Dear sovereign
Your worship	My commander	Great King (Queen)
Most royal majesty	Your highness	Most honored lord

Familiarity

Wench	Fellow	Kinsman
Mate	Sweet	Cousin or Coz

Disdain

Fool	Clown	Dunce
Sot	Wretch	Wretched One
Strumpet	Harlot	Hag
Whoreson, Villain	Foul devil	Viper
Minion	Idle creature	Dissembler
Knave	Rogue	Pedant

Table 5.2

Greetings

What ho?	Holla!	Hark!
I pray you . . .	Save you!	How now?
Well met	Happily met	Well o'erta'en
How dost thou?	Good morrow	Good day
Salutations	Happiness	Hail
Good day	Good even	Gooden
Good dawning	Good time of day	God save you
I bid you welcome	Joy and comfort	Greetings to you

Table 5.3

Good-byes

Farewell	Fare thee well	Peace be with you
Rest you merry	Give you good night	May we meet again
I take leave	I have done	I will anon
We will haste us away	Presently away	I go from hence
We will here part	I go	I will hie
To . . . will I	I am resolved	I must attend
Let us thither	Let us after	Come ho
Follow me thence	Let us remove	Let us not lack thy company

Table 5.4

Dismissals		
Be gone	Get thee gone	Away
Go thy ways	Remove thyself	Dispatch
Depart	Tarry not	No longer stay
I alone will stay	You have leave	I acquit thee
I weary of you	Get thee from my sight	Go tread the path that thou shalt ne'er return

Table 5.5

Commands

Action

Fetch him hither	Call her hence	Hie thee hither
Bear them thence	Call them forth	Give him tending
Attend him, her, them	Lend thy hand	Proceed
Approach	Let him approach	Stand forth
Bid them welcome	Prove it so	Apply thyself to our intent
Look to't	Provide yourself	I charge thee speak

Pause

Peace	Stir not	Relent
Forbear	Pause awhile	Cease
No more	Disturb me not	Leave . . . ing so
Speak not	Vex not	Press me not
Mend your speech	Mark me	Mark you that
Hear me	Give me audience	A word
Give us leave	Stay your thanks	Tarry
Behold	Repair thy wit	Await

Mood

Be of good cheer	Be merry	Live in hope

Table 5.6

Disagreement		
'Tis not so	A false conclusion	I think not so
Thou'rt mad to say it	Thou liest	I do defy thee
Believe not all	'Tis to be doubted	I know not that
That follows not	It cannot be	'Tis none of mine
Never	Talk not so	Not a whit
I do protest	Go to	Fie, fie
That is no matter	I care not	I will none
You do mistake your business	'Twould not do	Not a whit
I am for no more	I'll no more	Tempt me not
No, nor is it meet	Never so	Nay

Table 5.7

Agreement

Praise

Fairly spoke	Nobly spoken	Well said
Well urged	Worthily bethought	Roundly replied
Excellent!	A nimble wit	Thou hast hit it
I do commend thy choice	'Tis most credible	Amen

Assent

Perchance	Most like	'Tis thus
We are agreed thus	'Tis so then	I think it so
It likes me well	It pleaseth me	It shall suffice me
I am resolved	I embrace it	Yea, at all points
We judge no less	I doubt not that	Yea, in good faith
My physic says aye	I believe thee	'Tis probable
'Tis as thou sayest	That ever holds	I think it well
So shall I	I shall see it done	So be it
I am for you	Ay, marry	Amen

Table 5.8

Questions

Who

Who calls?	Who's within?	Who servest thou?
What's he comes here?	Of what parentage art thou?	Who hath done this?
What art thou?	Of what personage?	From whom come thou?

What

What cheer?	What sport tonight?	What is thy passion?
What is your will?	What find I here?	What would you?
What news?	What wilt thou do?	What make you here?
What means this?	What sayest thou?	Thy request?

Why

Why so?	Wherefore?	How follows that?
Why . . . you so?	Where's your argument?	Why dost thou?
Thy cause?	Thy reason?	Thy purpose?

Where

Where were you bred?	Whence camest thou?	Whither shall we go?
Whither bound?	What place is this?	Upon what ground stand we?

Table 5.8

Questions
continued . . .

How

| How fare you? | How know you? | How camest thou hither? |
| How is't with you? | How now? | How say you? |

Others

Wilt come?	Dost call?	Art thou resolved?
Shall'st go . . .?	Did'st note?	Is't come to this?
Dost thou hear?	Must it be so?	Say you so?

Table 5.9

Oaths

Alas!	Alack!	Jove!
Jupiter!	Zounds!	Cupid have mercy!
Od's my life!	Gramercy!	Woe the while!
Vexations!	Lord warrant us!	O ye gods!
Christ's mother!	A god's name!	A pox on you!

Table 5.9

Parentheses

As I do live,	As I bethink me,	Whilst we breathe,
In faith,	By my troth,	By mine honor,
I warrant you,	I'll stand to't,	In good earnest,
If there by truth in sight,	By this hand,	By yonder . . .,
If fortune please,	Sirrah,	In sooth,
Albeit,	Marry sir,	So please you,

Elizabethan lingo

Mr—Master

Ms—Mistress

Female(familiar but not at all insulting)—Wench

Ladies and Gentlemen—Gentles

Please—Prithee or Pray

No kidding or really—Forsooth

Excuse me—Pardon or Cry you mercy

Before—Ere

Wow—Marry

Maybe—Belike

Various or all different—Divers

Later—Anon

Nag, rag, scold—Chide

Bizarre or crazy—Antic

I said—Quoth I

She said—Quoth she

You (intimate) as sentence subject—Thou

You(intimate) as object—Thee

Your (intimate) before consonant—Thy

Your (intimate before vowel)—Thine (same with my and mine)

Thou and you in plural—Ye

Insult addresses comparable to Buddy, Pal, or Buster to a perfect stranger—Sirrah or Fellow

MUSIC AND DANCE

Every well-educated person in this period can sight-read music, often printed on a grand scale so several singers may read it at once. Minstrels are common at court and in the countryside. Extraordinary music pervades daily life, from glorious, sacred madrigals to bawdy tavern rounds. Composers work in all forms.

"Your eyes, your mien, your tongue declare, That you are music every where."
HENRY PURCELL

The most popular forms of song are the Ayre—composed for single voice, often self-accompanied by lute or viol—and the Madrigal—a complicated piece for two to eight voices, sung a cappella, often around a table, as part of a social function. Also popular are the consort or chamber music, and contrapuntal, polyphonic, and homophonic compositions.

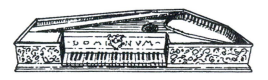

Popular instruments include the recorder (soprano, alto, tenor, and bass), a vertical flute, lute (small, pear-shaped harp with six to thirteen strings, some doubled),

virginal (a small harpsichord—often played by "virgins," including You Know Who), viol (forerunner of the violin, held in the crook of the arm instead of under the chin as now), cornetto (loud processional instrument, with clarinet body and trumpet mouthpiece), cithern, pandore, mandolin (forerunners of the guitar, with long neck and hollow sounding boxes), sackbut (forerunner of trombone), drum, tambourine, harp, and organ. In the theatre, the most popular musical choice is the broken consort, with wind and string instruments mixing tone colors for expressive, exciting, and moody effects.

Dancing moves from a loosely organized activity on the village green to an art practiced at court under tutelage of experts. Popular slow dances include processionals such as the basse (French promenade led by musicians), pavanne (grave and majestic dance) and alemdance (stately German dance moving from a pronounced goose step to a lighter, more delicate, triple-time step). Faster dances include la volta (risqué provincial couple dance, with men thrusting women into the air), corranto (Italian, faster dance, light and lively, low to the ground), galliard (most representative of the Elizabethan spirit, with leaps and plies in the air) and canaries (challenge dances, with each sex stomping and outdoing the other). Ring and round dances, such as the bralle, the jig, and morris dances, complete this rich tapestry of dance, from dignified to bawdy.

Dance is symbolic of the universe. Leaps and turns represent the cosmos, circles the continued passage of the globe and circling of the sun. Because it is believed that the sun moves clockwise, each dance begins on the left foot, and circles move to the left. Only witches "go round the wrong way," dancing in covens.

KEYS TO THE WORLD

IMAGES

When the word Elizabethan comes to mind, contradictory and lively images emerge:

"When the iron is hot, strike"
JOHN HEYWOOD

virile men, graceful women
men and women—dignified, hearty, robust, expansive, energetic, intimidating, bold, formal and informal, bawdy, flirtatious, sensual, powerful, fluid, balanced, and vigorous!
life as cause for celebration
violence as daily and inevitable
heavy perfume, sauces, fabric, rich, dense, voluptuous sensations

Figure 5.1

Hatfield House and gardens © Skyscan/ Corbis

blood and guts, thunder and lightning
exquisite, quiet dawns after turbulent nights
famous theatres: Rose, Swan, Globe, and Fortune
vocal music with echoes, alternations, and oppositions
Machiavelli's *The Prince*
Leonardo Da Vinci's pageant costume designs—Raphael's Vatican frescos—
Hatfield House—Benvenuto Cellini's *Saltcellar of Francis I*
furniture designs of Giovanni Nossemi
madrigals of William Byrd, Thomas Morley, Thomas Tompkins, Thomas
Weelkes, and Orlando Gibbons—Harpsichord compositions of Byrd and Morley
John Dowland's exquisite creations for the lute
individuality, virtuosity, zest, adventure

SOCIAL SUCCESS AND SUICIDE

Capacity to praise is so vital to simple survival that there is considerable competition
for the Ultimate Compliment:

"The heavens such grace doth lend thee, that thine eyes can cure the blind."

This line wins because the connection between the recipient and heaven also gives the recipient the power to perform miracles, with *very little effort*. In the devastating war of words, the Ultimate Insult might be:

"In his sleep he does little harm, save to his bedclothes about him."

The insult demolishes more than an overtly venomous, vituperative remark, because the recipient is regarded as inconsequential and silly, not even worth addressing directly. The subject probably drools and wets the bed. It is a throw-away, tossed en route to more significant altercations.

All aspire to excel at praise and verbal warfare. Here is a collection of lowest insults and highest praise from an age when everyone is expected to master both:

Insults

You cream faced loon

You bloody, bawdy villain

You whoreson, clap-eared knave

You remorseless, trecherous, lecherous kindless villain

You decrepid wrangling miser, you base ignoble wretch

You dwarf, you minimous

You brawling, blasphemous, uncharitable dog

You gross lout, you mindless slave

You caterpiller of the commonwealth, you politician

You worshiper of idiots

You dull, unfeeling barren ignorance

You wimpering, whoremaster fool

You mangled work of nature, you scurvy knave

You ignorant, long-tongued babbling gossip

You old withered crab tree

You irksome, brawling scolding pestilence

You base, vile thing, you petty scrap

You filching, pilfering snatcher

You injurious, tedius wasp

You common gamester to the camp

You country copulative

You tiresome, wrangling pedant

You fawning greyhound, you petty trafficker

You base, fawning spaniel

You infectious pestilence

You untutored churl

You son and heir of a mongrel bitch

You smiling, smooth detested parasite

You lunatic, lean-witted fool

You painted maypole

You thing of no bowels

You silly, sanctimonious ape of form

You low-spirited swain, you base minnow

You unlettered small-knowing soul, you shallow vassal

You rank weed, ready to be rooted out

You puffed and reckless libertine

You lascivious, fat-kidneyed rascal

You ugly, venomous toad

You foul defacer of god's handiwork

You tainted harlot, crammed with wickedness

You living dead man

You dull and muddy mettled rascal

You impudent, tattered prodigal

You contaminated, base and misbegotten sot

You close contriver of all harms

You cold porridge

You botcher's apprentice

You base, ignoble wretch

You juggler, you canker blossom, you theif of love

You puppet

Praise

Age cannot wither thee nor custom stale thy infinite variety.

Thou dost teach the torches to burn bright.

Thy beauty's majesty confounds the tongue and makes the senses rough.

Thou art far fairer than any tongue can name thee.

The all-seeing sun ne'er saw thy match since first the world begun.

To thine honors and thy valiant parts, I both my soul and fortunes consecrate.

Nothing ill can dwell in such a temple as thou art.

Thou hast the courtier's eye, the scholar's tongue, the soldier's sword.

Thou art as wise as thou art beautiful, as strong as thou art kind.

Thou walkest in eternal grace and with each step thy tread doth bless the ground beneath.

I gaze upon thee, adoringly, as the moon upon the water.

Thou mak'st each coming hour o'erflow with joy, each minute full of wonder.

Thou art a lion that I am proud to hunt.

If thou wilt not love me, I will not love myself.

My love for thee is dearer than eyesight, space or liberty.

Thou art as wise as thou art fair and true.

My wild heart could'st be tamed to thy loving hand.

The instant I first saw thee did my heart fly to thy service.

The four winds blow in from every coast renowned suitors, all vying for thy hand.

Thy hand is fair, yea whiter than the paper it writ on.

I bow to thee as a true subject to a splendid new-crowned monarch.

For you I would be trebled twenty times myself, a thousand times more fair, ten thousand times more rich.

I am giddy at the expectation of thy touch. Anticipation whirls me round and doth enchant my sense.

The silver moon shines not half so bright as doth thy face in giving light.

No book provides a study of such excellence, as doth the beauty of thy face.

Thine eyes spark the Promethean fire and nourish all the world.

To serve thee doth make labor pleasure and turns means tasks into noble delight.

Thou art perfect and peerless, created out of every other creature's best.

'Tis fresh morning with me when thou art by at night.

I might call thee a thing divine, for nothing in nature I ever saw so noble.

Except I be with thee, love, in the night, there is no music in the nightingale.

At the alter of thy beauty, I sacrifice my tears, my sighs, my heart.

Thy life is as tender to me as my own soul.

When my eyes did see thee first, I thought thou purg'd the air of pestilence.

Mine ear is much enamor'd of thy throat, so is mine eye enthrall'd to thy shape.

I'll pluck the wings from painted butterflies,
    to fan the moonbeams from thy sleeping eyes.

Each act of thine is crowned in present deeds
    so that, my love, all of your acts are queens.

Had I force and knowledge more than was ever man's, I would not prize them, without thy love.

Were I crown'd the most imperial monarch, I would not prize my crown above thy love.

Two of the fairest stars in all the heaven, having some business, do entreat thine eyes to twinkle in their spheres til they return.

Come what sorrow can, it cannot countervail the exhange of joy
    that one short minute gives me in thy sight.

To thine honors and thy valiant parts,
    I do my soul and fortunes consecrate.

More welcome are ye to my fortunes than my are fortunes to me. I give up all to have thy company.

I will live in thy heart, die in thy lap, and be buried in thy eyes.

Here comes my love, now heaven walks on earth.

O, thou that dost inhabit in my breast,
    Leave not my mansion so long tenantless.
    Repair me with thy presence.

My thoughts do harbor with thee nightly.
    Oh, could their master (mistress) come and go as lightly.

When I do look on thy perfections
    I lose all reason and I am struck blind.

Did my love til now? Forswear it sight.
    For I ne'er saw true beauty till this night.

The heavens such grace doth lend thee
    that thine eyes doth cure the blind.

To be successful, you must:

1. Excel in all Renaissance virtues: scholar, soldier, poet, lover.
2. Make music and verse at a moment's notice, with minimum provocation.
3. Master Italian, Spanish, and French fashion and philosophy while claiming to prefer plain English virtue.
4. Do all things fully, high or low, delicate or vulgar, angelic or animal. Go the distance.
5. Create a giant circular glow around yourself that gives off light. Make yourself resplendent any way you can.

Suicide may be committed if you:

1. Have an opportunity to speak, but fail to think of anything to say.
2. Get caught being false or feigning in your vows of love. Get caught breaking any promise.
3. Shrink away from a challenge. Be discovered as coward.
4. Fail to honor and reward excellence and loyalty in others.
5. Break your place in the cosmos and defy the stars.

Masking

Elizabethans do not wear theatrical masks except in a masque, a peculiar combination of mummery, pageant, and entertainment, which offers an excuse for court nobles (who are not otherwise supposed to "act") to dress in elaborate disguise and honor the monarch. The plot is always allegorical, with the queen, compared flatteringly to

Figure 5.2

A Masquerader on
Horseback, by Leonardo
da Vinci. The Royal
Collection © 2009
Her Majesty Queen
Elizabeth II

some classic mythological figure, triumphing over evil. The grand finale is a spectacle of choreographed dances, with Gloriana herself making occasional appearances. With the exception of great ladies, wearing a mask on a cord around their waists to protect white faces from the sun, a literal mask is not part of daily life.

Elizabethans value feelings, desire to share them, and hide them if not ready to express them *well*. Fear, cowardice, and indecision are most hidden because least rewarded. Social masks give identities to live up to. You portray yourself as *more* idealized and *less* vulnerable. The character always unmasks when alone with the audience in soliloquy.

Disguise is rampant. The five "breeches" heroines in Shakespeare (Rosalind, Viola, Imogene, Julia, and Portia) masquerade as boys (Ganymede, Cessario, Fidele, Sebastion, and Balthasar) for a portion of the play. The Navarrian lords in *Love's Labour's Lost* woo their ladies as Russians. Petruchio masks himself in boorish attire for his wedding. The masked Montague boys crash the Capulet ball in *Romeo and Juliet*. Beatrice uses her mask at the ball to talk about Benedick to his face. The mask of night is used for changing bed partners in *Measure for Measure* and *All's Well That Ends Well*. Edgar disguised himself as Poor Tom (in *Lear*) to keep from being killed. The Duke (in *Measure for Measure*) pretends to be a friar in order to examine up close the corruption in his city. Camouflage filters through the canon, where disguise is always for a good end. A character must don the new identity to save a life, uncover evidence, or fulfill destiny. Deception is a path toward freedom.

The production

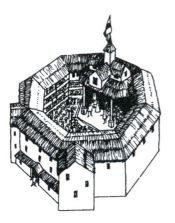

The reconstructed Globe Playhouse demonstrates a great open stage near 40 feet wide and 29 feet deep, with up to seven entrances and exits, where every corner of one's field of vision is filled with up to three thousand spectators, none farther away than 60 feet and some close enough to touch. A thrust stage and large audience rake come closest among modern spaces to the feel of the original.

Most productions are done on unit sets, with platforms, staircases, and ramps, but no attempt to suggest locale. Scenes overlap, with actors exiting while others enter. Lighting and music are used to smooth transitions, carve space, and shape time. Costuming is likely to be a period with a more relaxed and universal silhouette than Elizabethan. Costumes are often the single most important visual element in the production.

The perfect audience

The robust enthusiasm and active interaction of a modern rock concert or athletic event come closest to those passing between Elizabethan actor and public. The reverent, intimidated audience at some Shakespearean performances now is remote from the spirited original. Actors, though spared rude interruptions and distracting quarrels between groundlings, may miss the vitality of an audience that knows it is not in church.

Rehearse occasionally with interruptions from both ignorant louts and educated sceptics (played by other cast members, director, and staff) to get the feel of what could happen any moment. Think of tiers of people—some who've paid one penny to stand in the pit, others two pennies to sit in the galleries, and still others three for private boxes. You need passion and intensity to satisfy the groundlings, but must be noble and dignified enough for the private boxes. Imagine them all eating and drinking freely. Then consider that if you are not sufficiently involved, eloquent, *interesting* enough, you could be stopped. Or observers might turn to their own conversations. Or leave. Infuse the audience with boldness. Ask the questions in the soliloquies as if you really want an answer. Make them feel absolutely your best friend. They will reward you with energy and power, carrying you to new heights. Imagine listeners who virtually insist on electrifying action. Give it to them.

Figure 5.3

Interior of the Globe
Theatre, London
© PA Photos and/
Associated Photographers.
Used by permission

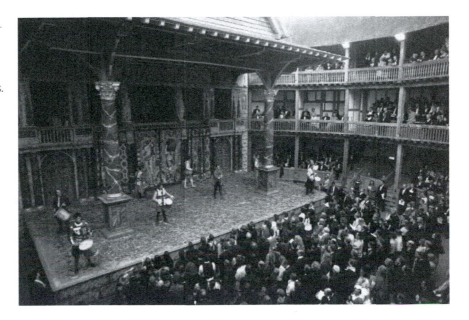

Figure 5.3

Interior of the Globe Theatre, London
© PA Photos and/ Associated Photographers. Used by permission

CONTEMPORARY PARALLELS

The early twenty-first century shares these conditions with the late sixteenth:

1. Music as a constant part of life, moving from background to foreground, but ever present, influencing and shaping events.
2. A great love of exploration and adventure, a genuine pioneer spirit, alert for new lands, planets or galaxies to discover, conquer and settle. Those who venture into unknown realms and return become heroes.
3. An understanding that basic body chemistry determines, to a remarkable degree, physical and mental health, that you are what you eat. For years we regarded the Elizabethan's body humours theory as one of their more quaint and naive. Now we know that fundamentally they were right.
4. Huge energy and expense expended in entertainment, in having a good time, an almost manic sense of creating (even working at) fun.
5. A plague, defying scientific knowledge and control, devastating a major portion of the population and creating unprecedented fear and paranoia.
6. Large cities, where the pulse beats faster and the action is, seen as center of life, but the beauty and peace of the country idealized. Constant turmoil over which we prefer and where we want to be.
7. Living comfortably with contradictions as science and high tech flourish along with astrology and spiritualism. Being at ease with both rational thought and superstition, looking in all directions to explain life, feeling no need to be the same all the time.

8. Self-knowledge seen as an important subject for study, and self-esteem as an important goal.
9. Belief in the individual, in assertiveness, spirit, and speaking out.
10. An explosion of information! Languages (English then, computer now) seem to have unlimited possibilities.

THE OPEN SCENE: Us and them

One way to embrace the Elizabethan Age is to experience an event from our world in their terms. The open scene is a common exercise in acting and directing classes. It stimulates imaginative subtext, since text is minimal. The lines below left can adapt to almost any situation, most obviously leaving home, substance abuse, or suicide, but myriad contexts are possible. In Elizabethan England, with magic, murder, royalty, and wonder in the air, possible situations for the lines below right compound even more.

Table 5.10

Contemporary Open scene	Shakespearean Open scene
"Oh"	"Alas"
"Yes."	"'Tis so."
"Why are you doing this?"	"Why dost thou this?
"It's the best thing."	"'Tis foremost among choices."
"You can't mean it."	"Thou cans't not speak from the heart."
"No, I'm serious."	"Nay, I am in earnest."
"Please."	"Prithee, note me."
"What?"	"Wherefore?"
"What does this mean?"	"What meaning has this?"
"Nothing."	"None."
"Listen."	"Hear me."
"No."	"Nay."
"So different"	"'Tis wondrous strange."
"Not really"	"Not in truth."
"Oh."	"So"
"You're good."	"Thou art good."
"Forget it."	"Think not on't."
What?"	"How now?"
"Go on."	"Proceed."
"I will."	"I shall."

Elizabethan language differs from ours, not just in word choice, but in the frequent choice of verse over prose:

Shakespearean open verse scene

"You're here I see. I had not thought to find you."
"I am intent to do the thing I must."

"Why do you feel that you must take this course?"
"It is the best that is now open to me."

"You cannot mean this truly in your heart."
"I mean it with my heart and my soul too."

"I ask of thee that thou wilt hear my words."
"What can'st thou say that I do not now know?"

"What meaning can this have to change our lives?"
"It means no more nor less than simply nothing."

"I do implore that thou wilt hear my plea."
"I do refuse because I am decided."

"This is most strange and unfamiliar."
"Not so in truth. It merely is the same."

"I see what is and that I must accept."
"You are as good as any human born."

"I do not wish for you to think on this."
'What shall, then, my friend, if not on this?"

"Go now and may God save you then from fright."
"I go and strong for I am in the right."

PLAYS AND PLAYWRIGHTS

Here are those scripts most likely to be produced. Almost any play by Shakespeare is more likely to enter your life than any single script by any other writer of the period. Do not discount his brothers, however. Some genuine thrills and chills exist in the rest of Elizabethan drama.

Beamont, Francis and John Fletcher	*The Knight of the Burning Pestle,* 1607
	The Maid's Tragedy, 1667
	The Two Noble Kinsmen, 1594
Dekker, Thomas	*The Shoemaker's Holiday,* 1599
Ford, John	*'Tis Pity She's a Whore,* 1625
Heywood, Thomas	*Woman Killed with Kindness,* 1603
Jonson, Ben	*The Alchemist,* 1610
	Bartholomew Fair, 1614
	Every Man in His Humour, 1598
	Volpone, 1605

Figure 5.4

A scene from *Volpone.* Used by permission of The Royal Shakespeare Theater Company, Washington, DC

Kyd, Thomas	*The Spanish Tragedy,* 1592
Marlowe, Christopher	*Doctor Faustus,* 1588
	Edward II, 1590
	The Jew of Malta, 1588
	Tamburlaine the Great, 1587
Middleton, Thomas	*The Changeling,* 1623

Shakespeare, William

All's Well That Ends Well, 1602–4
Antony and Cleopatra, 1605–6
As You Like It, 1599–1600
The Comedy of Errors, 1588–93
Coriolanus, 1607–8
Cymbeline, 1609–10
Hamlet, 1601–2
Henry IV, Part 1, 1597–8
Henry IV, Part 2, 1597–8
Henry V, 1598–9
Henry VI, Part 1, 1590–2
Henry VI, Part 2, 1590–2
Henry VI, Part 3, 1590–2
Henry VIII, 1612–13
Julius Caesar, 1599
King Lear, 1605–6
King John, 1596–7
Love's Labour's Lost, 1588–94
Macbeth, 1605–6
Measure for Measure, 1604
The Merchant of Venice, 1596–7
The Merry Wives of Windsor 1597–1601
A Midsummer Night's Dream, 1594–6
Much Ado About Nothing, 1598–1600
Othello, 1603–4
Pericles, 1608
Richard II, 1595
Richard III, 1592–3
Romeo and Juliet, 1594–6
The Taming of the Shrew,
    1593–4
The Tempest, 1611
Timon of Athens, 1605–8
Titus Andronicus, 1592–4
Troilus and Cressida,
    1601–2
Twelfth Night, 1599–1600
Two Gentlemen of Verona, 1593–5
The Winter's Tale, 1610–11

Webster, John

The Duchess of Malfi, 1612
The White Devil, 1608

Tourneur, Cyril

The Revenger's Tragedy, 1607

ELIZABETHAN SCENES

The Changeling

BEATRICE, DE FLORES

A game of sexual obsession is played between the beautiful Beatrice and her disfigured servant.

Doctor Faustus

FAUSTUS, MEPHISTOPHELES

As one of his experiments with magic, Faustus enters a dark grove where he conjures up a devil dressed like a friar.

The Duchess of Malfi

DUCHESS, ANTONIO

In spite of her brothers' warnings, the widowed Duchess decides to remarry and chooses her humble secretary.

DUCHESS, BOSOLA

Hired by her wicked brothers, Bosola brings more terror to the Duchess than she had imagined possible.

Edward II

EDWARD, ISABELLA

The King rejects his queen in favor of his "favorite," Gaveston.

The Jew of Malta

BARABAD, ABIGAIL, ITHAMORE

Not even the innocent love of his daughter can stop the ruthless ambition of unscrupulous Barabad.

The Maid's Tragedy

EVADNE, KING

Forced to become the king's mistress, even in the presence of her own husband, Evadne vows to kill him, using her known relationship with the king to get past his guards and take his life alone.

The Revenger's Tragedy

VENDICE, HIPPOLITO

Because of the violation of his sister, the revenger undertakes to even the score.

The Shoemaker's Holiday

LACY, RAFE

Disguised as a humble shoemaker, Lacy is able to enter the Mayor's home and pursue his beloved.

'Tis Pity She's a Whore

GIOVANNI, ANNABELLA

A brother and sister confront the fact that their love for one another is far more than sibling.

Two Noble Kinsmen

ARCITE, PALAMON

Sick of Thebes and the rule of Creon, the two kinsmen decide to leave.

ARCITE, PALAMON

Imprisoned, the two men profess undying loyalty to each other, then proceed to quarrel over a woman they see.

Volpone

VOLPONE, MOSCA, VOLTARE

A consummate miser and his crafty servant dupe a suspicious visitor out of one more gift, which Voltare gives in the hope of being remembered in Volpone's will.

The White Devil

VITTORIA, BRACHIANO

A duke makes the deadly mistake of falling in love with a famous Venetian courtesan.

SHAKESPEARE SCENES

Because actors are ever in search of Shakespearean material, often required to find it, and most intimidated by it, the following list is offered. For other periods and playwrights, only the surefire has been listed. Here, everything that might do for an audition or showcase is included, because "undiscovered" or rarely performed Shakespeare is, in some contexts, more admired than the familiar. Where an asterisk appears, some cutting of other characters or piecing from various parts of the scene is necessary.

All's Well That Ends Well

ACT I, SCENE I, HELENA, PAROLLES

An immoral rogue and clever heroine debate the relative use of virginity.

ACT I, SCENE III, HELENA, COUNTESS

Though below his station, Helena confesses her love for the Countess' son.

ACT III, SCENE VII, HELENA, WIDOW

Disguised as a pilgrim, Helena plots to trick her unworthy husband into getting her pregnant.

Antony and Cleopatra

ACT I, SCENE I, ANTONY, CLEOPATRA

Antony is too besotted with Cleopatra's taunting to attend messengers from Rome.

ACT I, SCENE III, ANTONY, CLEOPATRA

Feeling very sorry for herself, Cleopatra acknowledges she must allow Antony to pursue business in Rome.

ACT IV, SCENE XV, ANTONY, CLEOPATRA

A wounded Antony is brought to Cleopatra, where he dies in her arms.

ACT II, SCENE V, CLEOPATRA, MESSENGER

Pity the messenger, whose job is to inform Cleopatra that Antony has wed Octavia.

ACT IV, SCENE XIV, ANTONY, EROS

His servant holds the sword on which Antony, having false report of the queen's death himself, elects to kill himself.

ACT V, SCENE II, CLEOPATRA, CLOWN

The clown delivers the basket of figs with the asp, which will help the queen take her own life.

As You Like It

ACT I, SCENE III, ROSALIND, CELIA, FREDERICK

Two princesses joke merrily about the one falling in love. Next moment, the twisted father of one and uncle of the other expels his niece from his kingdom. They vow to stay together and to travel in disguise.

ACT III, SCENE II, ROSALIND, CELIA

Celia, disguised as Aliena, has spotted Rosalind's (now disguised as a boy, Ganymede) beloved in the very forest to which they have escaped.

ACT II, SCENE III, ORLANDO, ADAM

His faithful old servant informs Orlando of his older brother's plot on his life. The two agree to escape and to share their lives together.

ACT III, SCENE II, TOUCHSTONE, CORIN

The city clown lords it over the country shepherd, but the old man more than holds his own.

ACT III, SCENE II, ROSALIND, ORLANDO

Rosalind/Ganymede tries out her disguise on the man she loves, and he doesn't recognize her. In fact, he agrees to allow her/him to help cure him of his love for this person named Rosalind.

ACT IV, SCENE I, ROSALIND, ORLANDO

Orlando learns how to woo and even pretends to wed his teacher.

ACT III, SCENE V, ACT IV, SCENE III, ROSALIND, PHEBE, SILVIUS

In trying to get vain shepherdess Phebe to accept the wooing of her young shepherd swain, Rosalind misfires, and Phebe falls in love with her/him instead.

The Comedy of Errors

ACT I, SCENE II, ANTIPHOLUS OF SYRACUSE, DROMIO OF EPHESUS

Master beats the wrong servant for losing or stealing his money, not knowing the servant has a twin.

ACT III, SCENE II, LUCIANA, ANTIPHOLUS OF SYRACUSE

He tries to seduce her; she is shocked, thinking he is her brother-in -law, not realizing it is his twin.

ACT II, SCENE II, ANTIPHOLOUS, DROMIO OF SYRACUSE

Master quarrels with other servant (his own), not realizing that this time he has the other twin.

ACT III, SCENE II, ANTIPHOLUS AND DROMIO OF SYRACUSE

Servant informs master of his encounter with Nell, a woman of global proportions.

Coriolanus

ACT I, SCENE IX, CORIOLANUS, COMINIUS

After a brilliant victory at Corioli, Marcius is given his new surname of honor, Coriolanus.

ACT IV, SCENE V, CORIOLANUS, AUFIDIUS
Banished from Rome where he was formerly revered, a champion warrior offers his services to his old enemy in order to avenge himself on his ungrateful city.

ACT II, SCENE I, SICINIUS, BRUTUS
Two tribunes plot to disgrace Coriolanus whom they considered overproud.★

ACT V, SCENE III, CORIOLANUS, VOLUMNIA
As he is about to destroy Rome, the warrior's mother pleads with him on her knees to spare the city.★

Cymbeline

ACT II, SCENE IV, IACHIMO, POSTHUMOUS
A crafty Italian bets a trusting Briton that he can seduce his wife, Imogen.

ACT I, SCENE VI, IMOGEN, IACHIMO
Iachimo attempts to seduce Imogen. She rejects him outright; he claims to have only been testing her, then arranges to have himself delivered secretly to her bedchamber in a trunk.

ACT II, SCENE IV, IACHIMO, POSTHUMOUS
Iachimo presents falsely acquired but overwhelming evidence of Imogen's unfaithfulness, a bracelet she vowed to Posthumous never to take off and knowledge of a mole on her left breast.

ACT III, SCENE IV, IMOGEN, PISSANIO
Posthumous' servant reveals that he has been ordered to kill Imogen, falsely believed by her husband of being unfaithful. They plan a way to save her life.

ACT II, SCENE III, IMOGEN, CLOTEN
The princess rejects the romantic advances of her crude stepbrother, and he vows revenge.

Hamlet

ACT I, SCENE II, HAMLET, HORATIO
Horatio tells Hamlet about seeing his father's ghost on the castle watch.

ACT I, SCENE V, HAMLET, GHOST
Hamlet meets his father's ghost, who informs him of his murder by his own brother.

ACT III, SCENE I, HAMLET, GERTRUDE

Called to Gertrude's closet, Hamlet upbraids her for her marriage, kills Polonius thinking he was Claudius, and is visited by the ghost of his father.*

ACT III, SCENE I, HAMLET, OPHELIA

Ophelia tries to return Hamlet's gifts; he responds by destroying the last threads of hope for their relationship and advising her to "get thee to a nunnery."

ACT II, SCENE I, POLONIUS, OPHELIA

Ophelia tells her father about Hamlet's wild appearance in her chamber.

ACT IV, SCENE III, HAMLET, CLAUDIUS

Hamlet taunts Claudius about the murder of Polonius and is ordered out of the kingdom.

ACT V, SCENE I, GRAVEDIGGERS

While working on Ophelia's grave, the two clowns joke about death.

ACT V, SCENE I, HAMLET, GRAVEDIGGER

The prince discovers the grave and skull of the court jester, Yorick, he knew as a boy.

Henry IV, Part 1

ACT II, SCENE III, ACT III, SCENE I, HOTSPUR, LADY HOTSPUR

Lady Percy argues with her husband because he will not tell her his plans; they reconcile in their way and bid each other good-bye.

ACT I, SCENE II, HAL, FALSTAFF

The Prince of Wales and his large, dissolute friend trade friendly insults.

ACT II, SCENE IV, HAL, FALSTAFF

Learning that a rebellion is being mounted against the king, the two tricksters take turns imitating him.

ACT I, SCENE III, HOTSPUR, WORCESTER

Hotspur and his uncle plan the rebellion; the older man handles most of the strategy, the younger most of the anger.*

Henry IV, Part 2

ACT I, SCENE II, FALSTAFF, JUSTICE

The lord chief justice of London advises Falstaff to stay away from the prince.

ACT II, SCENE II, HAL, POINS

The two friends tease each other about their position in the world and read an outrageous letter from Falstaff.

ACT III, SCENE II, SILENCE, SHALLOW

Two old codgers discuss the good old days.

ACT IV, SCENE IV, HAL, KING HENRY

On his deathbed, the king and his son reach a final reconciliation.

Henry V

ACT IV, SCENE I, HENRY, WILLIAMS

Henry disguises himself at camp the night before the Battle of Agincourt and argues with a soldier about the lives of kings and troops and their obligations to each other.

ACT III, SCENE IV, ALICE, KATHERINE

Speaking mostly French, the princess and her gentlewoman attempt an English lesson.

ACT V, SCENE I, PISTOL, FLUELLAN, GOWER

Troublesome Pistol gets a deserved comeuppance and is forced to eat a leek.

ACT V, SCENE II, HENRY, KATHERINE

Though more soldier than master of love or languages, Henry manages to woo and win the French princess.

Henry VI, Part 1

ACT IV, SCENE V, TALBOT, JOHN

Father and son both die on the battlefield, one of wounds, the other of a broken heart.

ACT V, SCENE III, MARGARET, SUFFOLK

Sent to woo for the king, Suffolk finds himself strongly drawn to Margaret.

ACT I, SCENE II, JOAN LA PUCELLE, CHARLES

Joan of Arc wins over the French Dauphin by literally proving more skilled at swordsmanship than he.

ACT II, SCENE III, COUNTESS, TALBOT

The Countess has ambitious plans to capture the rebel leader until she finds how strongly supported he is.

Henry VI, Part 2

ACT IV, SCENE X, IDEN, CADE
A starving man is killed for breaking into the garden of another.

ACT I, SCENE II, ELEANOR, GLOUCESTER
Husband and wife reveal their dreams and boundless ambitions to one another.

ACT I, SCENE III, MARGARET, SUFFOLK
Suffolk is banished. The queen, who is in love with him, vows that she will somehow see him again.

Henry VI, Part 3

ACT III, SCENE II, EDWARD, WIDOW
Lady Grey refuses to sleep with the King, then accepts his offer of marriage.

ACT V. SCENE VI, GLOUCESTER, HENRY
King Henry VI is killed by the future Richard III.

Henry VIII

ACT IV, SCENE II, KATHERINE, GRIFFITH
Ill and no longer queen, Katherine tries to envision some kind of peace in her life.

ACT I, SCENE I, NORFOLK, BUCKINGHAM
Two lords respond differently to the pomp displayed by the cardinal.

ACT II, SCENE III, ANNE, OLD LADY
Henry's eye has fallen on Anne, and her old friend claims she will not refuse the crown.

ACT IV, SCENE I, WOLSEY, CROMWELL
Completely fallen from power, the cardinal tries to assess his life and pass some wisdom on to his secretary.

Julius Caesar

ACT I, SCENE II, BRUTUS, CASSIUS
Cassius attempts to get Brutus to join the conspiracy against Caesar.

ACT IV, SCENE II, ACT IV, SCENE III, BRUTUS, CASSIUS
Great strain is put on the friendship of the two leaders as the Battle of Phillipi approaches.

ACT II, SCENE I, BRUTUS, PORTIA

Reminding him that she is Cato's daughter and knows politics well, Portia asks to be told what her husband is up to.

ACT II, SCENE II, CAESAR, CALPURNIA

Because of troubling omens in the night's storm, Calpurnia begs her husband not to go to the senate today.

King John

ACT IV, SCENE I, HUBERT, ARTHUR

An imprisoned young prince persuades his keeper not to execute him.

ACT IV, SCENE II, HUBERT, JOHN

Hubert reveals to the king that he has not obeyed his order to kill Prince Arthur, and John is much relieved.

King Lear

ACT I, SCENE II, ACT II, SCENE I, EDMUND, GLOUCESTER

The Bastard fools his father into believing his brother, Edgar, intends to kill him. Later he gives himself a wound to "prove" his brother's treachery.

ACT IV, SCENE VI, EDGAR, GLOUCESTER

Disguised as Poor Tom, Edgar leads his blind father to Dover and makes him believe he has survived leaping from the cliffs.

ACT IV, SCENE II, ALBANY, GONERIL

Husband accuses wife of treachery, she accuses him of weakness, and each accuses the other of unworthiness.★

ACT I, SCENE IV, ACT I, SCENE V, LEAR, FOOL

The old king's fool attempts to counsel and mock him and to help him avoid madness.★

Love's Labour's Lost

ACT I, SCENE II, ARMADO, MOTH

Fantastical Spaniard and precocious page discuss Armado's infatuation for a peasant girl.

ACT III, SCENE I, ARMADO, MOTH

The page sings and jokes to offer solace to his lovesick master.

ACT III, SCENE I, BEROWNE, COSTARD

A courtier commissions a loud rustic to deliver a message to the woman he loves.

Macbeth

ACT I, SCENE VII, LADY MACBETH, MACBETH

He has second thoughts about committing murder to seize the crown, but the Thane's wife both shames him and spurs him on.

ACT II, SCENE II, LADY MACBETH, MACBETH

Between the two of them, Duncan is murdered, and his guards implicated.

ACT IV, SCENE III, MALCOLM, MACDUFF

Loyal warrior recruits Duncan's rightful heir to return and seize the Scottish crown from Macbeth.

Measure for Measure

ACT I, SCENE IV, ISABELLA, LUCIO

An impish rogue informs his friend's sister about his danger.

ACT II, SCENE II, ANGELO, ISABELLA

A young novice pleads with the deputy governor for the life of her brother, condemned to die for impregnating his fiancée.

ACT II, SCENE IV, ANGELO, ISABELLA

If she will offer him her sexual favors, he claims he will spare her brother.

ACT III, SCENE I, ISABELLA, CLAUDIO

In prison, Claudio pleads with his sister to put his life above her virtue and to save him.

ACT III, SCENE I, VINCENTIO, LUCIO

Not recognizing the Duke, who is disguised as a friar, Lucio slanders the Duke relentlessly.

ACT IV, SCENE II, VINCENTIO, PROVOST

A plan to save Claudio's life involves executing a reprobate drunk in his place.

The Merchant of Venice

ACT I, SCENE I, ANTONIO, BASSANIO

The Merchant agrees to loan funds to his young friend to help him court the beautiful Portia.

ACT I, SCENE II, PORTIA, NERISSA

An heiress's lady in waiting reviews with her the qualities of all the suitors who have pursued her since her father's death.

ACT I, SCENE III, ANTONIO, SHYLOCK

Antonio agrees to strange terms involving a pound of flesh in order to secure a loan from Shylock.*

ACT III, SCENE II, PORTIA, BASSANIO

The suitor whom she loves passes her deceased father's test, chooses the right casket, and wins her hand.

ACT II, SCENE II, LANCELOT, OLD GOBBO

The incorrigible young Gobbo teases and confuses his blind old father at their reunion.

ACT V, SCENE II, JESSICA, LORENZO

On a beautiful night in Belmont, two newlyweds contemplate the power of moonlight and music.

The Merry Wives of Windsor

ACT II, SCENE I, MISTRESS FORD, MISTRESS PAGE

Two housewives realize they have received the same love letter from a large, aging lothario.

ACT II, SCENE II, FORD, FALSTAFF

Pretending to be a Mr Brook, Ford hires Falstaff to attempt to seduce his wife.

ACT III, SCENE III, MISTRESSES FORD AND PAGE, FALSTAFF

The ladies foil Falstaff by having him hide in a basket, which they then have dumped in a ditch.

ACT III, SCENE V, FORD, FALSTAFF

Falstaff reports to the disguised Ford about his seduction attempts and basket misadventures.

A Midsummer Night's Dream

ACT II, SCENE I, HELENA, DEMETRIUS

She pursues her beloved into the woods, but he will have none of her and pursues Hermia instead.

ACT II, SCENE I, PUCK, FAIRY

The rhyming servants of the warring king and queen of the fairies discuss the war.

ACT II, SCENE I, OBERON, TITANIA

The battling couple encounter each other, fail to negotiate, and go their separate ways.

ACT III, SCENE II, HELENA, LYSANDER, HERMIA, DEMETRIUS

A love potion plays mischief with four lovers for hysterical misadventures in the woods.

ACT III, SCENE II, OBERON, PUCK

The king checks the not altogether successful efforts of his servant.

Much Ado About Nothing

ACT IV, SCENE I, BEATRICE, BENEDICK

Difficult as it was to admit their love for each other, Beatrice now presents Benedick with a very difficult challenge in order to prove his—he is asked to kill his best friend.

ACT V, SCENE II, BEATRICE, BENEDICK

The two battling lovers agree that they enjoy each other's company enormously and will probably continue taunting each other forever.

ACT III, SCENE I, HERO, URSULA

While Beatrice listens in hiding, her two friends "set her up" by pretending to discuss how much Benedick loves her.

Othello

ACT I, SCENE VIII, DESDEMONA, EMILIA

Her lady in waiting attempts to console Desdemona over her husband's wild jealousy.

ACT II, SCENE III, IAGO, CASSIO

Iago lures Cassio into asking Desdemona to plea for him to save his reputation.

ACT III, SCENE III, ACT III, SCENE IV, ACT V, SCENE I, OTHELLO, DESDEMONA

She innocently pleads for the life of a captain and loses her handkerchief. He later asks her for it, enraged with suspicion she has given it to the captain and that they are lovers. Finally, possessed, he takes her life.

ACT III, SCENE III, OTHELLO, IAGO

Iago subtly poisons Othello's mind and undermines his faith in his beautiful wife.

ACT I, SCENE III, ACT IV, SCENE II, IAGO, RODERIGO

While pretending sympathy for Roderigo's pursuit of Desdemona, Iago takes his money and fills him with false hopes.

Pericles

ACT V, SCENE I, PERICLES, MARINA

Father and daughter are reconciled after being separated for almost all of her life.

ACT IV, SCENE III, DIONYZA, CLEON

A queen confesses to her husband ordering the murder of Pericles' daughter because she so far outshone their own child.

Richard II

ACT I, SCENE III, GAUNT, BOLINBROKE

Father tries to ease the pain of banishment for his son.

ACT II, SCENE III, YORK, BOLINBROKE

The regent tries to dissuade the rebel from causing civil war in the king's absence.

ACT V, SCENE I, RICHARD, QUEEN

Waiting for him on his way to prison, Richard's queen bids him farewell for the last time.

Richard III

ACT I, SCENE II, RICHARD, ANN

She begins by cursing him for the deaths of her father-in-law and husband and ends seduced and won by him.

ACT IV, SCENE IV, RICHARD, ELIZABETH

Most of her children are dead because of him, and now he persuades her to woo her daughter for him.

ACT III, SCENE VII, RICHARD, BUCKINGHAM

Richard and his compatriot in crime stage a public scene where he is "persuaded" to accept the crown.

ACT IV, SCENE II, RICHARD, BUCKINGHAM

The two plotters begin to realize they cannot trust each other.

Romeo and Juliet

ACT I, SCENE IV, ROMEO, MERCUTIO

On the way to crash a ball at the Capulets', two friends make merry.

ACT II, SCENE IV, NURSE, ROMEO

Juliet's nurse meets him and helps set up their wedding.

ACT II, SCENE V, JULIET, NURSE

Fretting over her nurse's lateness in going to meet Romeo, Juliet is then frustrated by her teasing and her petulance.

ACT III, SCENE II, JULIET, NURSE

Bringing the dreadful news of Tybalt's death and Romeo's involvement, the nurse at last agrees to bring Romeo to spend one night with Juliet before his banishment.

ACT II, SCENE II, JULIET, ROMEO

The star-crossed lovers declare their love in the balcony scene outside her chamber.

ACT IV, SCENE I, JULIET, FRIAR

The friar saves Juliet's suicidal desperation by agreeing to help her with a magic drug.

ACT II, SCENE III, ROMEO, FRIAR

At first balking at his request to marry them, the friar changes his mind and decides this may provide a way to end the dispute between the two households.

ACT III, SCENE III, ROMEO, FRIAR

Romeo is frantic over his banishment, but the friar helps him realize those things for which he can be glad.

The Taming of the Shrew

ACT II, SCENE I, KATE, PETRUCHIO

Who is the immovable object? Who the irresistible force? This is their first meeting.

ACT IV, SCENE V, KATE, PETRUCHIO

En route to her sister's wedding, Kate learns how to play Petruchio's game.

ACT I, SCENE I, LUCENTIO, TRANIO

New in Padua and infatuated with Bianca, Lucentio trades identities with his servant so he may be near her.

The Tempest

ACT I, SCENE II, ARIEL, PROSPERO
While acknowledging his success with creating a shipwreck, Prospero informs Ariel he will have to perform more services before achieving his freedom.

ACT II, SCENE I, ANTONIO, SEBASTIAN
The two plot to kill Alonso for the throne of Naples.

ACT I, SCENE II, ACT III, SCENE I, MIRANDA, FERDINAND
She has never seen a young man, he has never seen a creature so lovely. They fall in love.

ACT II, SCENE II, TRINCULO, STEFANO, CALIBAN
A monsters and two clowns, frighten each other, get drunk together, and agree to scheme together.

Timon of Athens

ACT IV, SCENE III, TIMON, APEMANTUS
Two old friends call each other names and try to one-up each other in terms of who is angrier against mankind.

ACT II, SCENE II, ACT IV, SCENE III, TIMON, FLAVIUS
Too generous to all, Timon finds out, from his servant, that he is bankrupt. His faithful servant finds him in the woods and attempts to offer him comfort.

Titus Andronicus

ACT II, SCENE III, TAMORA, AARON
The queen and her lover plot death and rape for others.

ACT II, SCENE II, TAMORA, TITUS
Disguised as Revenge, Tamora tries to get Titus to do her bidding.

Troilus and Cressida

ACT I, SCENE I, TROILUS, PANDARUS
Troilus' adoration of Cressida is both encouraged and mocked by her cynical uncle.

ACT I, SCENE III, ULYSSES, NESTOR
The two try to devise a way to motivate Achilles to action.

ACT I, SCENE II, PANDARUS, CRESSIDA

While watching all the Trojan heroes march by, Pandarus praises Troilus. Pretending disinterest, Cressida admits later that she loves him.

ACT III, SCENE II, TROILUS, CRESSIDA

The two lovers, after much pandering by Pandarus, are brought together and declare their vows of faith.

ACT III, SCENE III, ULYSSES, ACHILLES

The famous warriors discuss the elusive nature of fame.

Twelfth Night

ACT I, SCENE IV, ACT II, SCENE IV, VIOLA, ORSINO

Disguised as a boy, Viola achieves service for the Duke of Illyria, and is sent by him to help him woo the Countess Olivia, but she has fallen in love with him herself.

ACT III, SCENE I, VIOLA, FESTE

The clown and the disguised young woman discuss the strange ways of the world.

ACT IV, SCENE III, MALVOLIO, FESTE

In disguise as a crazed curate, the clown mocks the imprisoned Malvolio.

ACT I, SCENE V, VIOLA, OLIVIA

The countess is not interested in the Duke's suit, but is very smitten with his messenger.

ACT III, SCENE I, VIOLA, OLIVIA

This time she confesses her love for the page and is rebuffed.

Two Gentlemen of Verona

ACT I, SCENE I, VALENTINE, PROTEUS

Two best friends part, as the one leaves their hometown of Verona and the other seeks adventure in Milan.

ACT I, SCENE I, PROTEUS, SPEED

Proteus cannot get a straight answer out of his servant over whether he did or did not deliver a love letter.

ACT I, SCENE II, JULIA, LUCETTA

An intercepted love letter is the source of much banter and teasing between mistress and maid.

ACT I, SCENE VIV, JULIE, SILVIA

Disguised as a boy, Julia, against her own heart, delivers a letter from her beloved to the daughter of the Duke.

ACT II, SCENE V, SPEED, LAUNCE

Two comic servants discuss the women with whom their masters are in love.

ACT III, SCENE I, SPEED, LAUNCE

The two consider a letter regarding the attributes of a woman with whom Launce is in love.

ACT III, SCENE I, DUKE, VALENTINE

The duke tricks his daughter's suitor into revealing his plans to elope with her, then has him banished.

ACT II, SCENE I, VALENTINE, SPEED

Speed offers his unique observations on Valentine's new love.

The Winter's Tale

ACT I, SCENE II, LEONTES, CAMILLO

A trusted advisor tries to persuade his king that his jealousy is unfounded.

ACT II, SCENE I, LEONTES, HERMIONE

A possessed king accuses his noble queen of adultery and that the child she is carrying is that of his best friend.

ACT II, SCENE I, LEONTES, PAULINA

Cursing him for his crazed jealousy, Pauline reveals that the king's wife is dead, and shocks him into recognition of his own madness.

ACT IV, SCENE IV, PERDITA, FLORIZEL

Prince dressed as shepherd and shepherdess dressed as goddess pledge their love. Neither knows that she is actually a princess by birth.

ACT III, SCENE III, SHEPHERD, CLOWN

Father and son find an abandoned baby and vow to give it a home.

ACT IV, SCENE III, AUTOLYCUS, CLOWN

Counterfeiting himself as a victim of robbery, a rogue steals the purse of the man who helps him.

A complete listing of monologs from Shakespeare's plays is available on the book's companion website, at www.routledge.com/textbooks/9780415485739.

(Note: Group exercises exploring ideas in this chapter are located in Appendix E.)

SOURCES FOR FURTHER STUDY

Aykroyd, J.W., *Performing Shakespeare*, New York: Samuel French, 1979.

Barton, John, *Playing Shakespeare*, London: Methuen, 1984.

Beckerman, Bernard, *Shakespeare at the Globe*, New York: Macmillan, 1962.

Bentley, Gerald E. (ed.), *The Profession of Player in Shakespeare's Time*, Princeton: Princeton University Press, 1984.

Berr, Ralph, *On Directing Shakespeare*, New York: Macmillan, 1977.

Berry, Cicely, *The Actor and His Text*, New York: Macmillan, 1988.

Bethell, S.L., "Shakespeare's Actors," in *Review of English Studies*, 1950.

Birch, Dorothy, "Vocal Interpretations with Reference to Shakespeare," in *Training for the Stage*, London: Pitman, 1952.

Boas, Guy, "The Speaking of Shakespeare's Verse," *Essays and Studies by Members of the English Association*, 1964.

Boyd, Morrison C., *Elizabethan Music and Musical Criticism*, Westport: Greenwood Press, 1962.

Bradbook, Muriel C., *Elizabethan Stage Conditions*, Connecticut: Archon Books, 1962.

Brissenden, Alan, *Shakespeare and the Dance*, Atlantic Highlands, NJ: Humanties Press, 1981.

Brown, Ivor, *Shakespeare and the Actors*, London: Ivor Brown, 1970.

Brown, John Russell, *Shakespeare in Performance*, New York: Harcourt Brace Jovanovich, 1976.

Burtin, Elizabeth, *The Elizabethans at Home*, London: Secker & Warburg, 1958.

Burton, Hal, *Great Acting*, London: British Broadcasting System, 1967.

Cohen, Robert, *Acting in Shakespeare*, California: Mayfield, 1991.

Davis, W.S., *Life in Elizabethan Times*, New York: Harper & Brothers, 1930.

Daw, Kurt, *Acting Shakespeare and His Contemporaries*, Porsmouth, NH: Heinemann, 1998.

Driver, Tom F., *The Sense of History in Greek and Shakespearean Drama*, New York: Holt, Rinehart, 1960.

Fletcher, Anthony, *Elizabethan Village*, Harlow: Longman, 1967.

Gurr, Andrew, *The Shakespearean Stage*, New York: Cambridge Press, 1980.

Harbage, Alfred, "Elizabethan Acting," in *PMLA*, 1939.

Holmes, Martin, *Elizabethan London*, New York: Fredrick A. Prasger, 1969.

Joseph, Betram, *Elizabethan Acting*, London: Oxford University Press, 1951.

La Mar, Virginia, *English Dress in the Age of Shakespeare*, Charlottesville: University Press of Virginia, 1969.

Linklater, Kristen, *Freeing Shakespeare's Voice*, New York: Theatre Communications Group, 1993

Playford, John, *The English Dancing Master (1651)*, London: Cecil Sharp House.

Reese, G., *Music in the Renaissance*. New York: Norton, 1959.

Reeves, Marjorie, *Elizabethan Citizen*, Harlow: Longman, 1961.

Rodenburg, Patsy, *Speaking Shakesperare*, New York: Palgrove Macmillan, 2004.

Tilyard, E.M., *The Elizabethan World Picture*, New York: Vintage Books.

Tucker, Patrick, *The Secrets of Acting Shakespeare*, London: Routledge, 2002.

Tynan, Kenneth, *He That Plays the King*, London: Longmans, Green & Company, 1950.

Van Tassel, Wesley, *Clues to Acting Shakespeare*, New York: Allworth Press, 2007.

Welford, Enid, *The Court Masque*, New York: Russel & Russel, 1962.

Williams, Neville, *The Life and Times of Elizabeth I*, New York: Doubleday, 1972.

Wilson, J.D., *Life in Shakespeare's England*, London: Cambridge University Press, 1949.

Woodward, G.W. O., *Queen Elizabeth I*, London: Pitkin Pictorials, 1975.

Acting in Tragedy (Brian Cox), *Acting in Shakespearean Comedy* (Janet Suzman): Master classes in which veteran performers coach novices and illuminate the extremes of Elizabethan performance.

DVDS

Elizabeth I (Tom Hooper), *Elizabeth* and *Elizabeth: The Golden Age* (Shekhar Kapur)

Two of the greatest actors alive, Helen Mirren and Cate Blanchett, portray the incomparable monarch.

Henry V (Kenneth Branagh) and *Henry V* (Laurence Olivier)

Seeing both films is a major lesson in changing tastes in Shakespearean performance over fifty years, since each represents its own era brilliantly.

Playing Shakespeare (John Barton)

Ten videos containing roughly the same as the book of the same title and corresponding to chapter titles, but with the invaluable addition of seeing some of the Royal Shakespeare Company's greatest actors in action.

Macbeth (Trevor Nunn)

This production, featuring Judi Dench and Ian McKellen, embraces the ritual, high intensity and audience (camera) confidences favored by the Elizabethans.

Romeo and Juliet and *The Taming of the Shrew* (Franco Zeferelli)

No other filmmaker has captured the Elizabethan sense of festival, celebration, and unbridled excess as well as Zeferelli, whose eye for lavish period detail is amazing.

Shakespeare in Love (John Madden)

A rollicking depiction of the theatre scene in London and the launching of Shakespeare's career as a writer.

COMPARING GREEKS AND ELIZABETHANS

Greeks and Elizabethans share, in spite of scientific "progress," a belief in the possibility of magic and a connection to the elements. Theatre is largely outdoors, with an audience surrounding the actor on three sides and on various levels. Nature, the world, and the cosmos are constant factors. As theatre moves indoors, largely at night, the concern also moves away from the universe towards social relationships.

Before we leave these two, let us compare them:

Table 5.11

Greeks and Elizabethans

Issue	Greek	Elizabethan
Time		
Written	5th cent. BC	late 16th, early 17th cent. AD
Set	mythology/13th to 5th cent. BC	Ancient Greece through imaginary times
Beginning	begin near end, draw in past events	story begins and ends
Climax	high emotional intensity, mental struggle	battle, duel, reconciliation— usually physical
Past	binding us in necessity	door to the future
Future	difficult to bear	full of promise
Change	characters do not change veil is lifted	sometimes metamorphosis all become more of what they truly are
Space		
Theatre	up to 30,000 spectators	up to 3,000 spectators
Ritual	formalized and ordered	unbounded
Movement	still	active
Tension	balance	motion
Change	action is fearful	action is highly desirable
Place	single, important gathering spot	anywhere/everywhere on the globe
Values		
Sin	hubris, against nature	disloyal to sovereign, people
god	multiple, personal	single Christian deity
Belief	Fate	Providence
Conflict	good vs good, or lesser of evils	good vs evil
Tone	high	high and low together
Structure		
Script	unities	freewheeling five acts
Pattern	event to knowledge	knowledge to event
Scenes	standardized	all lengths
Beauty	statuesque	polarized
Sex	survival, seed, ecstasy	bawdy, robust, deserved
Recreation	categorized	public celebration

Table 5.11

Greeks and Elizabethans continued . . .	*Sight*	striking simplicity	colorful splendor
	Sound	direct, clean, soulful subject to translation	eloquent, loquacious, mercurial

Restoration Period Style

Decadence as one of the fine arts

THE WORLD ENTERED

AN IMPORTANT, brief interlude precedes this era. While the death of Shakespeare alone does not send the English theatre into a state of mourning, his demise coincides with a downward spiral from theatrical greatness. Politics replaces art. Those for and against the monarchy struggle for power. The 1649 execution of Charles I proves that Parliament disagrees with him on the question of the divine right of kings. Oliver Cromwell and the Puritans take control, establishing the Commonwealth. A repressive atmosphere pervades. Theatre is officially called corrupt and eventually outlawed (1652). But with Cromwell's death, the Puritans are no longer strong enough to control the Loyalists, and Charles II, who has been living in comfortable exile in France, is invited back to reclaim the throne for the Stuart dynasty. After years of self-denial, a longing for diversion and indulgence resurfaces. The Sin Squad Puritans wear black. Many now long for color. What follows is the reign of a king far more wild and licentious than his father ever was.

THE INTERVIEW

There are two classes now, US and THEM. WE are the aristocracy and we do not care enough about THEM to discuss them. Theatre is only for US.

The following interview is with a court insider. Aside from assurances of impeccable credentials, the expert wished no more details revealed.

Time: 1660–1710

> We live in the eternal now. Nothing before us, or after, can measure up
> to what we are tasting.

How would you describe your sense of time?
"We have just survived a dreary period of *no* theatre. While it lasted less than twenty years, it *seemed* an eternity. Some dutifully wore those charming, if stiff, white collars, and tried to be as puritanical as Cromwell, but the effort was overwhelming and, quite frankly, tedious. Thank God the Protector (who was, just between the two of us, not all that attractive) has gone to heaven, where he will be much happier. Now, *our* idea of heaven, after wearing black forever, is to play and to forget the consequences, in this life or the hereafter. Today is the Age of Possibility, with a new king, new court, and new set of rules."

In what point in history are your plays set and performed?
"Our plays are set here and now, because everything else is less interesting. This is what your century might call 'country club theatre,' written by, played by, and presented to, the elite in exclusive environs, safely remote from the ill-informed, unwashed masses."

> *"The multitude is always in the wrong."*
> JOHN WILMOT, EARL OF ROCHESTER

How far does the audience or play move out of its own time?
"If the current age is at all decadent (and yours is, my dear), our plays might be updated, but usually you, the audience, will be asked to travel all the way back. You will be privileged to pretend you are a wicked, worldly citizen of our own incomparable era."

How rapidly does it move for most people?
"There never seems to be sufficient time to learn all the gossip or to engage in playful trifles. Life is a whirlwind. Only when I am trapped in the company of some bore, does it suddenly stand still. Therefore, time moves rapidly when I am amused and interminably when I am not. When I look long and hard in the mirror, I am suddenly sadly aware of the years.

I can get lost forever in the moment, but I see all around me those with brighter eyes, smoother skin and (can it be true?) more alluring auras? I must remember only to stare at my reflection in candlelight."

How do you note time? What is your tempo/rhythm?
"Time is arranged by periods of preoccupation or assignation, as chapters in a lurid memoir. Mostly we remember our lives according to love affairs or scandals of note. We must get on with life or we shall yawn and yet . . . If the moment or temptation is sufficiently delicious, let the world go by and let me savor. Life is an erratic game,

whose pace veers from frenetic to languid, allowing delightful diversion before jumping back into the fray."

Do people focus mainly on the moment, on whole lifetimes, the future, the past?
"Absolutely on the moment! Forget the past and defy the future! You may quote me, at least among people of quality and without using my name. What is the latest novelty there across the room? Our interest in the future only extends to immediate desires. The past is absolutely forgotten, with the exception of course, of grudges and vendettas."

> *"We all labor against our own cure, for death is the cure of all diseases."*
> GEORGE VILLIERS

What lengths of attention span do your people have?
"What was that question again? Ah, yes. Well, it depends on how delicious or obscene the details, does it not? What were we talking about? Let me just say that, if you are interesting enough, I will stay with you forever. Who is that divine creature who just walked into the room?"

Is age revered or feared? What is the relationship between youth and maturity?
"If only I could know all I do, without wrinkles, bitterness, and carping. Never mind, I much prefer knowing to *not* knowing, but wish I were still translucent. It does take longer to prepare to go out nowadays it seems. God-a-mercy, look over there. Who invited those old crones? Take them away; they depress me."

> *"Age is deformed, youth unkind, We scorn their bodies, they our mind."*
> THOMAS BASTARD

How important is this issue? How uniform are views?
"We endeavor not to think about time; that is how important it is. And we are, my dear, in complete agreement."

Space

How can I invade and how shall I respond to invasion?

How is it defined and viewed?
"Wherever I am is the center of the universe, and all forces move out from this central force, which is moi. We do delight in mind games, yet are infinitely more social than philosophical."

In what ways do personal bubbles alter?
"We desire enough space to *display* ourselves, but also love to sidle up closely for flirtation, so the 'bubble' as you so charmingly put it, is flexible, continuously 'popping'

and re-forming. We are secretive, but once discovered, no detail is considered beneath reporting. We often go out masked, desiring privacy *and* conducting our assignations in dangerously public places."

How is space violated?
"The hands do wander, no doubt about it, but all must be done with beguiling delicacy and panache. Enough skill will avail you anything you desire."

> *"Love ceases to be a pleasure when it ceases to be a secret."*
> APHRA BEHN

How do these beliefs translate into movement?
"I require considerable room around me to express myself sufficiently. Since, in performance, I am competing with socializing, what I do is pronounced, extroverted, presentational, and clear. I accomplish all this without seeming to push for effect or to overstate. I will prolong both my appearances and withdrawals from the stage. It is more important to me to make a stunning, clear, and authoritative impression than it is to be believed.

Our theatres are intimate and small. Standing room is a thing of the past, benches are backless, but three galleries of boxes provide 'comfort.' The apron is the invention of this time period, and we are proud of it, so proud that we use little else. At last there is a special, diminutive 'stagette,' if you will, to allow the actor closer proximity to the audience. All entrances are made through stage doors built right into the proscenium arch. All scenery is relegated to the upstage area, which is employed for little more. The actor may be fully, closely scrutinized and joined on-stage. I note you have kept the apron all these years. A wise move."

Place

Every detail must be perfect, whether God created it thus or not.

Is the setting rural or urban?
"Pshaw! Need you ask? The city is the source of all worthwhile, the country intended for occasional diversion. One must maintain a home there, but seldom use it, except as a place for sport. We remove ourselves from the forces of nature in all matters."

What influence does weather have? To what extent is your environment controlled?
"As little weather as possible, if you please. Our hedges say it all—painstakingly shaped domes, hearts, diamonds, not simple, vulgar vegetation. Our rooms are large and grand, with huge staircases, tiled floors, vaulted ceilings, and detailed surfaces. Furniture is not comfortable, but rather an array of lovely display pieces, the more ornate and gilded the better."

How aware are you of other places?
"We are infatuated with all things Oriental and adore travel. Chinese furniture and Peking scrolls upon one's walls will engender multifarious compliments. We do now acknowledge the French as style masters, particularly as our own monarch has so many French tastes, including the appearance of women on-stage, a recent and titillating development. Many are altering their names to sound more French."

Values

> Since I am the center of the Universe, my commitments are secondary to my desires.

What are the beliefs most widely shared?
"Life is a sumptuous, meticulously prepared meal, more enjoyable if nibbled than devoured. Self-gratification is to be pursued at all cost, unpleasantness to be avoided at all cost."

How important is tradition?
"The restoration of the monarchy means a return to old customs associated with old rank and old money. *Noblesse oblige*. There are no other impediments to personal pleasure. Etiquette is all. You may do what you desire, if you do it with the correct statement, finger, or gift."

What is the predominant mood?
"Giddy, hedonistic playfulness."

Who are your idols? What are shared fantasies?
"While the King and his current mistress set the tone, we greatly admire anyone clearly living out lives of limitless, but demurely pursued, pleasure. Perpetual amusement, youth, and gratification would be any notable person's view of rapture. Personally, however, I cannot abide anyone feeling better than I do."

How do people define sin and forgiveness?
"We forget easily, but do not forgive easily. Revenge for a personal slight is de rigueur. All else is negotiable."

What gets and holds attention?
"Startling, devastating wit and beauty. The capacity to shock without offending. The ability to continuously surprise and delight. It is inappropriate for the actor, no matter what his character's plight, to ask that the audience pity him, feel

"I must confess I am a fop in my heart . . . I have been so used to affectation that . . . what is natural cannot touch me."
SIR GEORGE ETHERAGE

"When all is done, human life is . . . but like a forward child that must be played with and humoured a little to keep it quiet, till it falls asleep, and then the care is over."
SIR WILLIAM TEMPLE

"I can endure my own despair, but not another's hope."
WILLIAM WALSH

compassion for him, or feel that their altruistic (pardon the word) natures have been broached. We abhor this cloying vexation. Instead, what must be appealed to is the audience's libertine, rational, unsentimental side, their love for satire, their delight in the outraging of conventions and in tweaking the nose of piety. *Comprenez?*

> *"For money has a power above*
> *The stars and fate, to manage love."*
> SAMUEL BUTLER

And money?
"Ah! A florin discreetly pressed into the appropriate palm. Money is freedom. Money is power. It can buy you anything, except youth. And it *can* buy you youths."

What is the place of God and the church in your life?
"God has been, quite frankly, overrated, and the church can be a bore. The clergy is truculently myopic, and the services simply lugubrious. Everyone is a potential god, and life itself is to be worshipped."

What kind of humor dominates?
"Wit is the means by which all is accomplished. Humor is cerebral, studied, arch, and biting. It is lovely to laugh at another's expense and, on occasion, useful to turn the laughter towards oneself. A slight titter is considered more appropriate than a howling guffaw. And it is far better to refer to another's 'odorous fondness for breathing through his mouth' and 'unpleasant, vaporous dampness' than to his bad breath and sweat."

> *"All men would be cowards if they durst."*
> JOHN WILMOT, EARL OF ROCHESTER

How is fear defined?
"Disgrace, public humiliation, poverty, disease, and pathetic old age are our terrors. Suppression, repression, and political maneuvers are survival tactics. We try not to dwell on fear and we certainly do not acknowledge it, but all abhor the thought of the scorn of one's peers and the grave of a pauper. It is acceptable to express controlled delight and occasionally a finely edged rage, but never vulnerability, uncertainty, or vulgarity.

Structure

Those In the Know lead those out of it.

Who rules and who follows?
"The aristocracy constitutes an exclusive fraternal order. We collectively decide the destiny of others, and the King decides *our* destiny. Since we are still reeling from the experiment in individual rights, we are quite reactionary and inflexible. Your only

hope for advancement is noble birth, fortunate marriage, or fortunate 'arrangement.' The King, at his discretion, may pluck a title and estate from a recalcitrant anti-monarchist, consign this person to oblivion, and place the awards in the lap of a favorite. Nel Gwynn, the best-known actress of our era, begins as a lowly orange wench, achieves great stage success, leaves the theatre to become the King's mistress, and bears him children whom he bestows with titles."

How is justice brought about?
"While there is talk of a constitutional monarchy, at the moment it is absolute. The King or one of his deputies decides what is right. It is, in my opinion, a burden lifted."

How is daily life ordered?
"The surprise of life comes not by what one is doing at a given time, but with whom one is doing it and where. The day begins with an elaborate, lengthy ritual of preparation. In a sense we are all actors in our own lives, and our attention to detail, before venturing on-stage, is considerable. The entire morning is given over to one's toilette. The hair and face are mended endlessly, and one may entertain in one's own boudoir, even upon one's own bed, provided one has an appropriately attractive morning gown. Remember, the bed is the only comfortable piece of furniture in our home. Dressing is an arduous task. The rest of the day is spent in a combination of receiving and paying calls, in the hopes that the evening will produce an occasion."

How are family and marriage defined?
"Must we speak of it?"

How are etiquette and education set?
"We look to the French court and to our monarch's whims for winds of change, but *volumes* are published on the appropriate way to go about almost any endeavor. Change slowly filters ever so gracefully down from the throne. The motions of classical education are pursued for both sexes of the aristocracy. Intelligence and literacy are greatly prized, but academic rigor is low, since these virtues are more valued for their resulting skill to charm and entertain than for their capacity to enlighten. Verses are no longer ends, but means."

> *"The world is made up for the most part of fools and knaves."*
> GEORGE VILLIERS

> *"Such was the happy garden-state While man there walk'd without a mate."*
> ANDREW MARVELL

> *"Strange to say what delight we married people have to see these poor fools decoyed into our condition."*
> SAMUEL PEPYS

> *"Here lies my wife; here let her lie! Now she's at rest, and so am I."*
> JOHN DRYDEN

> *"Poetry's a mere drug."*
> GEORGE FARQUHAR

How are groups created and work defined?

"What you call the clique (and I prefer to call coterie) comes into full flower. Those with similar self-interests become allies in pursuit of influence and information. The closer to the throne, the stronger. To not work is still *infinitely* preferable than to work. It is the 'work' (it pains me to speak the word) of the aristocracy to ensure that we will never have to work. That is why so many of our plays are all about the quite necessary pursuit of fortune and estate. The professional actor and musician emerge. If one must have 'work,' this is the best category for getting near the elite, but please do not assume you will become part of it, Mme Gwynn's good fortune not-withstanding. The ownership of land, managed by someone else, is absolutely the only acceptable way for a gentleman to earn an income."

How is information spread?

"The primary means of course is gossip. While word of mouth is astonishingly effective in our society, the use of hand-delivered notes is widespread, and news gazettes (not unlike your scandal sheets) are relied upon as well. To be the last to know is to feel deeply humiliated."

Beauty

Smooth, altered, and utterly, divinely calculated

What is the look, most aspired to, in this group?

"An elegance that defies one's sternest critics. In your era, such phrases as 'drop dead chic' summarize what we seek. A slender personage, topped off by a mane of curly hair of similar length for men and women, the women's considerably more contained. Pale skin and delicate features are prized. A great beauty is like a fine wine."

What part does physical fitness play in attractiveness?

"Physical what? Do you mean fit to be tied? Just a little sex joke. Health and comfort are really quite irrelevant. One will endure anything for splendor. Men's garments happen to be an encumbrance, while women's corsets are merciless. We believe frequent bathing is unhealthy, and only a very few of us have lavatories. We do not brush our teeth until the end of the century and then only the upper front teeth, because, of course, those are the ones seen. The newest rage from France is the

> *"She that is with poetry won Is but a desk to write upon."*
> SAMUEL BUTLER

> *"Her lips are two brimmers of claret, Where first I began to miscarry, Her breasts of delight Are two bottles of white, And her eyes are two cups of canary."*
> RAINS FROM EPSOM WELLS

silver toothbrush. I have two, each presented me by a different paramour. And, of course, one must examine one's countenance at regular intervals."

Which colors and shapes are favored?
"We love deep, rich jewel tones: greens, blues, vermilions, and crimsons, in velvet, brocade, and satin. The feeling is of towering height, gradually descending in a bell-shaped line. Ribbons, ruffles, feathers, fringe, and lace may cascade from almost any point, momentarily distracting attention as the eye descends. In both our persons and surroundings, it is surprising that so much ornamentation can be present and still communicate clear lines and spaciousness. Keeping up is simply essential, and, speaking of up, the King is one of the tallest men in England. I believe this is a cause for the desire we all now share to become longer."

> *"Why hast not thou a (looking) glass hung up here? A room is the dullest thing without one . . . In a glass a man may entertain himself."*
> DORIMANT IN *THE MAN OF MODE*

To what degree is nature altered to create beauty?
"Must we discuss nature again? Wigs, paint, and embellishment are fundamental. Nature did not leave the skin white enough nor the other features bright enough, and one must compensate. And let me just say, while we are on the subject, that your plastic surgeons would be the most successful creatures at court if they could manage some time tunnel travel.

Part of the morning ritual is the application of heavy white zinc oxide, which reduces one's features to an immobile mask. For the many unfortunate, this is an attempt to cover the ravages of small pox. The hands may be covered as well. The lips are painted Spanish red, and the cheeks inlaid with a shiny red gum. Next, the definitive symbol of our vision of beauty—the patch! A little black taffeta cover (usually circular, but possibly star-, moon-, crown- or heart-shaped), which may cover pox marks or simply attract. Place near the lip (for flirting), the nose (for roguishness), the eye (for passion), or, later, on either side of the face to indicate political affiliation (Whig or Tory). A lady's headdress may alter the shape of the head beyond recognition. We called it a 'commode.' Why are you smiling?

We use the term 'undress' to mean any state short of fully attired. A lady may be in undress when she is simply without a manteau, a gentleman without his wig. Undressed is therefore a normal stage, and it is possible to be undressed out of doors. Since both sexes may employ obvious make-up for daily life, a challenge for actors in your century may be to make up for the stage so that both the character and the fact that the character is deliberately made-up are clear to the audience. So much for nature."

How is taste defined?
"Taste has nothing to do with morals and all to do with refinement. The approach must be refined, but not the appetite. Fluidity is fundamental. What you will call

classical ballet is emerging as an art form, and much time is spent training with the ballet master on simple deportment for life as well as the dance. Ladies should be able to sing and play either harp or harpsichord. The instrument creating the most interest is the viol da gamba. Men who compose music and paint are highly regarded. An intellectually facile mind and a way with words are considered artistic accomplishments."

Sex

The chase is far more important than the act.

How significant a part of the collective consciousness is sex?
"We think about it constantly. We talk about it unceasingly. We believe in pleasure. Have I said that?"

What is considered a turn-on and turn-off by most people?
"Verbal facility is captivating, as are long, swan-like necks, exquisitely shaped shoulders, and lovely breasts for the women, and curly manes of hair and strong, well-shaped calves for the men. Any of these may be aggressively displayed. A sudden twist of a gallant's leg may send a damsel swooning. A little glimpse of her ankle *en passant* is truly provocative. The decolletage, often teasingly enhanced by Venetian lace at the edges of the bodice, is employed to store letters and other small, secret items. We are, as you so bewitchingly put it, 'turned off' by dullness, prudery, age, shyness, and overt, unrefined vulgarity.

"Women let me with the men prevail, And with the ladies as I look like male. 'Tis worth your money that such legs appear; These are not to be seen elsewhere: In short, commend this play, or by this light, We will not sup with one of you tonight."
EPILOGUE FROM
THE GENEROUS
ENEMIES

It is a rare Restoration play that does not, at some point, now feature the leading lady in male disguise, so that all may see her hips, calves, and ankles."

The King was most clever in quenching the howl of Puritan protest at this phenomenon. He argued that it is at least as offensive for the male sex (à la clergy) to wear skirts in public, as for the female to display herself. As I was saying to him just last Tuesday week, "Sire, you are a fount of wisdom and gladsome cunning."

"While we seem artificial to you, and our men do bedeck themselves with ornament, our desire is still for male virility and female delicacy. We have great tolerance for fops and crones, but tolerance is not the same as 'turn on.'"

How is seduction accomplished?
"The veil and mask are in words, looks, and moves. The double entendre and hidden agenda are deeply appreciated.

The fan sends out a series of provocative messages. Secrecy is essential. Seduction is a game of skill, intended for the masterful."

"The chase is so sweetly savored that achieving success is very near, but not quite, disenchantment. Yet, even as your beloved acquiesces and the rapturous Act of Oblivion grows near, you do not go hastily toward consummation but precede it with well-paced tiny kisses, caresses, nibbles and teasing words."

Is emphasis on pleasure or procreation?
"Pleasure is deserved; procreation a mere responsibility. We are not fond of children, but the world must go on."

What is the courtship ritual?
"A lengthy series of notes, gifts, and delicate gestures constitute the pursuit. Steps forward and backward and reorganization of strategy are all common. It is an endlessly fascinating game of cat and mouse. One proves oneself a worthy lifetime adversary and companion in the game of life."

Is there tolerance for deviation, infidelity, or promiscuity?
"We are an overwhelmingly, some would say exhaustively, heterosexual society. It is our primary interest, and our fops are very interested in assignations with women. We would probably tolerate almost anything done discreetly, however. Infidelity is almost inevitable. Promiscuity is all but expected from men and tolerated from women."

What degree of suppression or expression of sexuality occurs?
"I have no idea what you mean. Come sit closer and explain it to me carefully."

Recreation

Gossip, intrigue, flirtation, nibbling, tasting, and testing are the delights that make life tolerable.

What is most people's idea of fun?
"We love to play, without innocence, to be bad boys and girls. The words 'naughty' and 'saucy' come into widespread use in our era. We love a large gala gathering and a private rendez-vous better than anything in between, and particularly enjoy mixing these two. Creating one in the midst of the other is pure bliss."

"Perhaps the kind
attendant (damsel)
shall display
Her waving
handkerchief, to court
your stay.
If the white flag flies
waving to the field,
The warrior knows the
charming fort will
yield."
CHARLES HOPKINS

"Courtship to marriage,
as a very witty prologue
to a very dull Play."
WILLIAM CONGREVE

"Her arms by her side
are so formally
posted,
She looks like a pullet
[chicken] trussed up
to be roasted.
The swell of her bubbies,
and jut of her bum
To the next brawny
stallion cries, 'Come,
my dear, come!'"
NED WARD

What would be an ideal social occasion?

"An all-day celebration at Whitehall palace, with continuous feasting, culminating in a magnificent masked ball, would be perfection. Falling in and out of 'love' with someone and finding a new 'love' would be 'lovely.' Since clothes and lovemaking are the two great pleasures of life, a delectable day should involve both."

> *"I cannot think God would make a man miserable only for taking a little pleasure out of the way."*
> CHARLES II

"A less auspicious, but equally enthralling, day would include extensive discussions of my wardrobe with my valet or boudoir maid, my milliner, seamstress, and shoemaker, all of whose lives are devoted to my own personal splendor. I would take dancing, music, or fencing lessons and receive as guests some members of the royal inner circle. I may even ask them to join me in my 'Withdrawing Room.' (I am told you have now dropped the 'with' from the designation. Do you use the room for sketching now?) I would somehow manage to take in the court, royal park, salons of friends, a coffee shop, an eating house, the theatre, and some card game. I would promenade, employ my own carriage, a sedan chair—the newest and most prestigious French import—or hire a hackney coach. One keeps oneself amused."

> *"Men are but children of a larger growth."*
> JOHN DRYDEN

Are you doers or watchers?

"We do both. Although we would rather do and be watched than watch and not do. Our refinement requires allowing others to take a turn."

> *"I am always of the opinion of the learned, if they speak first."*
> WILLIAM CONGREVE

And your intellectual life? Are you thinkers or mindless hedonists?

"But, my dear, thinking can be hedonistic. You must *have* ideas in order to *fulfill* them. To feast and to indulge, one must know all that can be ordered from life's menu. Intellectual *playfulness* is requisite. Endless philosophizing, ethical pondering, and metaphysical voiding are as boring in their ways as an utter vacuum."

What are common shared pastimes?

"Beyond the musical endeavors I have described, we love to write letters and to promenade. Cards are now accepted addictions; the gambling table beckons like a demon. Ladies enjoy experimenting with magic potions designed to subdue or bring out the ribald in their gentlemen. Women do whatever men do, but with greater anonymity or more elaborate disguise.

Everyone seems, of a sudden, to have a little dog. The King has eighteen, and they have their own court physician. His favorite and mine (dog not doctor) is named Bibillou, but, in confidence, I must tell you it elates me His Grace allows me to call the darling creature, BiBi and occasionally even Lou-Lou."

What are favored food and drink?

"Consumption is both sensual gratification and art form. The dining hour is now quite late—two or three o'clock in the country and four or five in the city. We largely reject implements in order to eat with our fingers, making art a necessity. And delicate dribblings on chins and breasts are irresistible. Our small meals involve four courses, average ones up to twelve, and a true celebration must have twenty-four. Such an occasion would last five to twelve hours and move through separate rooms for fish and soup, roasts and fowl, sweets and desserts (I adore marzipans!). Then, after games in the salon, coffee, hot chocolate (recently the rage), or liqueurs in yet another room. Ten fine wines are minimal if you wish to set a good table, and the recent invention of the bottleneck [corkscrew] has vastly expanded the range of ports, sherries, burgundies, champagnes, and punches to savor.

We prefer richer and heavier than you and would find your chardonnays and your salads pathetic. A pleasing light snack? Some claret and sweetmeats, and perhaps a fig or two. Or one of the very new white wines, accompanied by the latest invention, a delectable cheese, produced in the otherwise quite boring village of Cheddar."

And the importance of recreation in life? The standard view of indulgence?

"'Pshaw. Life *is* recreation, so I never indulge myself. If my purpose is pleasure, how could any act I commit be construed as self-indulgent? I prefer to think of it as simply measuring up to my responsibilities. Now, I have some scribbles to share with you, but I would prefer you read them in the next room, so I may have a moment of reflection in solitude. When you return, I will have something utterly delicious to tell you."

(I acquiesce. When I return, the subject has disappeared and has not, at this writing, returned.)

END OF INTERVIEW

The subject did however leave this document:

Restoration warm-up

A few more touches and I think I may
Be ready to embark upon my day.

My wig's resplendent, to perfection curled.
My face a masterpiece to show the world

And this new glorious garment which I wear
Is very near too exquisite to bear.

When out upon the promenade I tread,
My enemies will wish that they were dead.

They all will feel so plain, so drab, so mortal
I must make certain they don't see me chortle.

Though I have often hovered near perfection,
There has been no day in my recollection,

When I looked so alluring, fine, and bright.
I know this will be my day and my night!

Although the day has not quite yet begun,
I feel my battles are already won.

I've ordered new hats, lace, shoes, songs and coats.
I've sung, danced, primped, fenced, gossiped and sent notes,

And most important, in one slight endeavor,
Learned some information that may sever

From off a pedestal a libertine,
Whom I have always known to be obscene.

When I so subtly share this tiny fact
The court from top to bottom will react!

I'm armed, festooned, prepared in every way,
I now make haste to leap into the fray!

SIGHT

Painted, bright, shameless and proud of it.

Personal splendor must be attained at any cost, and artifice is certainly expected. A wig is more likely than natural hair as the period progresses. You are a work of art that must be recreated daily and put on active exhibition.

WOMEN

Head—Hair is arranged in ringlets, longer in the back than in the front, although it may be styled similar to what we call pigtails. Long curls off the face (heartbreakers) and short curls on the face (confidents) may be embellished by ribbons, pearls, feathers, or a headdress (fontange) of lace and wire (resembling a Spanish mantilla).

Torso—The neckline is cut low, wide, and revealing, the corset boned in front and laced in back, the gown (manteau) bell-shaped. A long, full skirt is open and caught up in the front (revealing an underskirt and perhaps a small, heavily laced apron. Sleeves come only to the elbows, so the lace of the chemise can be seen below them.

Elbow-length gloves may have rings worn over them. A train is likely in public, not at home.

Feet—Stockings may be brightly colored and are held with garters just above or below the knee. A half-inch heeled shoe closed with a bow. The first high heels, which only cover the toe and instep, appear.

Personal props—The most fundamental prop is the fan. For going out, a reticule, pomander, and parasol may accompany. If the weather threatens, a fichu, hood, and muff may be added, and of course, a vizard mask.

MEN

Head—Hair is loose and long beneath a splendiferous, beplumed hat. One's wig will move from tousled (spaniel) to corkscrew formal (high horned) as the century ends. The face is clean-shaven, except for a possible thread moustache.

Torso—Clothing is an oversized prototpye to the three-piece suit. A long, embroidered coat is loosely shaped to the body and reaches down to the knees, as does the vest. Cuffs are wide and pockets large. The shirt is embellished with lace and ribbons. Breeches come to the knee. The look grows tighter as the period progresses, moving from full breeches to narrow.

Feet—The shoe is the same height as the ladies', but somewhat larger in shape, and a prominent buckle may top it off.

Props—Any or all of the following may be carried—snuffbox, hankerchief, perfume vial, walking stick (with elaborately carved head and perhaps a loop for ribbons), round or egg-shaped watch hung from a neck ribbon, and a small dress sword hung from a baldric.

BOTH

Both sexes may carry muffs, also hung from the neck. For royalty, the heels of shoes may be red and possibly the tongues as well. Ladies are known to adapt men's clothing with great abandon, for walking, riding, hunting, and shopping. For rehearsal, women should purchase a fan that snaps open and shut with great ease. For both sexes, a handkerchief is useful—the larger and heavier the material the better.

MOVEMENT AND CONTACT

Since artifice is desired, you need not fear being called unnatural. Calculate each maneuver, moving from pose to pose to pose. Imagine that models are trained in classical ballet and that only positions derived from ballet are ever used. This is the first period in which the feet are turned outwards, with the chest as center of energy. Fourth position is considered the most graceful. The others widely approved are long or short (feet apart or close) second for the man and first or short second for the woman. Some thought is given to the hands being governed by the feet, in imitation or attractive counterpoint.

A lady moves in sweeping curves, head held high, and heels slightly off the ground, so that the moves are silent. It is expected that one lead with the bosom, as if the breasts are the first and foremost art work in the moving gallery that is you. Steps are tiny and smooth, as if any move from one location to another were part of a dance. One leaves a pose by pivoting on the ball of the foot.

Men must command clothing by strongly flicking lace ruffs off hands and hair off shoulders. Power shines through embellishments. The flourish abounds. Hands never hang at the side because the hand disappears into a sea of lace. At every possible occasion, "make a leg" (flash a calf), without appearing to notice that you are doing so. Men are now often removing hats inside. After doffing it extravagantly, subtly showing off how clean the interior is, turn it inside towards yourself and place it under the left arm or in front of the left hip. Men are now standing up when ladies enter rooms or approach them, as well as opening and closing doors for ladies.

While there is little mobility from the shoulder, this is probably the loosest-jointed period in terms of movement at the elbow, the wrist, and within each finger (all can move in circles) used to colorfully enhance an impression of delicate refinement. Everyone is aiming to be irresistible. Movement is like a sentence, and stopping is like punctuation, with each stop as different as a comma from a question mark. For the first time in history, an acting book (by Betterton) appears. It is highly prescriptive, to the point of telling which hand to put over your heart when you speak of yourself. He concentrates, however, on the playing of tragedy, since everyone sees himself as playing a comedy all the time and therefore in need of no instruction.

FANNING: The language of the fan

The fan is a primary tool and even, on occasion, weapon. While the following signals have evolved historically and are worth practicing, what matters is that you and your partner understand each other. Invent your own signals. Command your fan and communicate clearly with it.

> Tip of fan touching the lips—Hush!
> Touching the right cheek—Yes!
> Touching the left cheek—No!
> Touching nose—I do not trust you.
> Yawning behind fan—You bore me.

Figure 6.1

Lady with the Veil
by Alexander Roslin
© Copyright The National
Museum of Fine Arts—
Stockholm. Used with
permission

Pointing fan to heart—You have my love.
Hiding eyes behind fan—You attract me.
Brushing open fan towards person—Go away.
Carrying in left hand—I desire your acquaintance.
Placing near left ear—You have changed.
Twirling on left hand—I wish to get rid of you.
Drawing across forehead—We are watched.
Shut—You have changed.
Carrying in right hand—You are too willing.
Drawing through hand—I hate you.
Twirling in right hand—I love another.
Drawing across cheek—I love you.
Closing fan—I wish to speak.
Carrying in right hand before face—Follow me.
Drawing across eyes—I am sorry.
Resting on right cheek—Yes.
Open and shut—You are cruel.
Dropping—Let's be friends.
Fanning slow—I am married, or, I am relaxed.
Fanning fast—I am engaged, or, I am upset.
With handle to lips—Kiss me.
Open wide—Wait for me.

> *"You can do almost anything with a fan, except fan with it."*
> EDITH EVANS

SNUFFING: Taking snuff

Take the box, which, if worthy, is of gold and encrusted with jewels. Hold it between your thumb and index finger and tap a bit of snuff onto the back of your hand or wrist or pinch some out with your fingers. Inhale! Close the box, return it, and flick errant particles from wrist, cuff, or sleeve. If offering it to a lady, who does not carry her own, allow her to take it in her fingers and snort it into each nostril.

HANDKERING: Handkerchief as weapon

You heavily perfume yourself to guard against your own body odors as well as those encountered on the street. You dose your handkerchief with scent and employ it as a kind of machete in your journey. You store it in your generous cuff or pocket, or a catch it in your ring and, when confronted with odiferous unpleasantness, whip it out and swoosh it in circles. There are elaborate guides to which fingers the point should be protrude between, which side of the hand the lace should appear on, and how to maneuver, most of the moves being circular.

TYPING: Playing into your image

Since your name is likely to reveal a dominant characteristic (Bull, Sir Clumsy, Constant, Lady Fanciful, Lady Fidget, Foible, Mrs Frail, Heartfree, Horner, Loveless, Manly,

Sir Novelty Fashion, Petulant, Pinchwife, Lord Plausible, Lady Pliant, Scandal, Mr Smirk, Snake, Sparkish, Mrs Squeamish, Sullen, Tattle, Waitwell, Lady Wishfort, Witwood), go deep into it, punching up animal images or emotional states. You probably have a function (gallant, rogue, prude, fop, courtesan, wit, cuckold, gossip, plain citizen, wooer, philandering wife, rich uncle, jolly old knight, country pumpkin, or city sophisticate) that allows you to follow a tradition. This typing can free creativity. The type gives a safe place to start.

DESCENDING: Sitting and reclining

A man needs to flip up his coat-tails and correct the fall of his sword as he sits. As you lower yourself with the back of one leg pressed against the chair, the other leg, toe pointed, slips under the chair to steady the descent. The positions of the feet may then be reversed, once seated, to nicely finish off the action. The whole thing is then reversed when rising. Ladies can sit and rise as in a plié.

REVERENCE: Bowing and curtsying

Since physical etiquette is taught by ballet masters, many maneuvers in the salon resemble those of the dance. There are contradictory sources regarding the correct bows. What follows is a frequent production choice.

MEN'S BOWS

The hat is swept off with the right hand and transferred to the left under the arm. The bow itself begins when the hat is at shoulder height. The right foot slides forward in a half circle a step before the left, with both feet turned out and both legs straight. The body inclines forward from the waist, spine and neck remaining straight. Both knees now bend outwards, with the front leg kept straighter than the rear, which in turn takes most of the body weight. Feet stay flat on the ground. The right leg is now swept back behind you in a half circle, before you shift your weight there. The right arm may sweep forward and down to your side. As you rise, the weight shifts onto the front foot, and you move into third position. One of many possible variations is to place either your hat or your hand on your heart (as if to say "My heart is yours") and then to gracefully sweep it towards the floor, palm or rim of hat upwards (as if to say "And I lay it at your feet").

WOMEN'S CURTSY

Take a step to either side and make certain this move calls attention to you before continuing. Now return the foot you have just moved back to the other foot, with heels touching as in first position. Bend knees smoothly and slightly outwards, inclining the body a bit forwards. Allow arms to fall easily at your sides. Heels remain on the ground, unless the curtsey is particularly deep, in which case they rise slightly. The move resembles a plié. If it is executed "en passant," you needn't stop moving for more than a split second to do it. A common variation is to sweep one foot, similar to the man's bow, forward for the "forward curtsy," back for the "back" and in either direction for the "deep curtsy," quite similar to that used by the Elizabethans.

Touching and being touched are matters of great care. The fingertips are primed and alert and may brush gently against another person or object before darting away. You are acutely sensitive to shifting maneuvers. The bulky clothing presents a challenge for getting close, but it is just that—a challenge. All the maneuvers of hand kissing, cleaving, kissing, and embracing hold true, except that some signal assuring compliance is likely prior to the action itself.

SOUND

Sly, playful, acerbic, sharp.

While Restorations may appear preoccupied with themselves, listening is terribly important. Not to have heard or understood is deplorable. You must have a lucid response but it must *be* a response. Calculated nonverbals (sighs, vaguely stifled yawns, laughter, subtle purrs, growls, and even hisses) usefully embellish verbals. Those nonverbals associated with basic body functions are, however, deplorable. Language is elevated, and the use of euphemism raised to a high art. Full use of the top head voice and the bottom chest voice and musical dancing between the two are essential for the sense of refinement and playfulness. Allow freewheeling melodic patterns and inflections. Consonants must be refined to razor sharpness to score points. The feeling of graceful gliding vowels arranged between dartlike clear consonants makes for devastatingly graceful speech.

There are skills of delivery that, while not exclusive to the Restoration, are most heavily employed in this style. They overlap.

1. Counterpoint—Speech requires a balance between nonchalance and precision, while points are made with pin-sharp crispness, but leave the impression they are exerting very little effort.

2. Asides—Whereas Elizabethans also do asides, theirs are generally shorter and less digressive. A complete shift in focus and upsurge in energy are necessary as you drive your interjected point home to the audience. Then you return to your scene partner, pretending it never happened.

3. Double entendres and pointing—Innuendo is constant. Statements usually have both an innocent and a sexual meaning. Usually, the double entendre needs just the slightest break or pause just before and after, with some vowel extension and perhaps a change in quality during to help load your statement. The more sexual the remark, the more likely you are to use false pause, stopping just before selecting the key word.

4. Verse interludes—The plays are mostly prose, so verse, when it comes, must be savored with pride and shaped with care. These people rarely create verse for its own sake but to achieve something and congratulate themselves on the effort. Play intention and pride in creation. The most common interlude is the epigram, a short (rarely more than eight lines) piece of verse ending in a clever summary, and involving puns, antitheses, paradox, or ironic counterpoint—some sort of set-up and a surprising pay-off built into the rhyme.

5. Negotiation—Contracts and deals are being made regularly. Observe the tone of negotiators and barterers in real life, which is unlike any other conversation. There is a constant presentation of self as powerless, so that the slightest compromise seems like a major sacrifice. Learn to martyr yourself to win the game.

6.   Echoing—Often you repeat your partner's line back to her with the slightest variation and continue this game in a series. You must give back as good and better than you get. Repeat each crucial word with a mimic's bite and then insert the *new* word with extra twist that tops choice your partner made.

7.   Love masks—Characters are often claiming to be enamored of someone to whom they are actually indifferent, or, vice versa, not admitting their love. The audience is allowed a glimpse of what you feel while your partner is not. As you speak, it is for two different listeners, each taking a different meaning.

8.   Repartee—Speaking cleverly for the sheer pleasure of doing so means a sensual tasting of language, an enormous relish in winning points, a sense of building triumph as an argument is developed, virtual caressing of your favorite images, and small orgasms of alliteration. This is particularly essential in building the longer speeches.

9.   Excessive politeness—Maggie Smith is one of the most accomplished living performers of Restoration comedy, moving past civility into a state of delicate endurance of the crudeness of others that is hysterically funny to watch, in part because she always appears to be somewhat sorry for the other person to whom she is speaking, sorry that they are so crude, so limited, so lacking in imagination. This attitude colors line readings and takes the vicious edge off biting lines. It is as if you simply have no choice but to put down the poor things with whom fate as forced you to interact, and so you insult out of a great sense of charity.

10.   Prologue and epilogue—These are now virtually constant in plays, usually the first spoken by a man and the second by a woman. They are usually in rhymed couplets and contain messages to ponder. They require intricate shaping and a very direct relationship with the audience. They are usually done as an actor relating to the public rather than as a character.

11.   Undercuts—The technique of deflating your partner by moving underneath his point is highly useful in Restoration dialogue. Usually, your partner feeds you something in a bright tone, perhaps a high pitch, and you respond, without seeming to push for effect, in a lower pitch/volume and a clear rejection of what has been said, coming in almost with no time at all, so that the other actor's point is starting to take flight but you ground it.

12.   Arcs—Lengthy speeches build in intensity and hilarity quite slowly. These require elaborate phrasing, with careful attention to breath, thought, and voice. While only practice will develop this skill, it is useful to think in terms of planting items around the room that you will then pull together into some glorious creation when you are ready. You drop a point to your audience and/or partner, make certain they have received it, and subtly promise them that you will get back to it and it will be worth their while to hold on a while, then sharply launch into your next. This way, you build and sustain interest until your work of speech art is complete.

MUSIC AND DANCE

Music is discovering an inventive, buoyant, self-confident spirit. For the first time, the publication of sheet music makes tunes available to anyone. Operas are loved, as are oratorios, cantatas, fugues, preludes, sonatas, suites, and concertos. Composers are becoming more attracted to (1) writing for one particular instrument or solo voice; (2) writing music for the first time in measures; (3) elaborate ornamentation comparable to decor; (4) expressing a wide range of emotions so that, for the first time, such feelings as rage and disdain are given full musical (controlled) expression; and (5) showing off, displaying virtuosity for its own sake. Favored keyboard instruments are the spinet, pianoforte, and perhaps the definitive instrument of the period, the harpsichord. Gaining attention are the oboe, cello, and, of course, viola da gamba, with winds and strings now coming into their own. The full orchestra is also now flowering, and art songs emerge.

Music matches ideals associated with speech—careful, exquisite tone and timing, assertiveness, buoyant attack, and a blending of French and English customs. The embellishment, called Baroque, literally means "irregular as a perfect pearl." Both speech and music are full of unexpected trills countered by long smooth swells.

While ballet influences offstage movement profoundly, the social dance of choice, the minuet, captures shared feelings about being alive. The style is formal, while steps are quick and light, demanding control, balance, clean lines, poses, stately and graceful moves, interspersed with pauses. While demanding correct deportment, it is full of searching and evading, with partners now facing, now side by side, now gliding past each other in elusive courtship. Skill in it is so highly prized that statesmen are said to have their careers and credibility in jeopardy if they cannot master the minuet. While both partners begin, as in the past century, on the same foot, it is now the right. Other popular dances are the sarabanda (using the entire body with controled arm movements), the gigue (a gentler version of the galliard with hopping steps), and the gavotte (another adapted French peasant dance in which each couple dances alone in the center and then each partner kisses all participating members of the opposite sex). Moves are now more limited and stylized, with less room for individual choice and more emphasis on correct form.

KEYS TO THE WORLD

IMAGES

Something you dislike: loathsome

Something you like: charming

Figure 6.2

Edward Montagu, 2nd Earl of Manchester, by Sir Peter Lely © National Portrait Gallery, London

Elegance—sensuous informality—decorous self-display—calculatedly casual—studied nonchalance—disguised artifice—consummate ease —effortless urbanity—brittle—satiric—flirtatious—veiled—deadly—wicked—delightful—proud, preening, brilliantly plumed exotic birds—paintings of Lely—philosophies of Descartes, Locke, Kant,

Figure 6.3

Thomas Betterton by
Sir Godfrey Kneller ©
National Portrait Gallery,
London

*"Next to coming to a
good understanding with
a new mistress, I love a
good quarrel with an
old one."*
DORIMANT FROM
THE MAN OF MODE

and Hume—acerbic observations of Jonathon Swift—music
of Purcell, Vivaldi, Lully, Scarlatti, Bach, Corelli, Torelli,
Handel—actors: Thomas Betterton, Charles Hart, Elizabeth
Barry, Anne Bracegirdle.

SOCIAL SUCCESS AND SUICIDE

You can quickly rise or fall from favor in the genuinely fickle environment of the
Restoration world. You will know you have succeeded if you should happen to
receive: the Ultimate Compliment.

"Your effortless wit has left me speechless and your beauty left me breathless. Allow me to bestow upon you any favor you desire."

"When you part with your cruelty, you part with your power."
MILLAMANT FROM
THE WAY OF THE WORLD

Your disgrace will be complete if someone to whom you happen to be particularly attracted bestows upon you: the Ultimate Insult:

"You are dull and old (stifled yawn here). Please remove yourself immediately from my path and permanently from my life."

To be successful, you must:

1 look stunningly and effortlessly turned out at all times;
2 make appearances at the best soirées with desirable companions and make everything done or said there look easy;
3 know gossip before anyone, or at least appear to;
4 be quoted with some frequency; be quoted often enough to be misquoted;
5 develop a reputation beyond your own actions or, even better, beyond human endurance.

Suicide may be committed by:

1 speaking directly, explicitly, and absolutely to the point;
2 exposure of country origins and animal tendencies through bodily noises or clumsy maneuvers;
3 have attention given you and somehow "drop the ball" by saying nothing, nothing noteworthy, or something stupid;
4 revealing your vulnerability in public;
5 get caught working, studying, trying too hard, being utterly faithful, enjoying the country or cheating at cards (any other type of cheating is acceptable).

MASKING

Socially, wearing a vizard out on the street is commonplace, as is remaining masked for the entire evening at a ball. There had never been such validating of hiding, while in public. While scenes are rarely played masked, life is a masked, deliberate presentation of self. Fans and other accoutrements noted earlier may literally hide one, while evaluation, recovery, and maneuvering occur. The best mask, of course, is to appear to have none.

Repeat the masked activities suggested in the previous two chapters, with this basic change in perception: the veneer never comes off in the Restoration. We might get a rapid-fire, fleeting glance beneath, but that is all. The relentlessly non-sentimental mask will vary in layers, in how opaque or translucent or even scrim-like in transparency it becomes, but it stays on. So Restoration playing is about how skillful, interesting, and varied your front is, rather than about when you have it on. Covering up is admired, and naked emotion abhorred.

THE PRODUCTION

Most Restoration productions attempt to recreate the ambience of one of the original performances, which had a consort in the gallery, with music preceding and following the play, as well as during interludes. Unrealistic wing and drop sets are often employed, along with some attempt to create the effect, through lighting, of candlelight, foot lights, and chandeliers.

Sometimes boxes are built onto the sides of the apron for aristocrats to sit in. Dandies may appear on the stage itself. The actor generally acknowledges the audience as "her public" and plays in a presentational way, even singling out favorite members of what might be termed her personal fan club. Proximity to audience means coming right to the lip of the stage for crucial speeches and asides. Not infrequently, the beginning

> *"A gallant ought always to testify an ardour and impatience: and though he be ice, he ought always to say, he burns."*
> ANONYMOUS AUTHOR OF *THE ART OF MAKING LOVE*

> *"No mask like open truth to cover lies, As to go naked is the best disguise."*
> WILLIAM CONGREVE

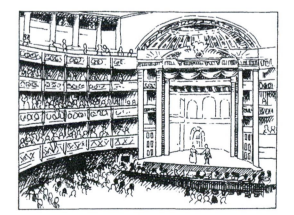

"Damn me, Jack, 'tis a confounded play, let's to a whore and spend our time better."
BULLY BEAU
QUOTED BY
TOM BROWN

"Lords come hither [to the theatre] to learn the a la mode grin, the antic bow, the new-fashioned cringe, and how to adjust their phiz to make themselves as ridiculous by art as they are by nature."
TOM BROWN

and end of performance are embellished by touches such as orange wenches and others peddling wares and themselves. A recent production always singled out the highest university official in the audience, and a wench publicly delivered an assignation note to him from one of the actresses, who would then peek around the curtain to blow him a kiss. Sometimes, actors dressed as the King and his entourage enter and are seated with honor. The more the audience is made to feel like the original, the more they will succumb to the playful, prurient spirit and leave prudery in the lobby.

THE PERFECT AUDIENCE

At no time in history has the action portrayed onstage been more perfectly matched to the daily life of the audience. You have come to the theatre as much to be seen, hunt for prey, socialize, and pass the time as to see the play. You have come to "chatter, toy, play, hear, hear not." You not only flirt outrageously and sometimes ignore the action of the play, but even attempt to top it because, as Sparkish in *The Country Wife* says, ". . . the reason why we are so often louder than the players, is, because we think we speak more wit, and so become the poet's rivals in his audience." If you feel more clever than the play, by all means sit in Wit's Row, on-stage or right up front. Or find other distraction. A scene rehearsal with this inter-action, while unnerving, can sharpen your attack and get you to win your audience and your points. Remember, however, this audience does not *oppose* you. It may lose interest in you or decide to top you, but it is not hostile or adversarial. See the action on-stage as a direct reflection of your own daily life and feel a participant in it, verbalizing to agree or compliment the charms of the performers. Men indicate approval by beating their walking stick or staff on the floor. Women applaud with the fan and use it to signal the players, or actually venture so far as to applaud with both hands.

CONTEMPORARY PARALLELS

1. Preoccupation with me first at all costs so that "I feel good about myself" becomes basis for major life decisions.
2. Conglomerates devoted to assisting in maintaining beauty and the illusion of youth.

3. Belief and resignation that corruption in high places is commonplace and almost inevitable.

4. While hardly as addictive, the ritual of snuff resembles cocaine, both in appearance and fundamental desire for a quick fix.

5. Establishments (singles bars, some fitness clubs, dating agencies) devoted primarily to hooking up strangers. In these spaces, the great opening line is all.

6. Greed as rewarded behavior.

7. Theatre-related social events (cast parties, receptions, awards banquets) where full bitchy artifice sometimes rules.

8. Preoccupation with food combined with desire for the very best, leading to such items as gourmet ice cream bars and hot dogs.

9. How-to-books that avoid ultimate ethical questions in favor of formulas for success.

10. A general softening of society, so that hard physical labor is unknown to many, and fitness must be achieved through equipment.

PLAYS AND PLAYWRIGHTS

Here are those scripts most likely to be produced:

Behn, Aphra   *The Rover*, 1667

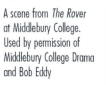

Figure 6.4

A scene from *The Rover* at Middlebury College. Used by permission of Middlebury College Drama and Bob Eddy

Congreve, William	*Love for Love*, 1695
	The Way of the World, 1700
Dryden, John	*Marriage a la Mode*, 1672
Farquhar, George	*The Recruiting Officer*, 1706
	The Beaux Strategem, 1707
Etheridge, George	*Love in a Tub*, 1664
	She Would if She Could, 1668
	The Man of Mode, 1675
Vanbrugh, John	*The Relapse* 1696
	The Provok'd wife, 1997
Wycherley, William	*The Country Wife*, 1675
	The Plain Dealer, 1676

SCENES

The Beaux Strategem

MRS SULLEN, ARCHER

Broke and seeking his fortune, Archer aims at a young, neglected wife. Though strongly attracted to each other, they feel compelled to pretend they have entered the gallery adjacent to her boudoir merely to "admire the art."

DORINDA, MRS SULLEN

A young woman, married to a drunken brute, meets with her sister-in-law to decide what to do with and about him.

The Country Wife

MARGERY PINCHWIFE AND MR PINCHWIFE

Fearing cuckoldry, Pinchwife tries to force his young wife to write a letter to her lover that will end their relationship.

The Man of Mode

DORIMANT, LADY LOVEIT

The affair is over, and Dorimant feels compelled to make certain his ex-lover understands this in no uncertain terms.

The Plain Dealer

MANLY, LORD PLAUSIBLE

A man of character tries to get rid of a fop with none.

The Recruiting Officer

CAPTAIN PLUME, CAPTAIN BRAZEN

Two recruitors in search of soldiers find more than they bargained for in a small English town.

The Rover

WILLMORE, ANGELICA

A rover and a rogue, Willmore is attempting to persuade Angelica, a high-priced courtesan, to bestow her wares upon him free of charge.

The Way of the World

MILLAMENT, MIRABELL

In drama's first pre-nuptial agreement scene, two sophisticates meet to negotiate the precise conditions of their future life together.

MIRABELL, FAINELL

Over a lively game of cards, two social climbers explore the foibles of the aristocracy and the need to hid one's true feelings in order to play the game.

The Relapse

LORD FOPPINGTON, YOUNG FASHION

On his way out to the theatre, a consummate fop is visited by his pleasant, but cunning, younger brother, who is in need of funds.

(Note: Group exercises exploring ideas in this chapter are located in Appendix F.)

SOURCES FOR FURTHER STUDY

Aitken, Maria, *Style: Acting in High Comedy*, New York: Applause Books, 1996.

Avery, Emmett, "The Restoration Audience," in *Philosophical Quarterly*, January, 1966.

Baur-Heinhold, M., *Baroque Theatre*, New York: McGraw-Hill, 1967.

Blitzer, Charles, *Age of Kings*, New York: Time-Life Books, 1967.

Boswell, Eleanor, *The Restoration Court Stage, 1660–1702*, Cambridge, MA: Harvard University Press, 1932.

Bracher, Frederick (ed.), *Letters of Sir George Etherage,* Berkeley: University of California Press, 1974.

Brown, John Russell and Bernard Harris (eds), *Restoration Theatre*, London: Edward Arnold, 1965.

Bryant, Arthur, *The England of Charles II,* London: Longmans, Green, 1935.

Callow, Simon, *Acting in Restoration Comedy,* NewYork: Applause Books, 2000.

Dobree, Bonamy, *Restoration Comedy, 1660–1720,* London: Oxford Unversity Press, 1924.

Elwin, Malcolm, *The Playgoer's Handbook to Restoration Drama*, London: Jonathon Cape, 1928.

Fujimura, Thomas H., *Restoration Comedy of Wit*, Princeton: Princeton University Press, 1952.

Gilder, Rosamund, *Enter the Actress: The First Women in the Theatre*, London: G. G. Harrap, 1931.

Henshaw, N.S., *Graphic Sources for a Modern Approach to the Acting of Restoration Comedy*. Ph.D. dissertation, University of Pittsburgh, 1967 (ETJ 5–68–157–70).

Hopkins, Charles, *The Art of Love: Dedicated to the Ladies*, London: Joseph Wild, 1700.

Hotson, Leslie, *The Commonwealth and Restoration Stage*, Cambridge, MA: Harvard University Press, 1928.

Knutson, Harold C., *The Triumph of Wit*, Columbus: Ohio State University Press, 1988.

"The Language of the Fan," in *American Heritage Magazine*, February, 1966.

Lester, Katherine Morris and Bes Viola Oerke, *Accessories of Dress*, Peoria, IL: The Manuel Arts Press, 1940.

Lewis, W.H., *The Splendid Century*, Oxford: Wm. Morrow & Co., 1954.

Loftus, John (ed.) *Restoration Drama*, New York: Oxford University Press, 1970.

Lynch, Kathleen M., *The Social Mode of Restoration Comedy*, Michigan: University of Michigan Press, 1926.

McCollum, John, *The Restoration Stage*, Boston: Houghton Mifflin Co., 1961.

Paine, Clarence B., *A Reference Guide to the Comedy of the Restoration*, Boston, MA: F. W. Faxon, 1941.

Palmer, John, *The Comedy of Manners*, New York: Russell, 1962.

Powell, Jocelyn, *Restoration Theatre Production*, London: Routledge and Kegan Paul, 1984.

Ramczyk, Suzanne, *Delicious Dissembling: A Complete Guide to Performing Restoration Comedy,* Portsmouth, NH: Heinemann, 2002.

Seyler, Athene, "Fans, Trains and Stays," in *Theatre Arts*, 31, 1947.

Styan, J.L., *Restoration Comedy in Performance*, Cambridge: Cambridge University Press, 1986.

Swedenberg, H.T. Jr. (ed.), *England in trhe Restoration and Early Eighteenth Century*, Berkeley: University of California Press, 1973.

Von Boehn, Max, *Modes and Manners,* Philadelphia: J.B. Lippincott Co., 1929.

Wideblood, Joan and Peter Brinson, *The Polite Society*, New York: Oxford University Press, 1965.

Wilson, J.H., *A Rake and His Times*, Oxford: Oxford University Press, 1952.

DVDS

Acting in Restoration Comedy (Simon Callow)

Masterclass, with scenes from *The Relapse* coached for ultimate clarity of language and varying levels of humor; companion to text of the same title.

The Draughtsman's Contract (Peter Greenaway)

Set in 1694, it is racy, arch, and filled with detail on daily life during the period.

Restoration (Michael Hoffman)

The story of a physician (played by Robert Downey, Jr.) in the court of Charles II, whose life is complicated by a request from the king to marry his mistress in order to provide a cover for their liaisons.

Stage Beauty (Richard Eyre)

A fascinating drama about the transition between the last of the male actors and the first of the females portraying women on the Restoration stage.

The Way of the World and The Country Wife (BBC)

Shortened scripts without most subplot action, these films are nevertheless effective in recapturing the period and are literally the only versions available of Restoration plays on film.

Dangerous Liaisons (Stephen Frears)

While set a hundred years later and in France, this film of Christopher Hampton's play is very much in the Restoration spirit of addictive decadence.

Ridicule (Patrice Leconte)

Also set later and in France, this film nevertheless captures the cruelty, irony, and wit of the Restoration.

7

RELATIVES OF RESTORATION PERIOD STYLE
Morals and manners

CRUSTY UNCLE AND CONSERVATIVE GRANDCHILDREN

TWO GROUPS of plays resemble those of the Restoration, but are different enough for a separate look. The term *comedy of manners* is often used for all of the plays of the Restoration, Molière, and the Georgians. In fact, the term often means *any* play involving witty banter among the elite. Since the setting is often a salon or parlor, a room designated for talk, the term *drawing room comedy* is also used. Some refer to any play of this kind as "Restoration," even though it is a specific English historical event depicting a unique world, never quite duplicated in any other time or place.

What ties the three groups of plays together is a new-found concern for appropriate behavior as the subject for plays. Questions of little interest to the Greeks and the Elizabethans are now considered important. What constitutes good manners? How important is it to have them? How do you get them? How do you display them? How far can you stretch them? These replace the cosmic issues of destiny and the meaning of life favored by earlier eras. The Greeks and Elizabethans defy mere rules or create their own; these later groups maneuver safely within structure. They play by the rules.

Whereas the Restoration involves elegant corruption, its two closest relatives are considerably more wholesome. Both Molière and the Georgians are interested in, not simply what behavior works, but what behavior is morally *right*. They are interested in the overall good of society at least as much as the individual in it. Molière *precedes* and influences the Restoration, writing from France during the earliest part of the movement. The Georgians *follow* the Restoration by nearly a hundred years, during which time enough sweeping changes take place in the world to cause a distinct kind of comedy, involving the middle class.

The three share many characteristics. Molière could be called the uncle of Restoration, the crusty but benign influence, always amusing, but with strict ideas about what is right. The Restoration takes his mordant wit and removes from it any discernible moral stance. The Georgians could be called, in turn, the grandchildren of the Restoration. A little embarrassed by their profligate ancestors, the Georgians become oh so concerned with what is proper and much less concerned with aristocratic privilege. The following sections are short, dealing only with answers that are *different* from the preceding chapter. If something is not mentioned, assume it is because there is no significant difference from the Restoration. Even the strangest families share genetic traits.

To keep these worlds clearly defined, you may wish to refer regularly to the comparison chart on pp. 208–9.

MOLIÈRE: Moral lessons sweetened with laughter

Figure 7.1

Detail of *Molière* by Jean-Antoine Houdon © Burstein Collection/Corbis

THE WORLD ENTERED

Why a section on a single playwright? Molière is the second most produced western playwright and most observers' choice for second greatest. While Shakespeare is surrounded by a half dozen other brilliant writers, Molière stands alone. Like Shakespeare, he steals or borrows plots everywhere, uses plots merely as something to which to attach his ideas, and embraces characters from the aristocracy all the way down to country bumpkins. In fact, Molière sometimes makes the play *about* the bumpkin. Also like Shakespeare, he dies in his fifties after creating over thirty plays and working primarily with one established company, under royal patronage. Both were investors or part owners of their companies and both were actors: Molière even acted on the night of his death in 1673, playing, ironically, the title role in *The Imaginary Invalid*. No one in his time and place touches his genius. And *absolutely* no one shares his particular voice. Today, *Théâtre Français* is rightly called the House of Molière.

Three important influences make Molière's work unique:

1. He writes when a movement called Neo-Classicism dominates France. Theatre is required to achieve a sense of decorum and appropriateness. Plays must not offend the sensibilities of audiences, must be morally uplifting, and adhere to the basic Greek unities. Molière manages to work within this framework and still write comedy. In fact, he is the first to give comedy true respectability and esteem, achieving subtle nuances in an art form thought to be loud, broad, and indelicate, surprising audiences with the idea that comedy can actually be polite. He creates *social satire* as we know it today and manages to get his audience to laugh at itself while being admonished.

2. Molière also writes out of the *Commedia dell'Arte* tradition, which employs the very broadest comic and improvisational ingredients. The *Commedia dell'Arte* had been a famous Italian acting company, led by the great Tiberio Fiorelli, also known as Scaramouche. The term gradually came to refer to the entire Italian improvisational movement. They work with stock characters, plots, and pieces of business—pratfalls, slapstick, and most of what we now see in broad farce, cartoons, and clowns. At one time, Molière's company shares a space with theirs. He observes and uses their great precision, carefully refining it and giving it sophistication.

3. A third significant influence on Molière is the reign of Louis XIV, a monarch with an incomparable ego and love for pageantry, laughter, and dancing. He appears early in his reign as the Sun King in the *Ballet de la Nuit*, and the name sticks. He desires more vehicles for more guest appearances. After first performing for the twenty-year-old Louis at the Louvre in 1658, Molière spent much of the rest of his life creating plays, interspersed with music and dancing, featuring His Radiance.

Figure 7.2

An etching from *Balli di Sfessania* by Jacques Callot, 1621. Fine Arts Museums of San Francisco, Achenbach Foundation for Graphic Arts

Figure 7.3

Madame de Ventadour, with portraits of Louis XIV and his heirs, reproduced by kind permission of the trustees of the Wallace Collection, London

Imagine a playwright of the twenty-first century managing to draw from vaudeville and the circus, to honor the strictest rules of etiquette and most repressive lobbying groups, to serve the whims of a major tycoon who believes himself the center of the universe, and to still write strong satire. This is the genius of Molière.

"Has God forgotten all I did for Him?"
LOUIS XIV

THE INTERVIEW

Our interview is with a member of Molière's own acting company, first called the *Illustre-Théâtre*. The actor has worked with the playwright from his humble days touring the provinces through his glory days at the Palais-Royal.

Time: 1658–73

How does this time influence your work?
"Mon Dieu! This age is full of changes. We first performed in Paris and were a flop. We toured the provinces and learned our craft. Now we are the most renowned company in Paris! The vastly overrated *Confrérie de la Passion (subject stops here to pretend to spit ferociously on the ground)* cannot even touch us. But we have many enemies, and each day is a new test. *C'est formidable!* There is always some group as ridiculous as the ones my dear Jean Baptiste mocks in his plays. Because they are about, how-you-say, universal foibles, they can be done anywhere, anytime.

"My friends we're wasting time which should be spent In facing up to our predicament."
CLÉANTE

Age is reviled, and youth has innocence, virtue, and a good heart. Both need to learn temperance! The old characters are often the most bigoted and easily duped, often exploding and yelling. Youth is sweet, but headstrong. It is not so wonderful to be young, but it is much worse to be old, *n'est-ce pas?* The disastrous Thirty Years' War, from 1618 to 1648, has wiped out half the people of Europe, so young, old, we are just grateful to be alive, you know? Time moves swiftly in our plays. Conflict is direct, with all action stripped down to bare essentials and the story strongly driven forward. A Molière play will be lively and brisk."

Space

*How is it **defined** and violated in the plays?*
"No one has any privacy, even at home, where visitors pop out constantly! Spying is common. Space is immediate, literal, social, close, and familiar. For long stretches, our characters give each other amounts of space, and there are many who never, ever touch. *Pas de tout.* But then, just when you think it is all talk, the *Commedia* (you know the Italians, *mon cher*) leaps in, and out comes the slapstick, cudgeling, delirium, physical jokes, "*lazzi*" (which you sometimes call "bits" or "schtick"), malaprops, echo-reply, and repetition of business.

While we were reduced for a time to renting tennis courts to play, our space at the Great Hall of the Hôtel du Petit Bourbon, adjacent to the palace of the Louvre, is 45 feet square. The theatre at the Palais Royal, our permanent home since 1660, is *magnifique* and *aujourd'hui* we are accustomed to playing to audiences of up to a thousand."

Place

*What is the **setting** like?*

"The play is in someone's home or just outside in the garden or street. We need several doors and places to hide for full effect, but little in the way of props. We are *artistes*! And remember, *mon cher*, we survived thirteen long years on the road and every *petit ville* from here to Marseille! *(Subject stops to cross self and look to the heavens, shaking his head as if to say 'Never again, please.')*"

How aware are people of other places and people?

"Casts are small. Characters have a narrow circle of acquaintances. Plays never expand beyond immediate community, neighborhood, court, or the circle in which the protagonist moves. It is Molière who takes comedy inside to the salon. As it moves inside, comedy focuses more on character, less on situation alone."

Values

*What **beliefs** are shared and what is the source of **humor**?*

"A war wages between decorum (natural elegance of thought and conduct) and baser behavior. At the extremes, *The Misanthrope* is dominated by aristocrats and stays quite dignified, except for the invasion of one crazed servant. At the other end, *The Doctor in Spite of Himself* is all rustic bumpkins and license for *lazzi*. Characters in Molière's plays often deny reality out of blind egotism or stupidity and seek to impose false visions of themselves."

"The humor comes from the way characters vigorously contrive to frustrate each other's plans. *Beaucoup de* tricks are played! Molière pokes fun at mistaken ideas of what is dignity, and the servant is often far more sensible than the master of the house. This character walks through the play taking *plaisir* in pricking the balloon of pretension in others. Remember, the balloon is our invention. The clever brothers Montgolfier create it, and Molière metaphorically pricks it. *C'est magnifique!*

> *"Common sense is not so common."*
> VOLTAIRE

Shared truth is that everyone can be frail and stupid, but the best thing to do is laugh at these human foibles. You cannot help liking even that Tartuffe, who is what you would call a 'sleaze.' This is a glorious role, and I could be glorious in it if only Jean Baptiste would . . . Never mind. There is a forgiveness in the plays that makes even the harshest judgments tolerable. We do not think of good and evil at their extremes. In the world of our plays, good means reasonable, not necessarily heroic. Evil means hypocritical and mean spirited, not necessarily corrupt. *Le roi* does not wish the subject of death discussed, *ever*. Are we alone just now?

Molière (not his real name you know—it used to be Pocquelin—he changed in order not to disgrace his *famille*) has known what it is to fail and to deceive the self. His *père* was one of eight court upholsterers, but he would not go into the family business!

Who would? To make love to a chair? *Pas moi*! He also dropped out of law school and spent time in debtors' prison after our first failed performances. Well, so did I to tell the truth *(stops to cross self again and clasp hands, this time shaking them at heaven)*. He tried repeatedly to play tragedy but to no avail. My beloved Jean Baptiste has a slight lisp, speaks very quickly, has short legs, wide-set eyes, a peasant face, swarthy skin, and heavy, black active eyebrows, not unlike your beloved Groucho. He managed to turn all his liabilities into grand assets, but not without some pratfalls along the way!

> *"It is an odd job, making decent people laugh."*
> MOLIÈRE

It was difficile almost beyond endurance. Just as Molière was released on bail, another creditor had him imprisoned again! Finally, we borrowed 522 *livres* and pawned everything, even our theatre wardrobe, our main working asset. So we took to the provinces at a low point. If we are now at the top, we have, as you say, 'paid our dues.' "

"We saw every type of person on the road! When we came back, Molière saw Paris with an eye sharpened by absence and experience. So the high and the low are all *stupide*, but what can you do but love them? And we are a huge success now, in part, people had forgotten farce, and now we make them remember. And we show them persons like themselves, with all their *petit* quarrels and foibles, and they are delighted to look into our mirror. Our work makes them laugh, makes them think, and sometimes makes them a little sad. This is as it should be."

> *"One is never as unhappy as one thinks, nor as happy as one hopes."*
> DUC DE LA ROCHEFOUCAULD

Structure

Who leads, and who are idols?
"Louis XIV dictates everything. Few kings have ever lived longer or ruled more powerfully. He took the throne at age five and has coined the phrase *"L'état c'est moi"* or "I am the state." The patronage of the King is essential to life, especially in a society that regards acting as a sinful profession. The King has even served as godfather to Molière's first *enfant*, who, it breaks my heart to say, died within the same year. *Pauvre petit bébé.* But past *Le Roi*, there are few deities. We see through the flaws in all and sometimes suspect it is better to be a peasant.

> *"The people have little intelligence, the great no heart . . . If I had to choose, I should have no hesitation. I would be of the people."*
> JEAN DE LA BRUYÈRE

What is the family and daily life like?
"The family! Ha! *Cherchez la femme*! My poor Jean Baptiste has married one of the most flirtatious, spoiled, and least affectionate women in Paris! And she is less than half his age. They fight continuously and worse yet . . . Oh, it is the worst *scandale*! . . . many think that she is his daughter!! *C'est effrayant!* Years ago, his

> *"No man is a hero to his valet."*
> MADAME CORNUEL

mistress was Madeleine Béjart. This coquette, Armande Béjart, has been presented as her sister, but the tongues wag. *Tout le temps*, they wag! Our arch-rival, Monfleury, he of the ranting and bombast (*a quick spit here*), has actually made the unspeakable accusation before the King! *Mon Dieu!* Well, enough of this petty gossip! Is it true? I know not. Does the frustrated relationship of the playwright and his *femme* enter the plays? Ha! All you have to do is read them!!"

How are the plays themselves structured?
"Plays are required to have four or five acts, of similar length and form. Verse was for tragedy and prose for comedy, so even in this category my brave Jean Baptiste pushes the limits and innovates. Language is required to be sonorous and appropriate.

Certain subjects are taboo. Our plays are structured so differently from yours that we invent something called the 'French scene.' A new scene always begins with the arrival or departure of a character, so our plays have many scenes even without changes of time, place, and action. There is always an opening exposition scene, where two characters explain all. Second, there is a demonstration of what they have been discussing. Third comes a series of cascading complications. And fourth and last, a group scene with the cast all present for the ending. *C'est parfait, n'est-ce pas?*"

> "*Let a single completed action, all in one place, all in one day, keep the theatre packed to the end of your play.*"
> BOILEAU

What is the role of friendship and trust?
"Our plays have concerned good friends (*raisonneurs*) trying tirelessly to save foolish central characters from self-destruction, offering patient, measured advice and comfort. The plays juggle excess against common sense, low farce with high wit, and emotion with reason. Of course, the advice is *never* taken, and the central character rarely grows or changes.

Molière has a close and lasting bond himself with the celebrated *homme* Cyrano de Bergerac, who has championed him on a number of occasions. A play about their friendship, now *that* would be worth seeing, *n'est-ce pas?* Why does no one write it? And our company understands true friendship. In all these years, only one actor has left us and we have the *best!*

Justice is always, *always* done in Molière's plays. Everyone gets just what he deserves. Family members often mistreat each other the most and are taught to forgive."

"The types that we play are as follows. (*Subject strikes a different delightful pose as each title is announced*):

> "*It is impossible to please all the world and one's father.*"
> JEAN DE LA
> FONTAINE

    Pantalone (duped father, often lecherous)
    Good friend (advisor)
    Good wife

Ingènue (both boy and girl)
Coquette (flirt)
Précieuse (learned lady)
Prude
Nagging wife
(Zanni) Tricky servant
Honest servant
Stupid servant
Honest courtier (a type I hope to meet someday!)
Dottore (doctor)
Marquis, Capitano (braggart soldier)
Tricky lawyer

These characters are more than your clichés. We *artistes* think of them as classic forms to be filled. Names mean little, and Molière often uses the same name for a single character type from play to play.”

Beauty

What are the favored look and modes of expression?
“Our plays feature the fluffier, larger, looser look of the period. We have a greater fondness than the English for the girl-woman who is not so sophisticated, or at least does not appear to be. While many in our society consider *les précieuses* (privileged young women who wish poetry, euphemism, and highly elevated talk to be a part of lovemaking—Roxanne in *Cyrano de Bergerac* is of this group) beautiful and fine, not Molière! How can such women be taken seriously? Women who call a chair ‘a commodity of conversation?’ They wish love to move through the following stages, quite slowly: *(again, strikes a pose for each précieuse phase)* Indifference—Disinterested Pleasure—Respect—Assiduity—Inclination—The City of Tenderness—and at last—The Dangerous Sea!!! Now how could Jean-Baptiste not make fun of them? And no wonder it is often a ‘simple’ servant who jabs!”

> *“The maid of the précieuse is always putting her spoke in the conversation.”*
> MOLIERE

“We are not attracted to those who violate social standards, and our sense of the beautiful is rather refined. We have a fondness for moral philosophizing. It shows the highest praise that Molière is called, by his contemporaries, ‘*le peintre*’ or the painter. His pen draws pictures with a beauty and clarity comparable to any executed in oil.”

Sex

“Cover that bosom, girl. The flesh is weak
And unclean thoughts are difficult to control.
Such sights as those can undermine the soul”.
                                        Tartuffe

How is sex viewed and communicated?

"Sex is, of course, *magnifique*, but also a bit funny, don't you think? And it can make you act *très* foolish. On the stage, *maintenant*, it is must be handled, if at all, with the utmost delicacy. We are limited by an edict, penned by Richelieu, forbidding us, on pain of dismissal, fine, or exile (only *le mort* is worse, *mon cher*), against the use of 'lascivious words', 'double entendres,' and 'indecent gestures.' We are required on the stage to remain 'completely free of impurity.' So be it."

> *"I could sooner reconcile all Europe than two women."*
> LOUIS XIV

Recreation

What are favored pastimes? How do people have fun?

"Fencing catches on with us in a way that never captures the hearts of the English. I believe they are fonder of greater brutality. The deft, quick touch, all dependent on the slightest flick of the wrist, gives us endless *plaisir*. And, of course, we never fatigue of discussing what is morally right. It is best, however, to say it quickly and sharply and leave a bit unsaid."

> *"The way to be a bore is to say everything."*
> VOLTAIRE

"But what is the *plus* 'fun' *de tout*? Why, to laugh, of course. It is the only answer for the reasonable man. Irrationality and excess are the best subjects for humor. Molière loves to mock complacency, extravagance, self-absorption, and vanity. He hates *les pedants* and quacks. Oh, and the doctors, whom everyone else takes so seriously and whom many fear. *Quelle* targets *pour la plume de Molière*!! *(Shouting forcefully at passers-by)* Down *avec les médecins*!!! *(Stopping, cringing, sitting)* Pardonnez-moi. I was momentarily carried away."

"While the pious are always trying to stifle our company, fortunately the King's idea of recreation is seeing others annoyed. We do that well."

> *"A learned fool is more foolish than an ignorant one."*
> MOLIÈRE

Sight and sound

What are favored shapes, movement, and speech patterns?

"We make a greater distinction between our stage costumes and those worn in life than the English. Brighter, bolder colors, with more reflective surfaces. We shine back on the audience a slightly more brilliant and vivid version of themselves. We actors must be verbal and physical acrobats, moving instantly back and forth between prankish contrivance and refined observation. Rhythms are often stichomythic, rapid-fire exchanges, involving repetitions, gradual exaggeration, set ups, pauses, 'straight' man responses, comic topping, undercutting, and general verbal warfare. Molière writes some plays in verse and some in prose, not mixing like Shakespeare. Jean-Baptiste's favored form of verse is the alexandrine, a line of four anapests or anapestic tetrameter, which simply does not translate to the ears of those who speak

English. A line of iambic hexameter comes closest in stress. *Mon Dieu*! Let me try to demonstrate. *Entendre*!

> I will now try to share with you the way in which
> Molière arranges his thoughts into lines that switch
> After twelve syllables, which may have an inner pause.
> After the sixth syllable, a caesura will cause
> A slight break in the total line of verse. They are
> Called alexandrines. Six iambs can somehow jar
> Your ears accustomed to Elizabethan lines,
> Which have only five feet and also fewer rhymes.
> Iambic hexameter might be the name to give
> This verse, through which Alexander the Great still lives.
> He is a favorite subject of many a French romance,
> But somehow his verse, when translated, does not dance!

Phew! *Quelle* task! It is, remember, *s'il vous plait*, Molière who is the playwright and the poet, not I. I am only an actor. What am I saying? *(Stops, hugs self, jumps up)* I am blessed and proud and ready to fly as an actor! Here is a summary of all I have told you, which we will call the

Molière warm-up

> The recipe for acting Molière?
> First ingredient? Comic timing to spare.
> Then for great Louis, the King of the Sun,
> A great feast of words, full of rhymes and puns.
> For the Académie, strict decorum.
> Stay 'appropriate' (but never bore 'em).
> Let your comedy seem to be polite,
> The mask of propriety veiling the bite.
> For the *Commedia*, we need slapstick!!!!
> Pratfalls, *lazzi*, an abundance of schtick!!!!
> Mix lightly together, stir until nice.
> Then sprinkle these sharp attitudes as spice:
> Sex? Ridiculous! Hypocrites? Vile pests!
> Trickery and deception we love the best!
> Old age we revile, yet youth is too green.
> Both can be tedious, or worse obscene!
> Fencing infuses the way that we speak.
> Sharp thrusts and ripostes, we perpetually seek,
> Our favored targets? Those in denial!
> First set them up; then charm and beguile.
> When they're full of themselves and start to swoon,

Then sneak up on them and prick their balloon.
Voilà! Social satire that stings and bites.
Laughter that teaches but mainly delights!

Oh *Mon Dieu!* And I am late for rehearsal as we speak, so if I wish to continue I must bid you *adieu. Bon chance avec votre performance de Molière!" (Exits running)*

> *"Anyone may be an honorable man and yet write verse badly."*
> MOLIÈRE

END OF INTERVIEW

KEYS TO THE WORLD

IMAGES

French words for standards in the theatre: *Bienséance* and *Verisimilitude.*

A point made in quick rhyme—the couplet—music of Lully—paintings of Poussin—Terboch's *Portrait of an Unknown Man*—Largillière's *Louis XIV and His Family*—Coysevox' bronze bust of Louis XIV—The Palace of Versailles's Hall of Mirrors.

For the serious side of the period: plays of Racine and Corneille—Jacques Callot's *Commedia* sketches—Eustache Lorsay's *Molière in Theatrical Costume*—Le Blond's

Figure 7.4

Bronze bust of Louis XIV by Antoine Coysevox. Reproduced by kind permission of the trustees of the Wallace Collection, London

Scaramouche engraving—Melingue's *Molière and his Troupe*—engraving of "the Players of the Hotel de Bourgogne."

MASKING

Molière's plays are about *un*-masking, taking characters' pretenses and stripping them away. At the same time, he derives inspiration from *Commedia* masked tradition, which involves inflexible, predictable masks and characters who do not necessarily learn from experience. Many of Molière's characters begin by being simplified to type, and then, in the unmasking, are simplified a step *further*, so that we recognize what is most basic and universal about them.

"Greatest fools are oft most satisfied."
BOILEAU

The *Commedia* troupes wore masks that were immediately recognizable to the audience, based on types listed earlier, and the French of this period are even more fond of wearing literal masks than the English. Farce involves pulling things *off*, one way or another, as stealing, hiding, deception, uncovering, gags, and practical jokes abound. Polite masks (spirit) are pealed away to show primitive urges (flesh). The *undoing* of others is crystallized by these mildly violent traditional pieces of business: the *gifle* (or small slap) in the face or the slapstick (or paddle split down the middle) used to spank or strike. Characters are often symbolically slapped or spanked into reality.

THE PRODUCTION

The major verse plays work best in a period that allows some aristocratic ennui or languor, where the look and feel of the designer's world is one where people have the time and money to simply hang out and tauntingly debate. The earthier prose farces are often set in a generic fairy tale or "ago," not unlike one might stage *Jack in the Beanstalk*, with a timeless sense of a more innocent world. Unlike Restoration comedy, Molière is very likely to be placed in the present time or near to it, since almost every element translates into contemporary life.

CONTEMPORARY PARALLELS

1. The hypocrisy of network censorship, allowing the most sordid topics on the air, just as long as certain words are not used and body parts are not revealed.
2. Exposure of the sanctimonious prude, as in TV evangelists and priests caught in the most lurid personal circumstances.
3. Accepted belief that common workers often know a lot more than those at the top.
4. Tolerant but condescending laughter at marriages or "arrangements" between persons of separate generations.
5. A strong desire for entertainment to be wrapped up with a message as well as a bow. A wish to be both amused and enlightened.

6.   A strong interest in exposing the failings of those in positions of power.
7.   A comfortable juxtaposition of philosophical discourse with circus antics. On a talk show, an innovative thinker may share airtime with trained seals.
8.   A tendency to type and generalize others based on first impression.
9.   A desire to have comedy instead of anything else, to have everything served up with the honey of laughter.
10.   An awareness that we all need to forgive each other, recognize each other's shortcomings and idiosyncrasies, and still invite each other to dance.

PLAYS

Here are those scripts most likely to be produced:

The Bourgeois Gentleman, 1671
The Doctor in Spite of Himself, 1666
The Imaginary Invalid, 1673
The Learned Ladies, 1672
The Misanthrope, 1666
The Miser, 1668
The School for Wives, 1662
Sganerelle, 1660
Tartuffe, 1667

SCENES

The Bourgeois Gentleman

JOURDAIN, MUSIC MASTER, DANCING MASTER
Desperately desiring to be regarded as a gentleman, Jourdain hires professionals to teach him the right qualities.

CLÉANTE, COVIELLE
A wily servant advises his young master on how best to win his beloved from his disapproving father.

The Doctor in Spite of Himself

MARTINE, SGANARELLE
A woodcutter and his wife perpetually try to outdo each other in tricks and insults.

The Learned Ladies

ARMANDE, HENRIETTE, CLITANDRE

Two sisters strongly disagree regarding matters of the head and the heart.

The Misanthrope

ARSINOÉ, CÉLIMÈNE

Célimène, the toast of Paris, is visited at her salon by Arsinoé, less youthful and popular, and wishing to tell her rumors of her "dear friend's" reputation.

CLITANDRE, ACOSTE

Two idle courtiers debate which of them comes closest to perfection of person.

ALCESTE, CÉLIMÈNE

The misanthrope tries desperately to get some degree of faithfulness from the hopeless coquette with whom he is infatuated.

The Miser

LA FLÈCHE, HARPAGON

A sharp-tongued servant, whose name means Arrow, is searched by his ever greedy, ever paranoid master.

The School for Wives

ARNOLPHE, AGNÈS

Arnolphe has selected and all but imprisoned an uneducated, naive woman, much younger than he. He hopes to prepare her to be his wife, but a young, handsome man has "found" her.

Tartuffe

ELMIRE, ORGON, TARTUFFE

The head of the household refuses to believe his wife's claims that his pious best friend tries repeatedly to seduce her. So she has him hide under the table and invites in the "friend" to prove it.

MARIANE, DORINNE, VALÈRE

An outspoken maid helps the daughter of the head of the household defy her father's wishes regarding whom she should marry.

GEORGIAN: Theatre welcomes the middle class

THE WORLD ENTERED

The population of England nearly doubles between 1650 and 1800. The group that procreates most? The middle class. Powerful citizens, who are neither upstairs nor down, emerge. They struggle to design their place in society, embracing some aristocratic and some lower class virtues. Plays of the period are often called *comedy of goodwill*. Most scripts are cloyingly sentimental, but two writers represent the period's true strengths. Richard Brinsley Sheridan and Oliver Goldsmith both react against the treacle of the times and in so doing reflect the best of the times.

In 1772, Goldsmith publishes his famous "Essay on Theatre," which decries sentiment and cries out for "laughing comedy." He does more than criticize. The next year, he produces *She Stoops to Conquer*. This play has so little in common with others of the time that only through the influence of the powerful and popular Samuel Johnson does it get produced at all. Both Goldsmith's plays and Sheridan's place more emphasis on character than Restoration theatre, while retaining some of the biting wit. They identify the difference between real and feigned virtue. By our standards, there is plenty of sentiment left in both playwrights' work—goodness is inevitably rewarded and gentility supported.

THE INTERVIEW

Our interview is with a member of the newly formed middle class, immersed in commerce and the arts, and often mentioned in the columns of *The London Tattler*. The subject was at pains to make certain I noticed the impressive coach and four in which he arrived, before sending it back in time. We discussed the quality and cost of the horses' bridles at some length before I could get the subject to turn to the issues of the interview, which was then embraced enthusiastically.

Time: Time for toys 1755–1800

Where do people focus their energy now?
"Your most obedient servant is pleased to reply. Egad! What a time this is! I vow, it seems not possible to me that any time ever could have been better! An astonishing number of recent inventions and discoveries have made the world our oyster: public clinics, the spinning mill, the cast iron bridge, the steam engine and both hydrochloric

> *"The arrogance of age must submit to be taught by youth."*
> EDMUND BURKE

and sulfuric acids! We even have the first encyclopedia, so it is now possible to look up all manner of learning. The young are lucky to be alive, say I, and they know so much!"

"Time not spent with these lovely new gadgets and such is spent planning parties, picnics, and balls. Even funerals have now become lavish displays and major occasions. Zooks! Got to do the dead right, you know! Do them up proud, say I. The plays are fast moving and lively. You must keep up. You just must."

> *"All that is human must retrograde if it does not advance."*
> EDWARD GIBBON

Space

Human being as ship afloat.

How is personal space defined?
"Zounds, but we feel big! We have big wigs, the ladies have big hips, we explode in every direction, as if we've been shot out of a cannon. Nowadays, we don't touch so easily and thoughtlessly as in the past. Only a thoughtless booby fails to show respect. But we all most definitely know how to put on a show of ourselves! A man's home is his castle, and his country is his pride. We would do anything to save the two.

> *"What a pity it is that we can die but once to serve our country!"*
> JOSEPH ADDISON

How has the performance space altered?
"The new theatre reduces the apron, and good riddance, say I. The lighting is much improved, so our scenes move upstage, creating a much larger distance between actor and observer. We can sit back and see the whole picture, not feeling intruded upon. And audience members are removed from the stage. It don't seem proper for a man to sit on a stage, so I'm devilish glad for the departure. The theatres are getting larger and larger and we are filling them to be sure. Mercy and miracles! Great scenic wonders are being displayed, cut out set pieces, fancy painting, much of it actually having something to do with the time and place of the *play* being performed in front of it! And we the people know what we like to see there, that let me tell you. We are The Public and you'd best serve us prudently."

> *"We that live to please, must please to live."*
> SAMUEL JOHNSON

Place

On the road.

What is your relationship to nature and how aware are you of other places?
"Well now, we finally put those old roads in order and made 'em more tolerably passable. It happens that travel and a new contrivance called the 'vacation' are

emerging as common practice. We are only just beginning to name the streets and put some numbers on a few houses. I protest it don't seem right to me to have a number on a man's castle, but it is starting to happen no matter. I own we most enjoy fixing up nature. The most important and fashionable of the arts is architecture! I confess we give more care to our interiors than our exteriors, with attention to every detail in mantles, doorways, and panels. I'll be sworn, we love domes. And we're painting everything white! If only it were possible to force the weather to be constant."

> *"The way to ensure summer in England is to have it framed and glazed in a comfortable room."*
> HORACE WALPOLE

Values

God as Engineer.

What are shared beliefs?
"The word that sums up how we feel about life, my boy, is Benevolence. Ay, this is what runs the universe and it is the basic guiding human quality. We don't ridicule vice anymore; we glorify virtue! Bad behaviors are simply mistakes in manners. Put a little charity in your face, say I. We are obliged to make manners better and to enlighten those less fortunate."

> *"To whom nothing is given, of him can nothing be required."*
> HENRY FIELDING

"In our time, God is seen in material, rather than spiritual, terms. He's the main engineer who designed the universe, set its laws, and started it running. Lud, the answer to all our problems lies in reason, and we call our time 'The Age of Enlightenment.' Oh, we still believe in sin, but also that man can move to enlightenment through reason. You will have to forgive me. It is *not* good manners to talk of this, son, so we must change the subject."

> *"Religion is by no means a proper subject of conversation in a mixed company."*
> EARL OF CHESTERFIELD

"I own that not everyone thrives in this system. And what about those who do not? Heigh-ho! We put 'em away. Debt is now an imprisonable offense, and the prisons are overcrowded. Since 'tis needful to pay jailor's fees to get out, many just go there and disappear! And the world is a cleaner place, say I. Only a very low, paltry set of fellows would allow themselves to get into such a state of affairs."

> *"The murmuring poor who simply will not fast in peace."*
> GEORGE CRABBE

"And then as to our theatres, there has been admirable atonement, and they are no longer the sinful citadels of cynicism and debauchery they were a century ago. They appeal to good, hard-working people, not just a drinking, philandering gentry. Our comedies have all the humor of the Restoration, without its decadence. Our greatest interest is in the natural man. A new, simpler, more direct human being defies the stuffy, arch old aristocratic order and ushers us into the future. Whereas many of our characters still have names that type them, we now have some fine young people called Charles, Maria, or plain simple Kate, who are pitted against the foibles and frivolities of the Snakes and the Sneerwells. Enough of trolloping and roguery, say I!"

Structure

A rule for everything.

Who leads and follows and how is daily life ordered?
"Heyday! For the first time in history, even the *French* attempt to emulate British art, fashion, and government! And goodness, do we teach those who are too Frenchified a thing or two! I dare say, we keep busy making up laws about what's proper and what's not, what's been done before and what must be done next."

"A precedent embalms a principle."
LORD STOWELL

"Now the Americans are a different matter. The impertinence! Wanting to be governed by themselves?! Plague me! Let me say that the only man from the Colonies (and I intend to use that term to my dying day no matter what they call themselves), the only one worth a half penny is jolly Ben Franklin. And the only reason Mr Franklin is enlightened, in the humble opinion of yours truly, is due to the time he spent on *this* side of the ocean. So say I. The revolutions in France and the Colonies, while lacking forbearance and good nature, have, I grant, gotten everyone arguing over the subject of freedom. And an interesting subject it is. There are still arrangements and mergers among families, but we all hope to find that we can think of our spouse as more than a business partner."

"Where there is marriage without love, there will be love without marriage."
BENJAMIN FRANKLIN

"Lud, our government is grand. Alack! Our huge middle class has economic power, but no real political clout yet. 'The two hundred' as we call 'em still own everything. Eh? Who are they? Zounds! The aristocracy families who really run the country. Psha! Ha'n't you read your history? In fact 5 percent of the population own 95 percent of the land."

"There is no art which one government sooner learns of another than that of draining money from the pockets of the people."
ADAM SMITH

"Young boys now attend private schools away from home, then try to get into Oxford or Cambridge. Then, I daresay, having completed their education, the young men must go abroad for a year to tour the Continent. Finishing schools are emerging for young ladies, who must know all manner of frippery to get on in the world.

"Beware you be not swallowed up in books! An ounce of love is worth a pound of knowledge."
JOHN WESLEY

Mostly, we want to know how things work. We have no wish for theory that just sits there as a confounded thought."

"Oh! And how I love my paper! Newspapers have gained massive popularity. I confess I am at a loss to recall how life was contrived before they came to pass. 'Tis fashionable to get your name in the columns, and political cartoons are a new delight, provided they are not about *you.*

And how are these changes influencing the theatre?
"Even *acting* becomes a respectable profession! Our much admired Mr Garrick has helped structure theatre, demanding far more regularly scheduled rehearsals than in the past, forcing actors to actually listen to each other, and to find natural rhythms. Since we prefer things tidy and positive, the plays themselves end happily, with all the loose ends tied up in a neat bow. This is the beginning of what you will call a 'star'. We go to the theatre to see our favorites! We cheer for them! In fact, we mostly think the players' personae far more important than the play."

Beauty

What looks are aspired to and how is beauty expressed?
"Now that even the French are looking to *us*, all proper persons are aware of image, so we fix things up proper. Topiary reaches even greater heights. Our bushes sometimes look like animals, chess pieces, even statues! But for real beauty, the new tree of choice is the elm!

Each person probably looks to you, my man, like an inflated balloon about to burst. A goodly portion of trumpery is needed to make a good showing. A woman's hair can add three feet one way (up), her panniers easily that the other way (sides), then her train another (back). Women appear as great ships sailing slowly in harbor. Men also add width with coats, higher heels, and wigs. By the laws, who would have thought a single human being could take up so many square inches!"

Sex

*How are sexuality and seduction **expressed**?*
"You alarm me with your questions. Well, truly, a hearty sort of eroticism exists, although a clear separation is made between women of quality and tarts! Make no mistake. Though a need is a need, if I may say so."

"Life is too short to study German."
RICHARD PORGON

"Authors owe more of their success to good actors than they imagine."
JOHN HILL, IN
THE ACTOR OR A
TREATISE ON THE
ART OF PLAYING

"Fashion—a word which knaves and fools may use, Their knavery and folly to excuse."
CHARLES
CHURCHILL

"O death! There is something new called burlesque, where, in private clubs, women are hired to dance naked for men. And Lud! There is a salacious interest in the memoirs of both the Marquis de Sade and Casanova, making them huge bestsellers. No one I know admits to reading them, of course, but the shops are always out of copies . . . Or so I have been told.

Whereas a young man's training may now involve a 'professional' to get him ready for the duties of husbanding, adultery is no longer a fit subject for discussion. Once harnessed together in matrimony, if passion cannot be founded in duty, then let discretion be your tutor."

"The Duke returned from the wars today and did pleasure me in his top-boots."
DUCHESS OF MARLBOROUGH

Recreation

Everything from restaurants to strippers.

"A miss for pleasure and a wife for breed."
JOHN GAY

What are favored pastimes and ideas of fun?
"Odd's heart, there is nothing to surpass a ball done proper. Unless it's a good game of lawn bowling. The newest diversions include cricket, horse races, fox hunting, and golf! Oons, gambling is so popular that even at a ball, a gaming room is provided for those who prefer the table to the dance floor."

"A man indeed is not genteel when he gets drunk, but most vices may be committed very genteely. A man may debauch his friend's wife genteely and he may cheat at cards genteely."
JAMES BOSWELL

Figure 7.6

Drury Lane Theatre, London, in 1776
© Bettmann/Corbis

On being encountered drinking in the street, while watching his theatre, Drury Lane, burn down:
"A man may surely be allowed to take a glass of wine by his own fireside."
RICHARD BRINSELY SHERIDAN

"Prize fighting is the sport of choice for young dandies. Lud, they often take lessons from the leading fighters of the day. Ladies do not participate in outside sports, except shopping! Shopping as diversion is new, and none of the shops of Europe can compare to ours! I understand you have eating places all over? Well, the restaurant as you now know it, is just emerging. Tea is added to the other beverages and is giving chocolate truly a run for its money as drink of choice. Serving tea is becoming a prescriptive art. Zounds, what a fuss in how each thing involved is held and used just so. Plague me if I can remember just how to hold the pot and my pinky all at once. We invent the real custom of tipping! In our coffee houses are placed boxes with the words 'To Insure Promptness,' eventually shortened to TIP. Please don't hate us for it."

"Women now take singing lessons. Every family who can afford one hires a dance master to teach us steps and deportment. He tells you how to walk and even how to embrace! Good breeding, you see, is in itself considered an expression of beauty. When being unkind, contrive always to appear to be discussing others not present."

> *"You should always except the present company."*
> JOHN O'KEEFE

"There's no denying it, we have even contrived fashionable maladies. If you wish to get ill with style, there is 'the spleen' among men and 'the vapors' among women. Lead poisoning, from both make-up and household items, is common. We now have the London season, fall to spring, with summers in the country, at Brighton or Bath, please. We even have country clothes, cut with more room to move, and of course we have country pleasures. Let me sum it all up for you:"

Georgian warm-up

Zounds! We are big, with panniers, jabots, and wigs to the sky.
Egad! We are white, pale, padded, and powdered.
Lud! We are wholesome, fresh, and respectable.
Pshaw! Good riddance to the Restoration wickedness.
Heigh-ho! Welcome to the robust and proper Middle Class!
For Gad! We love our gadgets and gizmos!
Heyday! We want to know HOW things work, not why.
Tilly Nilly! We want plain, simple good speech.
Gadzooks! Leave behind your fancy highfalootin' phrases.
Oh lordy! Our ideal state is Benevolence.
Tilly Tally! Your obedient servant tries never to be a thoughtless booby.
Harrumph! Let's be cheerful and at least PRETEND to be kind.
Ya-Hooh! If you must say something mean, always add "present
    company excepted."
Hail hearty! We love to go to the theatre to see our favorite stars!
Zooks! We cheer and shriek and applaud and guffaw!

By the Lud! We live in the age of Enlightenment!
Pish Posh! We're full of life and climbing up the hill!
Tish tosh! We'll fill you with Comedy of Goodwill!

"And now that I peruse my watch . . . See this? The finest gold and the best in craftsmanship, if I may be allowed to say so. Every time I wind it, I feel proud. Avarice is the vice of the age I must confess, but who would be a lackey when he may contrive not? . . . What was I saying? Ah, yes! My bags are packed, and I'm afraid, I cannot give you any more of my time because Brighton awaits me. Time is money you know. I must wish you a good morning. Heigh-ho!"

> *"God made the country and man made the town."*
> WILLIAM COWPER

(Subject summons coach and four, which have been equipped with new livery, and shows them to me with pride, even exposing the teeth of one of the horses so I will know what a quality steed it is. Subject jumps in, and the carriage lunges forward. Subject waves heartily from the window as carriage disappears around the corner and out of sight.)

END OF INTERVIEW

SIGHT

The look is large and pale, with powdered wigs, pastel garments, and a human silhouette sometimes nearly as wide as it is high. Make-up is still acceptable for both sexes, and fops might carry fans, but there is a movement against the use of both. Jewelry involves a revival of pearls, lockets, and jeweled buckles. You might call the total look "More is More".

MEN

Head—Men's hair is always tied back, and wigs are less common at the end of the period than at the beginning. Earlier on, men wear tricorn hats. Later, there are the beginnings of the top hat.

Torso—The waistcoat is the least comfortable piece of clothing, buttoned all the way to the neck. A short sword and cane are frequently carried. A jabot, a shorter waistcoat, tight knee breeches, and gartered stockings are standard. Cravats are worn high, and later collars on shirts stand way up.

WOMEN

Head—Women wear linen caps or large hats. Their hair is whitened and enlarged to great proportion. Above the hair, some great object, such as a bird or ship may be placed. Over this extravaganza may be worn a callash, a foldable sort of Conestoga wagon for the head. Later, hair is in loose curls, with shoulder scarves and enormous straw hats forming a softer look.

Torso—Heavy corseting restricts the upper body altogether. Use of busks or panels inserted into corset pockets can force posture, removal of them can allow some freedom. Panniers, a variation on hoops, project strongly right and left. Flowers, made of fabric, are now added to trim gowns, and floral patterns are widely used. A wide, deep neckline filled with a light scarf and elbow length sleeves with ruffles are favored. Later in the period, the hoops and panniers disappear, and emphasis shifts from sides to back, with a bustle arrangement. Women begin to choose plainer fabrics.

A man's wife is now considered a primary showpiece for his wealth. The finer and more elegantly dressed she is, the richer he is considered to be. Country clothes are cut with more room and comfort. In production, extremes may be used for comic effect, with "natural" women dressing more like our collective image of Martha Washington, while "extravagant creatures," such as Lady Teazle, Mrs Hardcastle, or Mrs Malaprop, might be festooned in the high excesses of a Marie Antoinette.

MOVEMENT AND CONTACT

Men may not approach married women directly, but may approach marriageable women with great discretion and minimal contact, and may do anything they wish with servants. Public displays of affection are not considered appropriate. Matrons are like monuments. The stereotype of women fainting emerges from this period, not as a result of their "weakness," but because the corseting makes only small, shallow breathing possible and impairs circulation. Maneuvering in panniers requires short mincing steps.

> *"I chose my wife, as she did her wedding gown, not for a fine glossy surface, but such qualities as would wear well."*
> OLIVER GOLDSMITH

Men greet with handshakes or slight bows. The same is true with women, who may also embrace. Ladies take gentlemen's arms, not hands, when walking. The fashion is to lift the heels slightly between steps. Armholes are particularly tight, restricting full range of motion, so arms are never straight at the sides. They are curved in various degrees and most gestures are made between the waist and the shoulders.

Bowing and curtsying

Bows are highly varied in this period, as they are starting to disappear. Some men are starting to simply bend forward slightly at the waist, not much more than a nod, and ladies to do no more than a small dip. For more traditional gentlemen, the bow involves moving the right foot to the side and putting weight on that foot, while the left is merely supported by the toe. Take off your hat and move it to the side, with a slightly inclined back. As you rise again, move the left foot up behind the right in the fourth position. The tricorn hat is removed in a robust and extroverted way. Extend your arm out nearly straight as it comes up to remove the hat. Let the thumb touch the forehead as the hat is take off and the arm straighten as it is removed, with the inside exposed to others around you. There is more fussing with clothing now, partly because of the sheer bulk, partly because so many people are new to dressing up. It is acceptable, and even recommended in behavior guides, for men to grasp a chair before sitting and rising in order to support themselves against ripping their breeches and for ladies to take skirts in their hands and rearrange them periodically. Unlike the svelte Restoration skirt, the Georgian hoop will not make it through a door without lifting each side to narrow your silhouette as you pass, or sliding in sideways. Early practice is advisable. I was once in a production where rented costumes arrived only just in time for a preview performance. An actress put on her panniers and entered, wearing them front to back, so she looked like she was riding a horse. Fortunately the play was a comedy.

While people fuss over how to greet *appropriately*, such concerns do not prevent this gregarious, outgoing, exhaustingly social group from greeting *enthusiastically*. The Georgians love to meet new people.

> *"Sir I look upon every day to be lost, in which I do not make a new acquaintance."*
> SAMUEL JOHNSON

SOUND

In comparison with the Restoration, language is consciously simple and direct. Decorum is important, but so is a collective need to drop pretension and "speak clear". The effort to avoid indelicacy in language often results in avoiding eloquence as well. Except for an excessive use of silly expletives and fractured grammar, the language is becoming very much as it will be for the next several hundred years.

The many guides to speaking and acting stress the need for a natural, unforced, unaffected delivery. What is uncertain is exactly what would be considered natural by these exuberant, puffed up, extroverted people. It seems less likely that natural means subdued or reserved, than rather open, robust, and unpretentious, striking a balance between bombast and boring.

"We should constantly use the most common, little easy words, pure and proper, which our language affords."
JOHN WESLEY

MUSIC AND DANCE

Music becomes fully available to the common man. Classical music becomes what it is today. Both opera and the mass grow in popularity. Haydn and Mozart perfect the symphonic form. Clarity, balance, order, refinement, control, and restraint all replace Baroque excess. Folk music spreads, and composers take popular street melodies as themes to use in symphonies. The age sees the rise of the professional dancer. There is more exhibition dancing. Contra-dances, however, are done by everyone. Popular ones include the cotillion—a four-couple circle dance, with weaving, often done at weddings—and the rigaudon—another circle dance, with hopping, pliés, and alternating leaps.

The real dance of choice and singular invention of the times is the waltz. Couples embrace and do turns about the room for the first time! The dance moves up from the middle class to intoxicate the aristocracy. Dropping rules and formality, it encourages individual expression. While the minuet emphasized social distinctions, the waltz breaks down all barriers. Moralists are quick to point out the danger of a dance that allows young women to be grasped by their partners, thrown into the air, and twirled about. Another similar and even livelier partner dance becomes popular. The polka involves a simple, up-tempo slide to the side, turn and hop.

"[Actors] who have feeling without fire are not able to express that very feeling; and those with whom spirit gets the better of sensibility, always run to excess . . . Insipidity is the general character of the inferior performancer and extravagance is too much that of the superior ones."
JOHN HILL IN
THE ACTOR OR A
TREATISE ON THE
ART OF PLAYING

KEYS TO THE WORLD

IMAGES

Architecture of the Adams brothers, Robert and James—Covent Garden and Drury Lane—operas of Gluck—symphonies and oratorios of Haydn, and the vast body of music of Mozart—Handel's *Messiah* and *Coronation Anthems*—paintings of Gainsborough and Watteau, large canvases, with perfect skies and clouds—Dequevauviller's *L'Assemblee au Salon*—Fragonard's *The Swing*—portraits by Lely, Kneller—engravings by Bosse, Hogarth, and Bouche—Chippendale furniture—Swift's *Gulliver's Travels*.

Figure 7.7

The Blue Boy by Gainsborough © Francis G. Mayer/Corbis

Figure 7.8

Mrs. Sarah Kemble Siddons, the undisputed queen of British theatre,
© Bettmann/Corbis

Outstanding actors: David Garrick, Charles Macklin, Spranger Barry, Thomas Sheridan, William Powell, Sarah Siddons, Hannah Pritchard.

MASKING

"Taste does not come by chance: it is a long and laborious task to acquire it."
SIR JOSHUA REYNOLDS

While the wearing of literal masks declines in popularity, the new social mask of choice is Middle Class Respectable, invented and shaped by the period. A solid outward show is employed. Lewd and power-mad impulses are carefully concealed and suppressed in favor of good-hearted decency. Everyone creates an appearance of joviality and good humor. Sentiment is often used as a personal mask, an increasingly popular choice among women. The middle-class code requires a shocked look for some moments, a deeply sympathetic one for others, and stern disapproval for quite a few. There is as much concern for personal image and outward appearance as at any time in history. "What will the neighbors think?," more than an idle question, becomes a guiding principle. Taste becomes a matter of study.

THE PRODUCTION

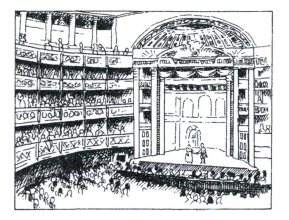

Most productions attempt relative authenticity. The spirit of the shows is comfortable enough that the peculiar clothes and props are not off-putting to an audience. Some allowance for comfort on the part of the actors is, however, frequently made. The language demands are fewer than in earlier plays, and character analysis is straightforward. These people are not difficult to understand. Much of the challenging fun in performance comes in the wigs, panniers, and general life as a human barge. Their motives are clearer and can be played with absolute directness.

CONTEMPORARY PARALLELS

1. The charge of government during the period was to "decrease the taxes of the rich and increase national defense." Sound familiar? Any administration within memory ever accused of these goals?
2. Newspapers represent a blur between fact and opinion.
3. Many view the entire world from an economic point of view.
4. Those with new money will go to extravagant, even ludicrous, lengths to display it and to prove they have the right to it.
5. An anti-intellectual aura combines with an interest in learning. The learning is based on how things work, not why.
6. The natural human form is expanded, much as with steroids.
7. The high-tech industry dominates, with machines and gizmos virtually a national addiction.

> *"Life is a jest, and all*
> *things show it.*
> *I thought so once, but*
> *now I know it."*
> JOHN GAY (HIS OWN
> EPITAPH)

8. A strong ambivalence exists towards sentiment, rejecting it, then turning around and getting downright cloying.
9. Plays are forerunners to modern sitcoms and screwball comedies, with formula plot, broad characterization, and hearty, robust humor.
10. The expanded middle class dominates the culture.

PLAYS AND PLAYWRIGHTS

Here are those scripts most likely to be produced:

Gay, John	*The Beggar's Opera,* 1728
Goldsmith, Oliver	*She Stoops to Conquer,* 1773
Lillo, George	*The London Merchant,* 1731
O'Keefe, John	*Wild Oats,* 1791
Sheridan, Richard Brinsley	*The Critic,* 1781 *The Rivals,* 1775 *The School for Scandal,* 1777
Tyler, Royal	*The Contrast,* 1787

SCENES

The Critic

DANGLE, MRS DANGLE
A drama reviewer's spouse wishes he would give up his calling, so that her house may be free of all sorts of riffraff, including actors.

DANGLE, SNEER, PUFF
An entrepreneur without scruple turns his hand to the calling of playwright.

The Rivals

MRS MALAPROP, JACK, LYDIA
Captain Jack Absolute (alias Beverly) has come to call on the niece of the woman more prone than any in history to misuse the English language.

JULIA, FAUKLAND
Two lovers insist on allowing pride and decorum get in the way of their love.

The School for Scandal

SIR PETER, LADY TEAZLE
A much younger wife, plucked from the country, has learned all too well how to spend her much older husband's money in the city.

SNAKE, LADY SNEERWELL
A leading gossip-monger prepares, with the help of her hissing servant, to take on the world.

She Stoops to Conquer

KATE HARDCASTLE, MARLOW (TWO SCENES)
Marlow is desperately shy in the presence of ladies, but bold in the presence of wenches. Discovering his malady, Kate disguises herself as a household maid in order to ease their courtship.

Wild Oats

ROVER, HARRY
A nobleman has been trying on the life of an actor, but now feels compelled to end his "vacation."

Figure 7.9

The Enraged Musician
by William Hogarth
© Historical Picture
Archive/Corbis

(Note: Group exercises exploring ideas in this chapter are located in Appendix G.)

SOURCES FOR FURTHER STUDY: Molière

Baur-Heinhold, M., *Baroque Theatre*, New York: McGraw Hill, 1967.

Chapman, R.A., *The Spirit of Molière*, Princeton: Princeton University Press, 1940.

Ducharte, Pierre Louis, *The Italian Comedy*, New York: Dover, 1966.

Grimarest, J.-L. de, *The Life of Molière*, Paris: Isidore Liseux, 1877.

Gordon, Mel, *Lazzi*, New York: Performing Arts Journal, 1983.

Gross, Nathan, *Aesthetics and Ethics in Molière's Comedy*, New York: Columbia University Press, 1982.

Howarth, W.D. and Merline Thomas (eds), *Molière: Stage and Study*, Oxford: Clarendon Press, 1973.

Hubert, Judd D., *Molière and the Comedy of Intellect*, New York: Russell & Russell, 1972.

Lawrenson, T.E., *The French Stage in the Seventeenth Century*, Manchester: University of Manchester Press, 1957.

Lewis, W.H., *The Splendid Century: Life in the France of Louis XIV*, Oxford: William Morrow & Company, 1954.

Matthews, Brander, *Molière: His Life and His Works*, New York: Kessenger, 2005.

Mongredien, Georges, *Daily Life in the French Theatre at the Time of Molière*, London: George Allen, 1969.

Oreglia, Giacomo, *The Commedia dell'Arte*, New York: Hill & Wang, 1968.

Scott, Virginia, *Molière: A Theatrical Life*, Cambridge: Cambridge University Press, 2000.

Tilley, A.A., *Molière*, Cambridge: Cambridge University Press, 1936.

Wilcox, John, *The Relation of Molière to Restoration Comedy*, New York: Benjamin Blom, 1964.

Wiley, W.L., *The Early Public Theatre In France*, Cambridge: Harvard University Press, 1955.

Wright, C.H.C., *French Classicism*, Cambridge: Harvard University Press, 1920.

DVDS

Aspects of the Commedia Dell'Arte (Giovanni Poli)
Clear demonstration of stock character types that so heavily influenced the writing of Molière.

Molière (Laurent Tirard)

A rollicking farce conjecturing adventures on the part of Molière that would eventually provide inspiration for his writing *Tartuffe*.

The Misanthrope (Edward Petherbridge)

Employing Richard Wilbur's translation, this production is highly stylized and compelling.

Tartuffe (Jean Meyer)

In French, with English subtitles. Thought to be very similar to the production style employed by Molière's own company.

Tartuffe or *The Imposter* (Anthony Sher)

A striking RSC production, translated by Christopher Hampton, in which the language is superbly spoken.

Tartuffe (Broadway Theatre Archives)

A less original but highly enjoyable New York production of the play.

SOURCES FOR FURTHER STUDY: The Georgians

Boswell, James, *Life of Samuel Johnson*, New York: Random House.

Boswell, James, *On the Profession of a Player—1770*, London: Elkin, Matthews, & Marrot, 1929.

Chesterfield, Lord, *Letters to His Son*, 1771.

Downer, Alan S., "Nature to Advantage Dressed; Eighteenth Century Acting, *PMLA,* LVIII, December, 1943.

Gay, Peter, *Age of Enlightenment*, New York: Time-Life Books, 1965.

Gray, Charles H., *Theatrical Criticism in London to 1795*, New York: Benjamin Blom, 1966.

Hill, Aaron, *The Art of Acting*, London: J. Osborn, 1746.

Hill, John, *The Actor or a Treatise on the Art of Playing*, London: 1755, reissued by Blom, 1972.

Lloyd, Robert, *The Actor, A Poeticle Epistle*, London: Dodsley, 1760.

Melville, Lewis, *Stage Favorites of the Eighteenth Century*, New York: Benjamin Blom, 1969.

Murphy, Arthur, *The Life of Garrick (1801)*, New York: Benjamin Blom, 1969.

Rude, George, *The Eighteenth Century,* New York: Free Press, 1965.

Russell, Gillian, *Women, Sociability and Theatre in Georgian London*, Cambridge: Cambridge University Press, 2007.

Shaftesbury, Earl of, *Characteristics of Men, Manners, Opinions, Times*, 1711.

Southern, Richard, *The Georgian Playhouse*, London: Pleiades Books Limited, 1948.

Thaler, Alwin, *Shakespeare to Sheridan*, Cambridge: Harvard University Press, 1922.

Wildeblood, Joan and Peter Brinson, *The Polite Society*, New York: Oxford University Press, 1963.

DVDS

Tom Jones (Tony Richardson)

Probably the consummate Georgian film in spirit and robust comedy, this adaptation of Henry Fielding's famous novel won an Oscar for best picture.

Barry Lyndon (Stanley Kubrick)

While more somber and cold than plays of the era, this film is filled with visual information and provides an indelible lesson in the class structure of the times.

Amadeus (Milos Forman)

Particularly in the numerous party and opera performance scenes, this film demonstrates period dress, manners, sensibilities, and pastimes.

The Madness of King George (Nicholas Hytner)

A dark-humored look at the descent of George III into dementia and the resulting political upheaval.

The Rivals, She Stoops to Conquer, The School for Scandal, The Critic (BBC)

Lovely, well-spoken renderings of all four plays are offered in these productions mounted for television. Each captures the peculiar balance of genteel exaggeration and proper audacity characteristic of the period.

The Rivals (Rachel Kavanagh)

A lively, rollicking production from the Bristol Old Vic, filmed before a live audience.

School for Scandal (Broadway Theatre Archives)

The most recent Broadway revival, featuring an all-star cast.

COMPARISONS OF MANNERS STYLES

Manners plays share a concern with social issues over cosmic ones, an interest in concrete, daily reality over mysticism, and a desire for a stable society over twists of fate. Because characters are completely preoccupied with themselves, scripts are always contemporary and local. Here are some areas of contrast:

Table 7.1

	Restoration	Molière	Georgian
Time	1660–1710 mercurial, quixotic	1658–73 rapid, impulsive occasionally stately	1755–1800 brisk, lively
Space	intimate displays, poses	court to court (tennis to King's)	large, well lighted scenic developments
Place	elegant urban	neutral, social	any city/country spot
Values	personal gratification	reason without hypocrisy	benevolent good humor
Structure	languid elite class erratic exclusive	absolute monarchy unities imposed all strata	representative government ordered, tidy middle class
Beauty	long, lean, painted	charming, demure, sprightly	fresh, fulsome, open
Sex	yes, please assignations	inappropriate topic ridiculous	categorized male outlet
Recreation	gossip flirtation	trickery deception	social events decoration
Sight	curls, ribbons, feathers decorative	same as Restoration	white, wide, symmetrical, architectural
Sound	arch, crisp, sly	sharp, bright, relished	simple, direct, proper

EXPLORING STYLE

THIS SECTION is about moving beyond historical styles to those that are still in flux and, in some instances, open to innovation. It is about how a work may be shaken up, and how fusion occurs as different styles interact. The eighth chapter deals with scripts written in one time but performed or set in another. It also addresses the varieties of translations, adaptations, and editions, and finally offers a system of connecting any script to the audience for which it is being presented. Just as in the third chapter, this one addresses style issues that influence the full range of periods and genres.

The ninth chapter surveys the genres (the *Isms*, from Romanticism through Post-modernism) that define today's theatre, their origins, manifestos, and the acting challenges involved in each of them. The final chapter brings all the material into the actors' off-stage life. It examines personal style, both in performance and in life, so that the text ends as it begins, with the actor's examination of self. The primary pragmatic issue dealt with in this chapter is the way lack of style self-knowledge may be blocking an actor's entry into the world of the play, and the way in which gaining such knowledge can offer power and freedom.

8 DISPLACED STYLE
PLAYS OUT OF THEIR TIME

TO SOME extent, every play gets displaced when it is performed outside the place or group for which it is intended. In classical drama, it is always an option to pull the play's audience back in time and to make them feel much like the *original* audience. But what about plays that do not reflect their own time to begin with? Or plays that do not travel well? Or that change radically, depending on which translator, adaptor, or editor gets hold of them? Displaced plays, like displaced persons, are searching for a home.

BLENDING STYLES

The audience comes with one set of answers to the ten style questions. The playwright comes with another, perhaps choosing answers from her imagination instead of her society. The play may be set in an era where a third set of answers exists. Sometimes, the producer decides to set it in yet *another* time and place. How to get the recipe right? Here are some suggestions:

1. Research all contributing worlds, being open to each having some part of the final product, even if that part ends up small.

2. Discover the purposes of the production, beyond simply serving the script. If the director is doing *The Taming of the Shrew* to show the systematic brainwashing and abuse by which spirited women are violated, everyone involved deserves to know. If the director is doing it to prove that men are stronger, wiser creatures, and that the

world is more civilized if these strong, wise men make the all–important decisions, everyone should know.

3. Examine reverberations from current events and controversies that can change the impact of the play. If a war is declared, a government overthrown, a new fad emerges, or a national lifestyle statistic is released, the play may suddenly take on unexpected reverberations.

4. At least consider doing the show exactly as it was done originally. But how much do we *know* about the original? How much is genuine knowledge vs scholars making good guesses? Each of the periods in previous chapters has been discussed in terms of the likelihood of authentic production, so it is clear that the closer the time of writing to the time of playing, the more likely is this choice. Georgian and Restoration plays are staged similarly to the originals far more often than are Greek or Elizabethan. The farther away in time and space, the more mist surrounding the originals, the more differences in cultural perspective, the less likely is an authentic recreation.

5. Historical research must come up against a "So what?" for relevance. An actress playing Titania, queen of the fairies, once stopped rehearsal to ask me if there were still rushes spread across the stage floor at this time in history. Good for her for reading about Elizabethan floors, but she is the queen of the fairies. She may be walking on gossamer speckled with soft diamonds, illuminated by fireflies, and spreading like a carpet of spider webs in her path. An imaginative choice is often more useful than a scholarly one.

The following "out of time" plays were written in one time and place and set in another, often earlier. Most classical plays are also set in eras *prior* to their dates of authorship. The ancient Greek playwrights were not much interested in fifth-century Athens as a source of drama. Only Aeschylus' *The Persians* is "contemporary" to the times, and only Aristophanes' satires are "local". The only play Shakespeare writes that seems to be at all about Elizabethan daily life is *The Merry Wives of Windsor*. The past, then as now, seems an irresistible source of inspiration.

The time of Shakespeare and the four hundred years before him (1200–1600) are the most popular choices for modern writers to "displace" new plays. Most of us look to these eras for our own Once Upon a Time fantasies.

DISPLACED PERIOD PLAYS

DISPLACED GREEK

Anouilh, Jean	*Antigone*
Giraudoux, Jean	*Electra*
	Tiger at the Gates

Jeffers, Robinson	*Medea*
	The Tower Beyond Tragedy
Sartre, Jean-Paul	*The Flies*
Walcott, Derek	*The Odyssey*

DISPLACED MEDIEVAL, RENAISSANCE AND ELIZABETHAN

Anderson, Maxwell	*Anne of the Thousand Days*
	Elizabeth the Queen
	Joan of Lorraine
	Mary of Scotland
Anouilh, Jean	*Becket*
	The Lark
Bolt, Robert	*A Man for All Seasons*
	Vivat! Vivat! Regina
Bond, Edward	*Lear*
Eliot, T.S.	*Murder in the Cathedral*

Freed, Amy   *The Beard of Avon*

Frye, Christopher   *The Lady's Not for Burning*
                                  A Yard of Sun

Gibson, William   *A Cry of Players*

Giraudoux, Jean   *Ondine*

Goldman, William   *The Lion in Winter*

Gressieker, Hermann   *Royal Gambit*

Herman, George   *A Company of Wayward Saints*

Maccoby, Hyan   *The Disputation*

Osborne, John   *Luther*

Shaffer, Peter   *The Royal Hunt of the Sun*

Shaw, Bernard   *St Joan*

Stavis, Barry   *Lamp at Midnight*

Synge, J.M.   *Deirdre of the Sorrows*

DISPLACED MANNERS

Balderston, John   *Berkeley Square*

Bond, Edward   *Restoration*

Hampton, Christopher   *Les Liaisons Dangereuses*

Hirson, David   *La Bête*

Jackson, Nigel   *Molière Plays Paris*

Jeffreys, Stephen   *The Libertine*

Marivaux, Pierre   *The Triumph of Love*

Rattigan, Terence   *A Bequest to the Nation*

Rogers, David   *Tom Jones*

Rostand, Edmund   *Cyrano de Bergerac*

Shaeffer, Peter   *Amadeus*

Shaw, Benard   *The Devil's Disciple*

Thomas, Eberle   *The Three Musketeers*

| Weiss, Peter | *The Persecution and Assassination of the Marquis de Sade . . .* |
| Wertenbaker, Timberlake | *Our Country's Good* |

BLENDS

Some scripts are clearly neither contemporary realism, nor directly inspired by a single historical period or culture. They are eclectic combinations, or they create a time that never existed. Knowledge of historical acting styles is still helpful because they often hearken back in some way. Some are set in modern times but written in verse, hardly the modern voice of choice. All create very specific style demands and opportunities. All create their own worlds.

Barnes, Peter	*Red Noses*
Barry, Philip	*Peter Pan*
Camus, Albert	*Caligula*
Coward, Noel	*Blithe Spirit* *Hay Fever* *Private Lives*
Daniels, Sarah	*Byrthrite*
Dunlap, Frank and Jim Dale	*Scapino*
Eliot, T.S.	*The Cocktail Party*
Fry, Christopher	*A Phoenix Too Frequent* *Venus Observed*

Figure 8.2

A scene from *Blithe Spirit* at the Chanticleer Theater, LA. Photo: Rob Williamson

Kopit, Arthur	*Oh Dad, Poor Dad . . .*
Kushner, Tony	*The Illusion*
Learner, A.J. and Frederic Lowe	*Camelot* *My Fair Lady*
Miller, Arthur	*The Crucible*
MacLeish, Archibald	*J.B.*
Molnar, Ferenc	*The Swan*
Richardson, Howard	*The Dark of the Moon*
Rogers, R. and O. Hammerstein	*The King and I*
Shaw, Bernard	*Androcles and the Lion* *Arms and the Man* *Caesar and Cleopatra* *Don Juan in Hell* *Heartbreak House* *Pygmalion*
Stoppard, Tom	*Rosencrantz and Guildenstern are Dead*
Webber, A.L.	*Phantom of the Opera*
Whiting, John	*A Penny for a Song*
Wilde, Oscar	*The Importance of Being Earnest* *Lady Windermere's Fan*
Wasserman, D.	*Man of La Mancha*

Figure 8.3

Scott Giguere and Shawn Telford as Guildenstern and Rosencrantz, directed by Josh Costello, MFA Thesis production, University of Washington, Seattle 2003

DISPLACED SCENES

Amadeus

CONSTANZE, SALIERI
Mozart's wife requests a teaching position for her husband. The court composer offers her terms, which she at first rejects, but later reconsiders.

Anne of the Thousand Days

ANNE, HENRY
Shortly before her execution, the king visits his wife to determine once and for all if the adultery for which she stands convicted is actually true.

Becket

BECKET, HENRY (TWO SCENES)
Young king and best friend frolic together with boyish abandon, then meet years later when "the honor of God" has made them adversaries.

BECKET, GWENDOLYN, HENRY
After promising his king and friend to return him an equal favor, Becket is asked to sacrifice his mistress, a conquered aristocrat, the thing he loves most in the world.

The Crucible

ELIZABETH, JOHN
Puritan wife searches her heart to find forgiveness and understanding for her unfaithful husband.

A Cry of Players

WILL, ANNE
Young Shakespeare can no longer endure the stultifying Stratford life and begs his wife to let him go to seek his destiny.

Cyrano de Bergrac

CYRANO, ROXANNE
He has loved her since their childhood, but she is beautiful, and he is a source of constant ridicule for the size of his nose. She has asked for a secret meeting and his hopes are high.

Elizabeth the Queen

ELIZABETH, ESSEX
The queen visits her rebellious young lover to attempt him to recant his treasonous acts and save his life.

The Importance of Being Earnest

GWENDOLYN, CECILY
When city sophisticate makes a sudden visit to the country home of her fiancé, she is greeted, much to her surprise, by a young, attractive, and not altogether naive young woman.

JACK, ALGERNON
Two London dandies debate appropriate behavior and the chances of the one to marry the other's cousin.

JACK, LADY BRACKNELL
A suitor for the hand of the formidable Lady Bracknell's daughter is interrogated as to his qualifications for marriage.

La Bête

PRINCE CONTI, VALERE
A consummate performer persuades his monarch that the court theatre cannot survive without him.

The Lady's Not for Burning

ALIZON, RICHARD
A young, convent-raised girl rejects her arranged marriage to a wealthy dolt, and chooses instead a poor clerk, whom she has just met today.

JENNET, THOMAS
He wants to be hanged, but no one will take him seriously. She wants to live but is about to be hanged for witchcraft. Together they find something larger than death—love.

Les Liaisons Dangereuses

VALMONT, MERTEUIL
Two decadent members of the French aristocracy plan new ways to corrupt the innocents around them.

The Lion in Winter

HENRY, PHILLIP
The young French king devastates the old English one by informing him that Henry's son has seduced him as a boy.

ELEANOR, ALAIS
The two women in Henry's life try to regain their own relationship and move beyond the battle of who is to be his queen.

HENRY, ALAIS

The king awakens his young mistress and promises to take her to Rome, for an annulment that will free them to marry.

A Man for All Seasons

HENRY, THOMAS

A dangerous, volatile king debates the relationship between church and state with his devout, principled, careful "servant."

Mary of Scotland

MARY, ELIZABETH

A rebellious, passionate queen is imprisoned by a crafty, political one. Now jailor visits prisoner.

Ondine

ONDINE, HANS

A young knight falls in love with a beautiful water sprite and unknowingly seals his own death warrant.

St Joan

JOAN, DAUPHIN

A peasant girl becomes the driving force behind the reticent young ruler and inspires him to action.

Tiger at the Gates

HECTOR AND HELEN, NEAR END OF ACT 1

The Trojan War is about to take place. The Trojan general is determined to stop it. The woman who caused it all is indifferent.

CASSANDRA AND ANDROMACHE, OPENING SCENE

The pregnant wife of the victorious general and his prophetess sister disagree on the prospects for peace in the land.

HECTOR AND ULYSSES, NEAR END OF ACT 2

The two generals meet to see whether Helen's infidelity is sufficient cause for war.

PERIODS AND PLAYS LESS CHOSEN

The first major omission you may have noticed is Greek comedy. Aristophanes was a comic genius on a par with the big three tragedians of the first flowering of drama. Of his eleven surviving scripts, the most popular (and the subjects of their satire) are:

Greek—Aristophanes	*Frogs* (Euripides)
	Clouds (Socrates)
	Birds (city life)
	Lysistrata (war)

The last, in which wives hold out sex on their husbands until the men stop fighting, is produced continuously, because its humor and wisdom are universal. Aristophanes managed to offer serious criticisms through rollicking wit and great fantasy. But his plays are about his *own* city in his own time. When they are done well, the *current* president, prime minister, mayor, policies, issues, and fads are all satirized. The plays are almost always updated so that the current *parallel* to the past target is zapped. The result is an acting style that is more Marx Brothers than classical.

No other periods have produced more than isolated instances of great vehicles for acting. The following scripts stand out along the road. They are all worth your attention and may enter your life at some time.

| Roman—Plautus | *The Menaechmi* |
| | *Amphitryon* |

These Roman plays have been adapted many times, with the device of mistaken identity used over and over. They are kindred to the work of Aristophanes, cruder, louder, more frantic. Acting in them feels like doing circus vaudeville with a plot.

Medieval—authors unknown	*The Passion Play*
	The Second Shepherd's Play
	Everyman
	The Nativity
	Master Pierre Patelin

The anonymous ancestors of Shakespeare grounded their plays in liturgical form, filled with Biblical characters, and they remained popular until Elizabeth I banned them as Catholic propaganda. Most have been adapted into very modern-sounding texts, but the originals offer all the challenges and much of the beauty of classical verse. They are far more simplistic than Shakespeare, but they bequeath him a legacy of blending comedy and tragedy in the same play. They share with the Greek tragedies the fact that the audience knows the plot and so watches the play to understand motivation (Why did Cain do that to Able, anyhow?) and to find reflections from sacred history to apply to their own lives. These are folk dramas. They are like folk music that precedes and inspires grand opera.

| Neo-classic—Jean Racine | *Phèdre* |
| Eighteenth-cent. Italian— Carlo Goldoni | *The Mistress of the Inn* *The Servant of Two Masters* |

Racine's work stays within the neo-classic confines and has much of the power of a Greek tragedy, written from a seventeenth-century perspective (he is a contemporary of Molière's). The two Goldoni plays have much in common with Molière in their *Commedia* influences, stock characters, dominating, busybody servants, and lively, non-stop action. They also share Georgian robust good humor and simplicity. Both hold up extremely well in twenty-first century production.

EASTERN VISION: Kabuki on the horizon

As a culture, we tend to stay focused on our own tradition, often missing a wealth of style wonders. There is a galaxy of Asian theatre, full of breathtaking stylization and conventions that can be fused into western production. We are going to focus on only one here, which is probably the easiest for westerners to understand.

Kabuki is a lively form of dance-like drama, dating back to the 1600s. Kabuki, from the verb Kabuku, means "incline," "slant," "tilt," or "trend." From the beginning, the form has been associated with the fashionable avant-garde, so it has lent itself to surprising new twists. It has come to mean, in popular usage, a break with the past. An outrageous and eccentric female dancer, Izumo-no-Okuni, was called by her audiences *kabuku* and *kabukumono*, meaning weird and flashy, which would be true of such a show even now. Although Kabuki began as seventeenth-century religious parodies performed by women, it ironically developed into a male-only theatre designed for demonstration of actor versatility, and recently came full circle with the revival of all-women companies.

The plays are epic and play fast and loose with history. They involve lightning-fast costume changes, freezes, and poses, juxtaposed with rapid, energized moves. Kabuki is popular because it deals with the joys and sorrows of common people living in a remote and fascinating past. It blends tragedy, comedy, realism, and romanticism all into one performance. The acting techniques, called *kata*, are passed from one generation to the next. The first kabuki actors were called *yakusha*, signifying one who officiates at a religious ceremony. The plays always teach some moral lesson.

Performance always relies on dance, music, and elaborate vocal effects. A guiding principle is *yatsushi*, in which the old is presented but at the same time modernized and parodied. Kabuki is a yatsushi of Noh, as haiku poetry is a yatsushi of tanka. Famous characters may appear in outrageous modern garb and predicaments. Narrators (joruri) frequently act as chorus for the play, and stage assistants (koken) dressed in black, act as invisible helpers, disappearing into the imagination, handing props to actors, holding garments out for display, and sometimes acting as scenery. Black is the color of non-existence, so a black curtain symbolizes night. Make-up also involves color symbolism.

Kabuki theatre uses a 90 foot proscenium opening, and important entrances are made on a *hanamichi*—a runway through the audience from the back of the auditorium.

The chorus (jorjuri) traditionally sits upstage on a raised platform. The traditional stage is made of cypress scrubbed with bean curd, which greatly aids movement on the resulting surface. A pull curtain (*hiki maku*) is standard, although revolving stages, lifts, and other spectacular effects occur in view of the audience.

Entrances and exits are made from the audience left, traditionally believed to be superior to right. Those entering on the hanamichi are of high rank or in some way due serious attention. Hanamichi exits are powerfully rhythmic. Great beauty of stage picture is sought, each scene ending with a striking pose. Stopping frequently to pose (called a *mie*) is preceded by energetic motion, then offset by the sudden stillness. This convention crystalizes the striking contrast within the form, between intense drama and utter tranquility. Acting veers from the stylized (*jida-mono*) to the realistic (*sews-mono*).

Music and percussion are heavily used to support actors. Ceremonial music involves stick drum and wooden clappers, special–effects (*geza*) music adds shamisen and flute, and *de-bayish* or song and chant music to accompany recitation. The flute is traditionally believed to have the power to bring back departed spirits.

Modern Kabuki has added everything from acrobatics to giant puppets to high technology. The scripts are not performed letter perfect, but are thought of as libretti or simply a blueprint for performance. Kabuki scripts are rarely performed by American actors, but the style itself has found recent increasing use for mounting other scripts, especially Shakespeare and Greek tragedy. Consider that Greek tragedy involves a mixture of drama, poetry, music, and dance and you see an immediate connection. Kabuki is often compared to Shakespeare, because of the sweep, grandeur, and sheer size of it. For those scripts by Shakespeare involving magic, storms, and high ritual (*The Tempest, Macbeth, A Midsummer Night's Dream, Lear,* and *Titus Andronicus* among others), the form offers an ideal way of handling these elements through striking theatrical conventions instead of high tech. A forest suddenly created and dissolved by koken and a wind by swirling chiffon are simple, highly theatrical possibilities.

ADAPTATIONS AND EDITIONS: Can this be the same story? Can this be the same sentence?

"It is important to be aware of all the editing that has gone on. The word we're revering may not be the playwright's intended word."
REX RABOLD

Myths and legends are fair game. Anyone may retell the story of Hercules, Arthur, or your Aunt Tillie if she is legendary. If the author significantly revises an old story, it is now regarded as a new play. Each of the three big Greeks writes an Electra startlingly different from the others. An editor prepares a work for publication, altering punctuation, spelling, and arrangement on the page for purposes of clarification. Editors are seldom actors, directors, or playwrights. They are often not even theatre-goers. They often read the line, not as it might be spoken, but rather as it might be silently read.

I was puzzled the first time a Shakespeare festival director instructed each of us in a cast to go back to the First Folio (the earliest collected works of the playwright) and check for differences between what appeared in that massive volume and the paperback single-script copy that we, for convenience, used in rehearsal. I was amazed first at how many differences there were, and at how often, after looking at both choices, I found the original more speakable and more intriguing as a line to be delivered. So, whenever you are in a play that has appeared in different editions, check out as many as possible. Every change of a comma or a colon may reveal some clue to meaning.

Do the same with any word not precisely clear, because words were not only being invented during many of these periods, but they often had multiple meanings. Because the first dictionary (*The Table Alphabeticall of Hard Words*) did not appear until 1604, and the first dictionary of all *English* words did not appear until 1721, there is no standard guide to definitions prior to these dates. Since Elizabethan and Restoration writers are particularly fond of puns, key words, therefore, may have multiple meanings.

TRANSLATIONS: Can this be the same script?

Here are some samples of ways in which translators have dealt with the same speech. This is the very first speech of *Antigone*, perhaps the most performed of all the Greek tragedies. The play is a debate between youthful desire for what is morally right and mature desire for order, betwen personal justice and justice for all. Antigone, has, in direct defiance of her uncle Creon, ruler of Thebes, buried her brother. Because her brother had been fighting against the government (in a battle with her other brother), he has been denied the rights of burial. She is asking her sister, Ismene, if there is any more grief possible that could come to their family.

> Ismene, O my dear, my little sister, of all the griefs bequeathed us by our father Oedipus, is there any that Zeus will spare us while we live? There is no sorrow and no shame we have not known. And now what is this new edict they tell about, that our Captain has published all through Thebes? Do you know? Have you heard?
>
> (Shaemus O'Sheel)

> My sister, Lov'd Ismene, of the ills
> Which sprung from Oedipus conceives there
> One, by the hand of Jove, not brought on us
> His sole-surviving children? There is nought

That sinks the soul with anguish, deep distress,
Shame, and disgrace, but in thy ills and mine
I see it all. E'en now what new decree
Is rumour'd by the Chief as late proclaim'd
Through all the city. Know'st thou? Hast thou heard?
(R. Potter)

Ismene, sister mine, one life with me,
Knowest thou of the burden of our race
Aught that from us yet living Zeus holds back?
Nay, for nought grievous and nought ruinous,
No shame and no dishonour, have I not seen
Poured on our hapless heads, both thing and mine.
Uttered, men say, to all this Theban folk?
Thou knowest it and hast heard?
(Robert Whitelaw)

O sister! Ismene dear, dear sister Ismene!
You know how heavy the hand of God is upon us;
How we who are left must suffer for our father, Oedipus.
There is no pain, no sorrow, no suffering, no dishonor
We have not shared together, you and I.
And now there is something more. Have you heard this order,
This latest order that the King has proclaimed to the city?
(E.F. Watling)

Ismene?
Let me see your face:
my own, only sister,
can you see
because we are the survivors
today Zeus is completing in us the ceremony
of pain and dishonor and disaster and shame
that began with Oedipus?
And today, again:
the proclamation, under the rule of war
but binding, they say, on every citizen . . .
Haven't you hard?
(Richard Braun)

Ismene, dear sister,
You would think that we had already suffered enough
For the curse on Oedipus:

I cannot imagine any grief
That you and I have not gone through. And now—
Have they told you of the new decree of our King Creon?
(Dudley Fitts and Robert Fitzgerald)

Ismene listen. The same blood
Flows in both our veins, doesn't it, my sister,
The blood of Oedipus. And suffering,
Which was his destiny, is our punishment too,
The sentence passed on all his children.
Physical pain, contempt, insults,
Every kind of dishonor. We've seen them all,
And endured them all, the two of us.
But there's more to come. Now, today . . .
Have you heard it, this new proclamation,
Which the king has made to the whole city?
(Don Taylor)

Read the six versions aloud. Let the differences in the words act on you. Ancient Greek is a strongly inflected language, with verse lines roughly equivalent to trochaic hexamater (six feet each, with a stressed followed by an unstressed syllable), a rhythmic pattern all but impossible to translate literally into our language. It seems tentative, uncertain, and overly inflected to our ears. The result is that many translations seem like adaptations, they veer so far from the original. There is almost every form of translation available: rhyming couplets, blank verse, free verse, flowery and curt, vague and blunt, romantic and sardonic, elevated and basic. One translation has the messenger in Antigone call her a "bitch."

"For such is our pride,
   our folly and our fate,
That few, but such as
   cannot write,
   translate."
SIR JON DENHAM

Differences are even sharper in two characters' exchanges. Experiment the same way with the following two tense Greek confrontations. Prior to the following exchange with Medea, Jason has married another woman, and Medea has retaliated by killing their two children. This is their first confrontation after the murder:

M: Think of thy torment. They are dead, they are dead!
J: No, quick, great God; quick curses round thy head!
M: The Gods know who began this work of woe.
J: Thy heart and all its loathliness they know.
M: Loathe on . . . But, Oh, thy voice. It hurts me sore.
J: Aye, and thine me. Would'st hear me then no more?
M: How? Show me but the way. 'Tis this I crave.

J: Give me the dead to weep, and make their grave.
M: Never!. . .

(Gilbert Murray)

M: The children are dead. I say this to make you suffer.
J: The children, I think, will bring down curses on you.
M: The gods know who was the author of this sorrow.
J: Yes, the gods know indeed, they know your loathsome heart.
M: Hate me. But I tire of your barking bitterness.
J: And I of yours. It is easier to leave you.
M: How then? What shall I do? I long to leave you too.
J: Give me the bodies to bury and to mourn them.
M: No, that I will not . . .

(Rex Warner)

M: See, they are no more:
       I can hurt you too.
J: They'll live, I think
       in your tormented brain.
M: The gods know who began
       this whole calamity.
J: Yes, the gods know well
       your pernicious heart.
M: Hate then: I spurn
       the wormwood from your lips
J: As I do yours; so let us
       be rid of one another.
M: Yes, but on what terms?
       That's also what I want.
J: Let me have the boys—
       to mourn and bury them.
M: Never!. . .

(Paul Roche)

M: The children are dead. That will sting you.
J: No! They live to bring fierce curses on your head.
M: The gods know who began it all.
J: They know indeed, they know the abominable wickedness of
       your heart.
M: Hate me then. I despise your bitter words.
J: And I yours. But it is easy for us to be quit of each other.
M: How pray? Certainly I am willing.

J: Allow me to bury these bodies and lament them.

M: Certainly not.

(Moses Hadas and John Harvey
McLeon)

Which translation is best? It depends on the kind of production, showcase, audition planned. Is it going to be formal, with masks, and highly theatrical costumes? Is it going to be simple, with minimal make-up and subtle playing? Wildly experimental? Text and production should match. If you are choosing a translation for a scene or monolog, consider your purpose. What is the impact you wish to make? If you are putting together an audition with two monologs, what do you need yet to show? A capacity for artifice? A direct, strong attack? Facility with language? Raw honesty? Many actors stop at the first translation they find. Many are disappointed, because they have been told that a certain work is deeply moving, but they read it, and it leaves them cold. It may be the translation that leaves you cold. These are great plays. They are survivors. Keep looking until you find the version that suits you.

Molière's plays, originally in French and often in a form of verse that is not quite alexandrines (see Chapter 7), have also been widely translated. What follows is a speech by Alceste, the title character in *The Misanthrope*. He is criticizing, as he frequently does, hypocrisy. He is unhappy when people claim to like someone whom they do not care for at all.

The original speech reads:

> Une telle action ne saurait s'excuser,
> Et tout homme d'honneur s'en doit scandaliser.
> Je vous vois accabler un homme de caresses,
> Et témoigner pour lui les dernières tendresses;
> De protestations, d'offres et de serments,
> Vous chargez la fureur de vos embrassements:

Some translations include:

> I call your conduct inexcusable, Sir,
> And every man of honor will concur.
> I see you almost hug a man to death,
> Exclaim for joy until you're out of breath,
> And supplement these loving demonstrations
> With endless offers, vows, and protestations.
> (Richard Wilbur)

. . . there's no excusing such an action, and every man of honour ought to be shocked at it. I see you stifle a man with caresses, and profess the utmost tenderness for him; you overcharge the transport of your embraces with protestations, offers and oaths.

(H. Baker and J. Miller)

There can be no excuse for such an action!
A man of honor should be scandalized!
I watch you load a man with compliments,
With protests of the tenderest affection;
You put your arm around him, uttering vows
Of aid and comfort and profound esteem.

(Morris Bishop)

There is no excuse for such behavior: every man of honour would shrink from it. I see you overwhelm a man with caresses and show him the utmost affection; you burden the wealth of your embraces with protestations, offers and vows of devotion.

(A.R. Walker)

. . . there is no excuse for such behavior, and every man of honour must be disgusted at it. I see you almost stifle a man with caresses, show the most ardent affection, and overwhelm him with protestation, offers, and vows of friendship.

(Waldo Frank)

Here is a lover's spat from *Tartuffe*. Marianne's father is insisting she marry a man she loathes instead of her beloved Valère. But their pride and stubbornness provide as much of a barrier as her father's plans.

V: Of course! You never really loved me at all.
M: Alas! You may think so if you like.
V: Yes, yes. I may indeed: but I may yet forestall your design. I
     know on whom to bestow both my hand and my affections.
M: Oh! I don't doubt that in the least, and the love which your good
     qualities inspire . . .
V: Good Lord! Let's leave my good qualities out of it. They are slight
     enough and your behaviour is proof of it.

(John Wood)

V: I'm sure
     you never really loved me.
M: You're entitled
     to your opinion.
V: Yes, I am entitled;

       and I may manage to forestall your plan,
       by taking my proposal somewhere else.
M: I wouldn't be surprised; you're so good-looking . . .
V: God, let's leave my looks out of it, shall we?
       They can't be that good, as you've just yourself
       demonstrated.

                           (Christopher Hampton)

V: Doubtless, and you never had any true love for me.
M: Alas! You may think so if you please.
V: Yes, yes, I may think so; but my offended heart may chance to be
       beforehand with you in that affair, and I can tell where to offer
       both my addresses and my hand.
M: I don't doubt it sir. The warmth that merit raises—
V: Lack-a-day! Let us drop merit. I have little enough of that, and
       you think so.

                           (H. Baker and J. Miller)

V: And I now see
       That you were never truly in love with me.
M: Alas, you're free to think so if you choose.
V: I choose to think so, and here's a bit of news:
       You've spurned my hand, but I know where to turn
       For kinder treatment, as you shall quickly learn.
M: I'm sure you do. Your noble qualities
       Inspire affection . . .
V: Forget my qualities, please.
       They don't inspire you overmuch, I find.

                           (Richard Wilbur)

While critics, actors, and directors disagree which translations of Greek plays are the best, there is wide consensus that the Molière works of translator Richard Wilbur are most effective. They are actable and come closest to both the metre and the rhyme scheme of the original. Your choice of translator depends on your style of presentation. A highly physical performance, *Commedia* inspired, with lots of slapstick, will suit a different text than an arch, still, and elegant presentation in the manner of the Comédie-Française.

When looking at a script, consider each of the following before making a translation choice:

1. speakability (trippingly on the tongue or just tripping?);
2. form (rhymed, free, or blank verse, prose, a mix? similar or removed from the original?);

3. phrasing (short to lengthy? smooth to choppy?);
4. vocabulary (common, elevated, clear, inaccessible?);
5. characterization (distinct or do all speak similarly?);
6. notes (none or explanations of alternate line readings and meanings?).

When tracking down multiple translations, aside from electronic searches, try *Play Index* for translations in anthologies; *Chicorel Theatre Index* for possible omissions in the above; play script catalogs from major publishing houses (Samuel French, Dramatists Play Service, and Dramatic Publishing Company), which may each have several separate translations; *Books in Print* to determine new editions recently published; as well as the *Arts and Humanities Index, The New York Times Theatre Reviews, New York Theatre Critics Reviews, Book Review Index, Book Review Digest,* or a reference librarian. If all else fails, you could become a translator or an adaptor yourself.

PLACING VS DISPLACING

How do you get over linguistic and cultural hurdles in period-style production? As literacy and vocabulary scores drop, and visuals replace conversation, it is the actor who has the stewardship to keep the classic plays alive and vital, keeping the words immediate and impossible to ignore. Start by returning to a point of innocence regarding the play, so that you can rediscover, step by step, to get back to the spirit and relationships at the heart of the play.

PLACING THE PLAY: Thirty steps to classical acting

Style plays are always potentially strange to an audience and potentially intimidating to an actor. Displacement is always in the air, ready to invade both sides of the footlights. Many actors get assigned a period-style monolog or scene and spend weeks "hating" it because they do not yet understand it. Or they get the general idea, but not the moment-to-moment riches. Here is the best way I have found for placing the work so that it makes perfect sense to both performer and observer. Some of these ideas were introduced in Chapter 3 as general principles. Try them here as rehearsal exercises connected to a specific text. These thirty steps will clarify and enlighten. Some can even thrill you.

1. SCANSION: Honor the meter

If the play is not written in verse, you can obviously skip this step. Otherwise, sit down with the script as if it is a musical score and count it out. The laborious effort of identifying stressed vs unstressed syllables, elisions, compensations, trochees, and iambs will pay off in a clear rhythmic pattern, with much information about pronunciation and interpretation. Once you understand the stresses, you can let the script's pulse work on you and free you. (See Chapter 3 and Appendix C.)

2. STANISLAVSKI-BASED CHARACTER ANALYSIS: Unearth circumstances and motives

These principles of the Stanislavski System are always present in any clear, sharp performance. Can you answer as your character would?

For any single encounter:

- Relationship? (What do characters mean to each other?)
- Objective? (What do I want?)
- Obstacle? (What is in the way?)
- Strategy? (What is my game plan to achieve my objective?)
- Tactics? (What are my plays within the overall game plan?)
- Text and subtext? (What do I speak out and what do I hide or imply?)
- Interior monologs (What is the "tape" running in my head saying?)
- Evaluations (What do I consider and reject, each time I choose something else?)
- Beats (What transactions occur? How many are there? What points are won? How does the encounter break into smaller encounters?)

For the full life of the character:

- Given circumstances? (What are the major influences shaping me?)
- Magic if? (What do I the actor need to project/change to play this person without judgment?)
- Objective hierarchy? (What does the character want most to least? In what order?)
- Through-line of actions? (What is the arc of my behavior? How do my events pull together into a pattern?)
- Score of script? (How can I mark and shape the script to help me map my work? How can it become my musical score?)
- Endowment? (Which props and people do I need to imagine possess more than they do? What do I need to enhance and fill in?)
- Recall? (What can I use from my own experience to illuminate that of the character?)
- Images? (How can I tap my senses to bring the performance to life?)
- External adjustments? (What do I the actor need to change about my persona to play the role and serve the script?)
- The creative state? (How can I relax and make myself available to inspiration?)

The most common complaint from coaches and directors working on the classics is that their actors skip these steps instead of adding new ones. What point is pointing your toe correctly if you don't know what you want?

3. RECORDING WHILE READING FROM THE MANUSCRIPT: Memorize and review

Listening to yourself can open your ears. It will assist you with memorization. You want to get the words right, especially since some are well known. The more you work on a role, the less likely you are to look at the text and see the unfortunate re-writes you are speaking. If you record it *early*, word for word, you will not only get to see how far you have come with time, but also ensure that you are text perfect. Play the tape while you do other activities at home. Let the *words* come to *you*. They will.

4. REFERENCE ROOM RESEARCH: Unearth new clues to meaning

OED and lexicons—multiple and contradictory meanings

Define every key word. Do not neglect the ones you think you already know, which may have double, triple, or more messages. You need to know if a word has lost some twist in time, so you can punch it to help the audience. The Oxford English Dictionary (the OED) is the most highly regarded as an authoritative source, with a wealth of historical detail. What seems like a purely scholarly exercise will reveal a wealth of suggestions for new line readings.

Other editions—punctuation, spelling, phrasing hints

Check out editions and translations beyond the one you are using. One comma can change a line. Learn how these traffic signals can re-direct and guide you.

Production histories—traditions in interpretation

Knowing what other actors did with the role is important. Keeping yourself pure is arrogant. As Brecht said, steal from the best. Do not study these actors' work relentlessly, but look at it once, on DVD, or track it down in production history sections such as the Shakespeare *Variorum*, summarizing performance choices actors have made throughout history. Keep what excites you. Then make it your own.

5. REGULAR TAPING AND PLAYBACK—Gain permission to do more

Many are afraid to tape themselves because they hate what they hear. The truth will set you free. Listen to yourself often enough to get past that first coy embarrassment and reach an objective assessment of that voice. What most actors discover in playback is that they are doing much *less* than they thought they were. You think you are making this tremendous drop in pitch for strength in a given moment, and you hear that you have merely dropped a few notes. What happens? Taping and listening gives you permission to go the distance. Video equipment offers even more possible feedback.

6. ANTITHESES—Try to overdo

Classical writers set words in opposition to each other. One word is set up, and another comes along to match it, slap it, or knock it down. Sometimes, four and five sets of words knock out or counterbalance each other. Consider this sentence: "The *actors* in white at the back are more interesting than the *jocks* in lime at the front." There are three sets of contrasts. Each requires a slight punching. The first word is pointed, and its "mate" is given a similar, but greater, twist to help connection and contrast. This is the single exercise that has clarified speeches for actors and audiences.

7. KEY WORDS—Punch up even more in long passages

Audiences hear about 70 percent of what is spoken from the stage and fill in the rest. In classical drama, this percentage drops considerably because of obscure language. It is likely that you are being too restrained in kicking the most important images. Fight the tendency to play general emotion and meaning, instead of finding each image anew. Serve up the images like great gifts.

8. ADJECTIVES—Giving them value. Make them modify, qualify, and change nouns

If the writer adds a word before a noun, it is probably intended to *work* that noun in some way. Let it. The temptation is to just dive into the phrase and get through all the modifiers as quickly as possible. Often, modifiers act *against* the noun and alter it. Honor the adjective for its power and use it.

9. METAPHORS—Set them mentally in quotations, underlined, or in capital letters

When you are not speaking directly but using metaphor, your delivery needs to help the listener so they don't think you're really talking about your dog when you mean the kingdom. The three techniques above can separate the thoughts from the more direct ones. If you putting something into quotations, you will retard slightly before and after the phrase and thrust it forward as you speak. If you put a line under it, you will stretch and sweep the phrase deliberately from beginning to end, finishing it off quite sharply. If you think of using capital letters, your attack on the initial letter of each word will be bold, big, and precise, as if you are putting it up on a marquee. All three techniques grab attention. Each gives a different edge to the line.

10. COINING—Refuse to play summaries or generalizations

A big temptation is to speak these famous words as if they have been written in granite and recited many times. For your character, they have *never* before been uttered. When you begin the most famous soliloquy, you have *no idea* how you will end it. You start a sentence unsure how it will develop. Mint the words and evaluate as you move through each thought. The more familiar the material, the greater the need. Consider always what your character might have said, but chooses not to. Almost choose to. This technique can lead you to startling, original readings.

11. ALLITERATION—Try to overdo matching letters

A series of words with the same first letter or sound is worth punching. Your character delights in her capacity to do this. Relish, twist, and turn the sound, instead of backing off from it. A series of matched sounds is just that—a series. Savor it.

12. VERBS—Punch up and relish action

Classical sentences are long. The trip from subject to predicate can seem interminable. By the time the period roles around, you can lose the drift. By thinking of the verb as a truly active word, breathing and full of energy, you can often bring the whole sentence to life. Grab each verb, feel it and free it.

13. HUMOR AND IRONY—Unearth all kinds

Don't forget the jokes, folks. These characters are wittier than you and I. They see sly smiles at every corner, little digs, undercuts, and twists that further delight on each hearing. Explore all possibilities and then go back and do it faster. When you first discover irony, you will be tempted to take forever with it, just in case anyone missed it. Once adept, you can flick it off. These little sparks will not light if labored.

14. AUDIENCE RELATIONSHIPS—Find the balance

Classical theatre often acknowledges audiences more overtly. Use your listeners the way you really use the people who are always there for you, no matter what. Most of the time, if you are alone on-stage, the speech will come to life if you turn to the audience and share it with them. Try going deep into yourself at extreme on the speech, then try thrusting it out in a very public way. Then blend, recognizing that even when you confide in a best friend, there are times when, in that friend's presence, you internalize and ponder. The audience is there to help you at every turn. When you turn inward, do so with the knowledge that they will come inward with you.

15. SENSE OF FIRST TIME—Expect the opposite of what you get

If the play is a tragedy, the characters rarely expect it to be.

Most people live in a state of hope. No matter what the past disaster, today may pull it all together. Forget that you have read the play, and work your way moment by moment through the character's life, just as you do your own. This frees you from a sense of self-importance. Return each sentence to a point of innocence.

16. INTERRUPTIONS—Speak as if audience heckling possible at any moment

The original audiences were rowdier than ours. Few listeners today will stop you mid-speech in defiance. But learn to play as *if* that is a possibility. Imagine that your thoughts are sound, the audience believes in you as a person, but they may take issues with any of the particular twists and turns of your observations. Really good friends do this. It will give you an energy, an immediacy, an impulse to keep it moving.

17. EXITS—Audience or partner exit is possible at any moment

In any moment, the person you are with may end the scene by just leaving. Rehearse as if each line may indeed end the scene. See what happens. A dynamic is set up if you realize that you need to be vital and compelling enough, or your partner and everyone else may move on to other pastures.

18. BOTTOM OUT—Explore mumbled, naturalistic, scratch and itch delivery

Reduce the speech from high-flying affectation to simple, direct, basic communication. Speak without any sense of the world of the play, but with a strong need for contemporary truth. Take the speech way "down" to find out what to throw away and what to simply let happen. The most electrifying performances are those with surprise, variety, and sudden unexpected contrast. Great actors know when to drop the grandstand play and get simple.

19. OVER THE TOP—Go for old-fashioned oratorical delivery, full of bombast and overplaying

If you listen to recordings of actors of the nineteenth century (Julia Marlowe, E.H. Sothern, Ellen Terry, Otis Skinner, Edwin Booth), it is clear that what was thought brilliant now seems ludicrous, but imagine yourself in an enormous opera house, with a public desiring the full romantic unleashing of dramatic passion. Let it rip. Feel the rush of going over the top, of giving the top balcony its money's worth. Discover those moments where nothing less than full out bravura, razzle-dazzle, tour de force will do. It is a great rush. Almost everyone who tries this finds isolated moments where they realize that diva delirium is just what they need.

20. SPEED-THROUGH—Determine if you have earned each pause

After working on so many of the techniques above, it is tempting to labor a performance, because there is now so much *going on* internally and technically for the performer that time has gone into slow motion. So, occasionally, speak the part as rapidly as possible. In speed-through, you may sacrifice projection, but keep other elements in place. Video can be crucial at this stage, because you may honestly feel you are going as fast as you can. Then you view the vid and marvel at all the dead air.

21. MUSIC—Sing it like an original musical or opera

Most of this language of classical drama is higher than day-today speech. Some of it is *much* higher. The words, rhythms, images, and phrases all come closer to song than speech at given moments. Polarize into that sphere. Imagine that the play is either opera or a contemporary "sing-through" musical. Let your pitch, volume, quality, and phrasing know no bounds where music is concerned. Afterwards, acknowledge where it felt and sounded good, and which operatic elements might feed your performance. In the case of ritualized drama, such as Greek tragedy, you may literally wish to chant, intone, or sing given passages.

22. CHANGES—Using shifts in moods, tactic, and attack

The big trap in long speeches is to find an overall mood and to play "in general." Avoid this. Name each section of the speech in a way that forces you to get clear how the character is different now than she was a minute ago.

23. LAYERING—Give shape to the performance

Elements relating to Stanislavski but developed by subsequent research in behavioral sciences can "layer in" a performance.

Conditioning forces—How hot, cold, familiar, unknown is the space? How light, safe, comfortable? How late are you? What thoughts may be distracting you?

Imaging—To make each line bright, what pictures, scents, sounds, and touches should you be considering?

Private audience—Which people in your character's life haunt him, no matter what? Which are always present? Who is his god, mentor, idol, deadly enemy? How are these the same or different than your own?

Grouping—What does the character think of the groups around her? Which does she judge and which does she join?

Rehearsed futures—How does she fantasize and plan the future? What does she fear and dream may happen?

Suppression—Which impulses does your character sublimate, feeling they are not appropriate to unleash?

24. ONOMATOPOEIA—Coloring your words

Since so much archaic language and convoluted phraseology can limit a modern audience's enjoyment, your job is to get them past these barriers. Imagine the show is written in a foreign tongue and try to make each word and sound comprehensible. Shape and taste each image. Then go back and try to do all of it as fast as you can. Push yourself to edit the air so that your speech is bright and seamless.

25. APPREHENSION—Understanding beyond simple comprehension

Recognize that rhythm, sound, and texture can clarify an audience experience beyond a direct, cognitive level. Get them to *feel* and *sense* the language as you do, experiencing what you are on an apprehending level beyond recognition. Brilliant writers create speeches that depend less on conscious computing of definition than an almost magical combination of rhythm, music, sound, and silence. Let the magic work through you.

26. CONTEMPORARY PARAPHRASE—Clarify the work in modern idiom

One of the best ways to bridge the language gap is to make certain that the subtitles in your own head are complete and accurate. If you know every word in your own terms, your chances are greater for making those words clear to your audience. The most effective exercise is to take the text and "translate" it yourself. Present your scene or monolog in entirely contemporary language. Update the situation and use as much slang or jargon as you wish. Paraphrase word by word and phrase by phrase. A big pitfall in this exercise is to go for the general "gist" of the line. Note places you have just skimmed and haven't a clue what you are saying. These are the passages that really need work. Fight the temptation to lampoon the script. After a few inevitable collapses of laughter, move past absurdity and work for simple word-by-word clarity. Use the exercise two ways. First perform the entire scene or act in paraphrase, and then go back and run the lines as written. Next time, alternate on individual lines and speeches. Say the paraphrase until you are clear and comfortable, then go back and speak the original, coining the words.

27. RHYMES—Give them extra pride and relish

Savor your cleverness. When your character completes a couplet, instead of backing off from the artificiality of rhyming, enjoy your imagination and connection. When you say brilliant things in conversation, don't you savor them? It is a significant source of pride to alliterate, and an incredible rush to rhyme! Instead of feeling put off, the audience will begin to share your relish and almost feel they are writing the couplet with you.

28. MONOSYLLABIC LINES—Give them air

When a line has words of only (or mostly) one syllable, it is a clear sign that a deliberate, measured, drumbeat of a delivery is required. No matter how light and mercurial you have been previously, this kind of line is a signal to measure and allow each word to breathe. It can offer an electrifying contrast to the multisyllabic complexity.

29. AMBIGUITIES AND CONTRADICTIONS—Look for them and play them

If your character analysis does not produce a tidy package, be delighted and intrigued. Find each moment where your character is headed in one direction, but veers in another. The very qualities that are most frustrating are often ultimately the most compelling. Each of us is a series of contradictions, and we all have areas no one can figure out. Big, brilliant characters have complex edges, so don't try to get them to fit too perfectly into your notebook.

30. TRUTH + POETRY + CHARACTER = Keep all three balls in the air

Rehearse them in alternate patterns. Speak and move with total *honesty*. Then shape the *verse* brilliantly. Then work on the detail of this particular *human being* down to the slightest mannerism. Honor each at various rehearsals with the knowledge that, if you do, they will all eventually honor each other in your performance.

(Note: Group exercises exploring ideas in this chapter are located in Appendix H.)

9 GENRE STYLE
The Isms

IN A STORE, the term *generic* means a low-cost, non-name brand product. In general usage, it means "average" or "typical." In drama, the term genre refers to type, class, form, movement or category. The individual product inside the genre may or may not end up "ordinary."

Realism is the dominant contemporary genre. The term "Realism" did not emerge until the 1850s. In a way, however, the dramas of all periods are "realistic," because performances on-stage reflect the way each period sees itself —not necessarily the way that its people really looked or lived, but their collective **self-concept**. Every period has its own vision of Realism. That vision can look quite "unreal" from the perspective of time.

The predominant Isms emerged during the nineteenth and twentieth centuries in approximately this order:

Romanticism: early 1800s
Realism: 1850s
Naturalism: 1873
Impressionism: 1874 +
Symbolism: 1890–1920
Expressionism: 1910 (or 01)
Futurism: 1910–30
Dadaism: 1916
Constructivism: 1921
Surrealism: 1924

Didacticism: 1927
Absurdism: late 1940s
Feminism: late 1960s
Postmodernism: 1980s

While most Isms are no longer produced in their pure form, elements continue to influence both playwrights and productions. Why should an actor know all this? Because the terms are batted (and battered) around by directors, designers, and critics attempting to explain what a show is striving to accomplish. Often a script is not written in a particular genre, but the production team decides to *present* it in that form. Sometimes this illuminates the text. Other times it destroys it. Some Isms began in art, music, literature, politics, or philosophy. The terms are not understood the same way by everyone, so there can be confusion when they pop up. You need to know enough to communicate well with others involved in a show and you need to know enough to protect yourself within the show. Many Isms are not actor concepts at all, but it is the actor who is expected to function within the "concept" all around her.

Most Isms begin with a manifesto or public declaration of principles, from someone who does not like the status quo and feels it is time for a change. Each manifesto is summarized here, followed by historical background, sight and sound characteristics, and images to help grasp the genre. Where relevant, performer skills required and representative play titles are listed.

ROMANTICISM

A rejection of classical order in favor of imagination and emotion.

Figure 9.1

Liberty Leading the People by Eugène Delacroix © The Gallery Collection/Corbis

MANIFESTO

Feelings are more important than thoughts. Anything that is natural is good. A true hero is often forced to stand outside society in order to live life as passionately and fully as it should be lived. Beyond mere earthly life lies a higher truth, found through art and feeling. True happiness can only be found in the spiritual realm. The sublime in nature and art must be worshipped. Everything exotic and picturesque has value. Even something ugly and grotesque has worth, if it stimulates powerful response. We long for the past.

Our heroes often need to die by the final curtain, as a result of following their hearts in an uncomprehending world too full of reason, machines, and rules, a world that has become spoiled by moving too far away from its natural state. Still, to die and leave the physical world is not too great a price to pay for being true to oneself.

BACKGROUND

By the late 1700s, neo-classical, strictly ordered works depicting the ideal, rather than the natural, are declining in appeal. German writers Goethe, Schiller, and Klinger develop a school of writing called *Sturm und Drang* (storm and stress), espousing the rights of the individual, the glory of nature, and the power of emotion. English poets Coleridge, Wordsworth, and Forrest catch the drift. A form of drama evolves that is still, in some ways, with us today.

IMAGES

Terror of the self—music of Chopin, Liszt, Wagner, Tchaikovsky—love through death—Byron's poetic drama *Sardanapalus*—poetry of Shelly, Blake—Brighton Pavilion—honor and duty above all practical consideration—an evil establishment trying to crush passion—Delacroix' operatic paintings—Turner's landscapes—rich, lush, heavy, sensuous, operatic.

Figure 9.2

Brighton Pavilion
© PA Photos

SIGHT

Often large casts, spectacle, settings long ago and/or far away, bold and fluid movements, flowing garments—think capes, scarves, billowing fabric, grand and graceful maneuvers. While romanticism is influential in bringing about historical accuracy in costuming, the look is likely to be flamboyant. The vision of nature tends toward glorious sunrises and tornados, not just a blah day. A romantic hero need not be beautiful, but should somehow be extraordinary.

SOUND

Plays are in verse or poetic prose on a grand level. Great variety of expressiveness is desired. Delivery should be defiant and sentimental, without becoming strident and cloying.

SKILLS

Great bravado and expressiveness. Willingness to hit operatic heights. Romantic acting is tour de force bravura playing, soulful and expansive. Training in classical ballet and great beauty of tone can help. Can you suffer deeply and defy society? Of course you can. This is full-blown melodrama and not for those who tend towards half-hearted attacks or who giggle easily.

WORKS

Dumas, Alexandre	*Camille*
Goethe, Johann Wolfgang	*Faust*
Hugo, Victor Hernani,	*The Hunchback of Notre Dame, Les Misérables*
Rostand, Edmund	*Cyrano de Bergerac*
Shelley, Mary	*Frankenstein*
Shelley, Percy	*Prometheus Unbound*

REALISM

Art based on nature and real life, without idealization or distortion.

MANIFESTO

It is time to reject the impractical and visionary. Theatre should show how everyday people react to their environments with multidimensional, internally motivated, and believably portrayed characters. Human psychology and the five senses should be employed to explore relationships on-stage. Only drama that has direct relevance to the *life* of the viewer has genuine *meaning* to the viewer. We have had enough plays about kings and lords, rebels and visionaries. What about grocers? Social and domestic problems are experienced by us all and need to be illuminated on the stage.

BACKGROUND

The French Revolution, industrialization, and Darwin's and Comte's theories of evolution sequentially lead to an interest in bringing social themes and scientific inquiry to theatre. By the mid 1800s, the extravagant characters and callow insights of melodrama are losing interest. Freud's work on the clinical analysis of personalities, Ibsen's scripts of carefully crafted social import, and Stanislavski's acting system all reflect an interest in seeing life portrayed on-stage as it is lived off-stage. The term achieves full validation when the Moscow Art Theatre names its Fourth Studio "the Realistic Theatre." For the first time in history, plays do not focus on people who are exceptional by title, power, beauty, intellect, or eccentricity of personality. For the first time, characters on-stage could be people next door.

IMAGES

Selected truth—the well-made play—relevance—democratic individualism—writing about what you know—life as model—explore, then reduce—photojournalism—paintings of Philip Pearlstein—novels of Steinbeck and Faulkner—poetry of Sandburg and Frost.

Figure 9.3

Rosa Parks sits in the front of a bus in Montgomery, Alabama, after the Supreme Court ruled segregation illegal on the city bus system on December 21, 1956 © Bettmann/Corbis

SIGHT

All scenic elements are as accurate as possible, with some editing of irrelevant details and some partial or skeletal sets. Settings look like modifications of actual locales. An attempt is made to create the feeling of a real living space, with considerable use of props. Largely through the influence of Émile Zola, the box set develops, though sometimes several settings are represented with a cinematic overlapping of action. Costumes and properties try to be true to both historical period and character personality. Movement is true to life, which may mean hesitant, unobtrusive, and occasionally random. Movement strives to appear motivated and honest.

SOUND

Use of pauses, nonverbals, incomplete thoughts, informal sentence structure—all the characteristics of speech on the street or in the home. Scripts are prose, barely heightened from normal conversation. Declamatory artifice in delivery is rejected, but clarity is maintained.

SKILLS

Capacity for public solitude and strong sense of natural interaction with other actors, props, and setting. Strong believability. Ability to tap internal resources and find truth. Working on character from motivations. Eye for contemporary detail, shading, and nuance. No ham actors allowed. Minimal scenery chewing allowed.

WORKS

Earliest and most influential plays and playwrights:

Chekhov, Anton	*The Three Sisters*
	The Cherry Orchard
	Uncle Vanya
	The Seagull
Ibsen, Henrik	*A Doll's House*
	Hedda Gabler
	The Wild Duck

Most of the works of the two most revered twentieth-century playwrights, Arthur Miller and Tennessee Williams, are realism. Elements are also strongly present in the works of Wendy Wasserstein, Michael Weller, Lanford Wilson, Marsha Norman, Tina Howe, A.J. Gurney, Aaron Sorkin, Beth Henley, and August Wilson.

NATURALISM

Life with details, including the ugly, the distracting, and the irrelevant.

Figure 9.4

A scene from David Belasco's production of *Tiger Rose*

MANIFESTO

Realism only *begins* to oppose artificial theatricality and does not go far enough! It chooses which elements of life it wishes to present. What is needed in the theatre is stark reality, with no compromise. Individuals cannot be held responsible for what they do, because heredity and environment overwhelm them. Plays should be more human and less social in orientation. No characters are specifically sympathetic; they just are. Plays do not need to progress rapidly, be briskly paced, or have clear climaxes. Endings can be pessimistic, ironic, cynical, and even disappointing, like life. Actors should *live* the life of their characters on-stage rather than *play* them.

BACKGROUND

All the forces influencing realism, with the addition of rising interest in socialism and the average working man, combine to form naturalism. Émile Zola coins the phrase "slice of life" (can we assume that realism was merely a bite or sip of life?) and writes *Thérèse Raquin*, the first consciously conceived naturalistic drama. His introduction for that play is the complete manifesto of the movement, which catches on in France (Antoine and the Théâtre Libre), Germany (Otto Brahm and Freie Buhne) and Russia (Stanislavski and the Moscow Art Theatre). An attempt is made to establish the movement in England by Shaw and Grein's Independent Theatre, but the British don't care for it. Eventually, the detail necessary for naturalism is adopted by filmmakers, but its impact remains in the theatre today. Naturalism is the alley behind realism's street.

IMAGES

Warts and all—don't look away—man as victim—effects of environment—David Belasco's sets—scientific scrutiny —Théâtre Libre—Dégas' last works—documentary—tight close-up—white noise—the uncensored mind —who needs an ending?—eavesdropping.

SIGHT AND SOUND

Set detail may be extensive—water runs, stoves cook, and (in a famous Antoine production), real flies buzz around real beef hanging in a meat market scene. A highly contained box set is likely. Real clothes are better choices than costumes. The environment is a major character. It has more influence than any human in the play. Movement needs to seem spontaneous. The fourth wall is very much in place, the audience never acknowledged. Actors are more likely to turn their backs to the house and generally drop theatrical conventions in favor of accuracy. All movement comes from inner experience.

One of the most vivid touches of naturalism in television history took place in the old series *All in the Family*, when the sound of Archie Bunker flushing the toilet was heard. This was not a naturalistic show, but that was a naturalistic moment. When a flush is heard on network TV, we think about all the off-stage noise and life sound usually edited in performance.

Speech may be muffled or even mumbled if it is true to character. Language is basic, gritty prose, often lower class in syntax. Conversations do not necessarily go anywhere. Snatches of dialogue may be lost or drowned out by background noise or distractions.

SKILLS

"Zola descends into the cess-pool to take a bath, I to cleanse it."
HENRIK IBSEN

Naturalistic acting demands great subtlety and a complete lack of artifice. The performer must have a willingness to drop charm, charisma, and the need to command an audience. A simplicity that belies technique is essential. It is much more difficult than it first seems, because actors are so accustomed to editing ourselves for performance. A complete concentration and an ability to play *in* the moment and to go *with* the moment are needed, as is a willingness to "let it all hang out." A director I once worked with referred to a role as a "scratch and itch and belch and fart" part. He meant naturalism. How does Ibsen, the father of realism, feel about all this?

WORKS

Gorky, Maxim	*The Lower Depths*
Hauptman, Gerhart	*The Weavers*
Steinbeck, John	*Of Mice and Men* *Grapes of Wrath*
Strindberg, August	*Miss Julie*
Zola, Émile	*Therèse Raquin*

IMPRESSIONISM

A higher world, artificially created and emotionally sublimated.

Figure 9.6

The Banks of the Seine at Argenteuil by Gustave Caillebotte © Christie's Images/Corbis

MANIFESTO

Theatre should attempt to capture the moment through feeling, mood, and atmosphere. We reject realism's need for identifiable motives. There is no need for a clear-cut climax, beginning, or end. Characters may be bewildered and indecisive, because that is what we all are. Human desires are half formed, our impulses rarely followed through. Violence and rage often smolder and remain unreleased. Art should reflect our pervasive passive and/or helpless state.

BACKGROUND

The movement evolves from a famous painting (*Impression: Sunrise*) by Claude Monet and develops first into a school of painting, beginning in Paris in the mid 1870s, then develops as a music movement. It is a reaction against the near-strident intensity of Romanticism and lingers in theatre as tolerance for mood pieces without recognizable structure. Its influence remains strongest in the scenic elements of a production.

IMAGES

Fleeting light—rough brush strokes—spontaneity—repetition of hue—small planes of color—quick rendering —filtered boulevard, distanced landscape—vantage point—juxtaposition—paintings by Pissaro, Caillebotte, Cassatt, Morisot, Renoir, Bazille, Sisley—Café Guerbois—scrim.

SIGHT

The foreground disappears into the background, with total emphasis on creation of mood. Movement is tentative, half formed, incomplete, often juxtaposed with tableaux.

SOUND

Overlapping dialogue, isolated fragments of speech, heavy use of background sounds may be employed and orchestrated. In the purest form, voices will blend with each other and with other sounds to become sometimes indistinguishable.

SKILLS

Sustaining a mood effectively and the capacity to perform compellingly, without a recognizable through line or sense of character development. Capacity to blend with environment, physically and vocally when required to do so. Since these works intermingle with both realism and expressionism, the actors may be asked to blend elements of all three. This Ism is more likely to involve the design team than the actors.

WORKS

Maeterlink, Maurice	*Pélleas and Mélisande*
Strindber, August	*The Father*
Zola, Émile	*Nana*

SYMBOLISM

Poetic, dreamlike theatre seeking the profound or mysterious in life.

MANIFESTO

Mood and atmosphere are far more important than plot or action. Let us drop a simple-minded cause-and-effect mentality. There is no need for characters to have personalities of their own, since they are symbols of the poet's inner life. Ambiguity is the key. Something on-stage is not necessary a *clear* symbol that the audience will recognize, but rather symbolic of the author's *consciousness*. Legend, myth, and spirituality come together to produce evocative theatre. Suggestion is far more powerful than explicit representation. Theatre should seek the profound and the unfathomable experience. Let us turn our backs on objective reality and move into the subjective and intuitive. The autonomy of art frees it from any obligation to deal with social problems in political terms. Art needs to move beyond truth.

> *"Lying, telling beautiful, untrue things is the proper aim of Art"* so that *"life will imitate art."*
> OSCAR WILDE

BACKGROUND

Maurice Maeterlinck and Edward Gordon Craig begin the movement in the 1890s, and it remains popular until the 1920s. Symbolism is a reaction against the growing popularity of realism. Appia and Reinhardt dabble in this movement through lighting and set design, respectively. The paintings of Gauguin, Rousseau, Toulouse-Lautrec, and de Chirico reflect the basic values. Wagner tries to fuse all the elements (music, dialogue, color, light, shape, and texture) together in performance. Film, because of the control it affords, embraces elements of this movement after it falls away from the theatre. The use of a single, monumental, symbolic (though not necessarily comprehensible) set decoration remains common today.

IMAGES

Irrational self—bizarre juxtapositions—projected light—mood music—filters—mixed analogies—your wildest dreams—Marie Lugne—Edgar Allen Poe—Alfred Jarry—Claude Debussy—decadence glorified—Fellini—omnipresence.

SIGHT

Movement may be enigmatic and often accompanies music. Static poses may alternate with ritualized, frenzied, whirling ones. The space is full of shadows, mists, possibly mirrors, with a dreamlike quality. Costumes draw on a range of tribal,

cultural influences, often draped and gauzelike. Much modern dance, in the Isadora Duncan tradition, relates strongly to symbolism.

SOUND

Strong emphasis on the voice and its music. New Age music suits a symbolist production. Language may be full of mysterious references. Statements may be simple nouns rather than completed sentences. Lines tend to be rhythmic, possibly poetic, with hypnotic use of cadence and intensity to build emotion.

SKILLS

Actors must function on a high level of abstraction to play situations associated more with dreams than waking experience, playing larger than life, personifying a quality or trait, and functioning sometimes like a puppet. They must have a willingness to drop the need for clarity in favor of distortion and exaggeration.

WORKS

Andreyev, Leonid	*He Who Gets Slapped*
Jarry, Alfred	*Ubu Roi*
Maeterlinck, Maurice	*The Intruder* *The Blind*

	The Bluebird
	Pélleas and Mélisande
O'Neill, Eugene	*The Emperor Jones*
	The Hairy Ape
O'Casey, Sean	*Within the Gates*
Strindberg, August	*The Dream Play*
	The Ghost Sonata
Wedekind, Franz	*Spring's Awakening*
Wilde, Oscar	*Salome*
Yeats, William Butler	Early plays

EXPRESSIONISM

Life seen through a single set of subjective emotions.

MANIFESTO

Other Isms are too passive and specialized. We need theatre that is forceful, urgent, and emotionally charged, capturing the inner struggle each of us goes through spiritually to develop into the new person of the future. Creating a character is much less important than presenting a strong argument on-stage. Nightmarish, anti-industrial, deliberate distortions of reality are perfectly acceptable ways to deliver a harsh truth. Real theatre is not literary drama, but instead explores consciousness through living performance. Dreams are a major source of truth, and the portrayal of the dreamlike state may illuminate life so that the subjective can be objectified. The real heroes are hidden among the common workers, stifled by a dangerous and dehumanizing system. It is time for fresh subjectivity that mirrors inner psychological realities instead of outer physical appearances. It is time to get serious.

BACKGROUND

The movement originates in the paintings of Auguste Hervé, exhibited in 1901 under the title "*Expressionismes*". Expressionism eventually influences all the arts. While Hervé intends his works to oppose those of the Impressionists, the movement ultimately revolts against Naturalism and Romanticism as well. Vincent Van Gogh and Edvard Munch are the best known of the painters involved, and George Kaiser is the leading dramatist working exclusively in the form, although the later, visionary works of Strindberg and Ibsen are significant contributions. The theatre embraces Expressionism most fully in the 1920s. Meyerhold and his "biomechanics" acting theories (involving gymnastics, ballet, and acrobatics) have influence, as does Freud's analysis of dreams. The movement's early idealism regarding change gives way to utter disillusionment after World War II and eventually becomes more a mode of production than playwrighting.

IMAGES

Author's message, author's message, author's message—sharp contrast and intense distortion—martyrdom—moody, atmospheric lighting—diagonal lines—leaning walls —colored light—nightmares—later dances of Nijinsky, Cunningham and Graham— music of Stravinsky.

SIGHT

Sharp angles, harsh and startling lighting and color. Walls may slope, windows and doors may be deformed, dark shadows may be juxtaposed with shafts of bright light. Platforms, ramps, scaffolding, and unexpected elements (such as a trapeze) may enter the playing space. Geometric images dominate. Movement may involve stark groupings of actors and choreographed histrionic business. Actions may be fragmentary, disconnected, puppetlike or robotlike. Masks and Asian stage technique may be employed. Costumes and props may be grotesquely exaggerated.

SOUND

Explosive language, with a startling contrast between lyrical passages and staccato, almost amputated dialogue. Full range of sound, including non-human noises, shouting, chanting, and barking may be asked.

Movement and dialogue may be repetitious and mechanical, with tempos shifting dramatically.

SKILLS

Actors need a capacity for volatile, emotional, sometimes flagrantly presentational playing, representing an alienated state of abstraction.

WORKS

Capek, Josef and Karel	*The Insect Comedy*
Capek, Karel	*R.U.R.*
Kaiser, Georg	*From Morn to Midnight*
Rice, Elmer	*The Adding Machine*
Shaw, Irwin	*Bury the Dead*
Strindberg, August	*The Road to Damascus*

Figure 9.8

Character sketch for Iris in *The Insect Comedy*, 1974. Courtesy of Robert Doyle Fonds, Dalhousie University Archives and Special Collections, Halifax, NS

Figure 9.9

Figura Nello Spazio, by Enrico Prampolini. Image courtesy of the Museum of Modern and Contemporary Art, Rovereto, Trento, Italy

FUTURISM

Actor as machine and totally integrated theatre.

MANIFESTO

Reject the past and glorify progress. Anticipate a great industrial future! Theatre needs to give formal expression to the energy and movement provided by new machinery. We need strong, broad emotions. Technology must rescue theatre from a deadly museum-like atmosphere and literary, logical bias. Machines and wars can be a source of great beauty. In fact, war is the world's hygiene, cleaning out unfortunate vestiges of the past. Barriers between arts, actors, and audience need to be smashed.

BACKGROUND

Filippo Marinetti's "Manifesto of the futurist synthetic theatre" is the document that most clearly defines the purposes, including the effort by some Italians to wake up their country and get it to leap into the Industrial Age. The concepts later influence Italian fascists. The movement runs from about 1910 to 1930. Eventually, Ionesco employs some of the techniques, as does Performance Art today.

IMAGES

Figure 9.10

Eleven Polychrome by Alexander Calder © Christie's Images/Corbis

War games—ideas that kill—kinetic sculptures—utilitarian objects—designs of Depero—psychology of machines —leather, chains, steel, cement— mechanical ballets of Silvio Mix— electric currents and colored gases— scenography of Enrico Prampolini —Mad Max macho movies.

SIGHT

Multimedia, high-tech wonders, with multiple focus and simultaneous action. Costumes favoring straight lines, metallic surfaces, and loose fit, turning the human silhouette into a mechanical one. Actors are totally integrated into setting, which may be controlled, or the event may occur as street theatre. The look is macho mechanical.

SOUND

Almost anything may be asked. Language tends to be blunt, simple, direct. Sound is masculine and militaristic. Lines may involve ideological diatribes, manifestos, shouting, and mechanical noises, mostly delivered in presentational fashion. The actor is the director's robot and may be asked to perform in a geometric, machine-like fashion. Sound can be just noises rather than lines. "Music" may be created out of sounds of sirens, machine guns, and other war sounds.

SKILLS

Highly developed technical skills, great patience, complete letting go of desire to portray realistically. Ability to completely eliminate your own idiosyncratic, detailed behavior in favor of total integration into surroundings. A strong masculine attack, along with the stamina to endure sustained, violent, high-energy, repetitive sequences.

WORKS

Balla, Giacomo	*Disconcerted States of Mind*
Canguillo	*Detonation*
Marinetti, Filippo Tommaso	*Feet*
Settimelli	*Sempronio's Lunch*

DADAISM

Expectations must always be contradicted.

MANIFESTO

Nothing is sacred! Theatre should take a nihilistic approach to life and a revolutionary attitude towards art. Anti-art is the way to think; "creative" acts are worthless. Audiences should be infuriated, enraged, and moved beyond rationality to passion. All elements of the past need to be destroyed. All beliefs have no reason. The future smacks of death, so the moment is all that matters. Spontaneity is the closest anyone can come to creating; the more shocking and violent the better.

BACKGROUND

Inspired by the writings of Franz Kafka, the movement is conceived in Zurich by Tristan Tzara and spreads to France, led by Hugo Ball. Dadaism itself defies the keeping of records, so its progress is randomly transcribed. The Dada Gallery is established in 1916, and the ideas are prominent until 1922. More a means of creating a theatrical event than of writing scripts, dadaism does not produce a body of work.

IMAGES

Anti-art, anti-reason, anti-thought—Kurt Schwitters—terrorism—fingernails scratching a screen door—eating garbage, worms, and excrement—your own personal worst gross-out—car horn locked into honk—freewheeling, unconnected, non-verbals.

SIGHT, SOUND

Largely improvisational and spontaneous. Incongruous dialogue, full of non sequiturs, shouting, singing, berating, gibberish, obscenities. Space tends to be vast, bare, un-localized, and abstract, but it may be buried in irrelevant items. Laughing at the audience is a common mode of attack.

SKILLS

Willingness to humiliate yourself and others aggressively. An imaginative sense of what will strike others as obscene and sacrilegious. Audacity and a confrontational, defiant nature.

WORKS

Concept discourages scripting. Some elements appear in these works:

Peter Weiss	*Marat/Sade*
Tom Stoppard	*Travesties*
Sam Shepard	*Unseen Hand*
e.e. cummings	*Him*
Gertrude Stein	*Four Saints in Three Acts*

CONSTRUCTIVISM

Build a story, don't tell it.

MANIFESTO

Sentimentality and individual feeling have no place in the theatre. Theatre has been too interested in illusion, and it is time to strip all that away. The unsightly clutter of the naturalistic stage needs to be replaced with an architectural vision. It is time for acting to turn back outward, replacing psychological and emotional nuance with gymnastic and acrobatic precision. A play is just a vehicle for examination and revelation.

Constructivism precedes today's deconstructivist theatre, in which a play is taken apart for revelation of a theme of current interest, with no regard to the playwright's intentions. The script may then be reconstructed in a new configuration.

BACKGROUND

A joint project between sculptor Lyubov Popova and director Vsyevolold Meyerhold in 1921–2 produces the idea for a "machine for acting." Meyerhold develops an accompanying approach to acting called bioenergetics. Frederick Winslow Taylor's research into efficiency finds a theatrical corollary. The movement reacts against the Moscow Art Theatre, in an attempt to go as far away from detailed, lengthy, painstaking internal work as possible. Meyerhold takes an engineer's approach to the stage, demanding purely functional use of space. While the acting approaches do not last in popularity, the idea of a bare-bones, skeletal set is still common.

IMAGES

Popova's sculpture and stage designs—costumes by Goncharova—message above text—biomechanics in action—social masks in relationships—script as mere libretto—El Lissitky, Naum Gabo, Kasimir Malevich—Vladimir Tatlin's *Model for Monument to the Third International*.

SIGHT AND SOUND

A production may involve circus techniques, acrobatics, highly physical performances, and machine-like sets that strip away traditional decor and illusion. The entire support structure is clearly in view, and all platforms are unfaced and unadorned. A curtain is never used, and the entire set will be completely in view from the time the audience arrives until it leaves. Ramps, wheels, ropes, pulleys, elevators, conveyer belts, may all be employed. Actors may be asked to use exaggerated, rhythmic, repetitive movements. Garments may be geometric creations or work uniforms. Sound is dominated and determined by movement. Sounds of wheels, pulleys, conveyer belts, or hammers may all be imitated by the actor.

SKILLS

The actor needs an intensely controlled, precise, athletic body, circus techniques, gymnastics, acrobatics, mime, dance training, and broad, farcical caricature ability.

WORKS

Since this is a production concept only, there are no scripts. The most famous early production was:

> Meyerhold's mounting of the Crommelynck's *The Magnificent Cuckhold*

A current deconstructivist production will always be controversial, because it will not be the same play many arrive expecting to see.

SURREALISM

Spontaneous creation, without interference from reason.

Figure 9.12

Woman Seated Before a Mirror by Pablo Picasso
© Bettmann/Corbis

MANIFESTO

Insanity is often true sanity. Freed from the need for reason, morals, or esthetics, the artist's mind is finally capable of creation. The subconscious mind is the source of the most significant perceptions. Once your logic and ego are neutralized, truth has a chance to surface. Elements that appear at first glance to be opposites can actually be reconciled into a new vision. Great theatre has plasticity (freedom to manipulate appearances) and musicality (freedom to allow the subjective mind to explore). The spirit can be liberated from the flesh, and the unreal can become real. True theatre has the power to disturb viewers to the depths of their being.

BACKGROUND

Antonin Artaud, working in the 1930s, is the major figure associated with this movement, but its origins go much farther back. Alfred Jarry's 1896 production of *Ubu Roi* strongly influences surrealists, as does Freudian psychology. The term is first coined by the French poet Guillame Apollinaire, in 1917. The manifesto is written in 1924 by André Breton, who claims that surrealism rises out of the ashes of Dadaism. Artaud evolves the movement from one with emphasis on words to one inventing new language to express psychic experience. He breaks away from others and creates a "Theatre of Cruelty," in which actor and audience are asked to suffer a painful psychic transformation in order to achieve purification. His work influences Genet, Camus, Grotowski and subsequent tribal, communal theatre experiments.

IMAGES

Jean Cocteau's blends of ballet and drama—Pablo Picasso—Salvador Dali —music of Pierre Boulez—grotesque as path to liberation—spontaneous gesture as key to true inner self—Guillaume Apollinaire—André Breton—Massine —Psychic automatism—plasticity.

Figure 9.13

Ballets Russes de Diaghilew. Poster by Jean Cocteau © Swim Ink 2, LLC/Corbis

SIGHT

A dream world and a realistic world are often both explored for contrast. High level of distortion, optical illusion, objects in unexpected sizes and juxtapositions are all possible. Scenes occur in unusual locations, and two seemingly unrelated scenes may be played back to back. A strong sense of lyrical ritual emerges.

SOUND

Dialogue favors poetic imagery. Characters often do not answer each other directly; one person's shared internal monolog may motivate but not otherwise connect with another's. Language is used, not for communication, but exploration, interweaving, and ritual. Musical tones may dominate. Sound attempts to free itself from traditional slavery of written word into full, nonverbal exploration.

SKILLS

Capacity to play archetypes and to blend sexual characterics is helpful. Characters are often androgynous or hermaphroditic. A full range of sounds beyond language may be tapped. A priestlike total commitment to the process is required.

WORKS

Apollinaire, Guillaume	*The Breasts of Tiresias*
Artoud, Antonin	*Jet of Blood* *The Philosopher's Son* *The Burnt Belly*
Cocteau, Jean	*Antigone* *Orpheus* *Parade* *The Ox on the Roof*
Frederico Garcia Lorca	*The Butterfly's Spell* *Blood Wedding*
Jarry, Alfred	*Ubu Roi*
Vitrac, Roger	*The Mysteries of Love* *Victor*

DIDACTICISM

Narrative theatre for the intellect, rather than the emotions (also called "Epic" or "Brechtian Theatre".)

MANIFESTO

Theatre should make you think and act. Actors should present characters instead of inhabiting them. Audiences should remain aware they are watching a performance, instead of losing themselves in the lives of the characters. "Alienation" destroys

Figure 9.14

Lotte Lenya plays
Mother Courage at the
Ruhr Festival in
Recklinghausen, 1965
© Ducklau/dpa/Corbis

theatrical illusion by frequently interrupting the action, so the audience can remain emotionally disengaged and capable of viewing the work intelligently. Critical watching discourages passivity. The *subject matter* is what is alienated (The term does not mean to be "offended" or "angry." The original German word is *"verfremdung,"* which is to see things in a new light, to step back and look again at what had become familiar.) Drama should deal with a human being caught in the midst of social or political conflict. Theatre should spread social ideology. Naturalism is to be rejected, because it fails to portray man within the landscape of the whole society. Other forms of theatre encourage audiences to idealistic attitudes with no relevance to real life. The stage is meant to narrate (not embody), to demand decisions (not feelings), to communicate knowledge (not experience), to present arguments (not suggestions), and to appeal to our reason (not instincts). "*Gestus*" involves the revelation of a relationship by deed, word, or look, the way all connections between people can be suddenly illuminated by some movement of the body, tongue, or eye. This is achieved through productions that are epic, with a loose, narrative form, and numerous separate episodes, sometimes presented in the past tense.

BACKGROUND

Erwin Piscator conceives of the idea of a "proletarian drama," which is developed and extended by Bertolt Brecht, who becomes the movement's main theorist and dramatist. He is strongly influenced by the expressionists, but works in a far more cynical mode, developing a dramatic economy, simplicity of language, mature vision, and depth of expression seldom seen on the stage before this time. He refines his work through his own company, the Berliner Ensemble. His arbitrary ideas modify with time. Delight becomes a major concern, but he defines delight as the pleasure that comes from discovering new truths, which he calls the perfect reconciliation between teaching and pleasing. His theories are subjected to many conflicting interpretations, but continually stimulate directors throughout the world.

IMAGES

Figure 9.15

Lithograph of industrial workers from *In the Shadows* by George Grosz © Stapleton Collection/ Corbis

Being forced to make a decision—clarity, strength, and reserve, nothing wasted—social significance above all—political focus—complete control—moving within and outside the mask—cartoons of George Grosz—Munch's *The Scream*—*Gestus*—Helen Viegel, Kurt Weill, Lotte Lenya.

SIGHT

A proscenium space is preferred, with a blank screen used to project images. Signs may describe scenes and remove suspense. Auditorium lights may be left on. Conspicuously theatrical props (such as a paper moon) may indicate time. Scenery is likely to be constructivist—simple stairs, scaffolding, possibly revolving stages. We now tend to disregard the naked mechanics of a show, so these traditional choices may be replaced by any constant reminder (cameras, amplification, multiple screenings) that the event is a theatrical one and not real life. Changes in time and place are frequent and abrupt.

SOUND

Clear, distinct, often harsh and strong language is employed. Dialogue is mixed with narration and singing interludes that have a vaudeville-like feeling. Music is used to neutralize emotions instead of intensifying them. Dialogue may be poetic in a blunt, colloquial way, full of both malice and wit. Strident prologues and epilogues are common. Direct address of audience is frequent, and a wide range of dialects may be employed.

SKILLS

Actors may be called upon to use the capacity to step in and out of character, to comment and "demonstrate" character with some flexibility, to be able to make an idea crystal clear rather than enforcing emotional involvement. Brecht recommends that actors train in mime, clowning, and Asian acting techniques, and develop the ability to think of characters in the third person and to "quote" their behavior.

WORKS

Brecht, Bertolt	*Mother Courage*
	Good Woman of Setzuan
	The Threepenny Opera
	The Caucasian Chalk Circle
	Gallileo
	The Resistable Rise of Arturo Ui
Kipphardt, Heinar	*In the Case of J. Robert Oppenheimer*
Tabari, George	*Brecht on Brecht*
Weiss, Peter	*Marat/Sade*

ABSURDISM

An irrational world where truth is unknowable and life is nonsensical.

MANIFESTO

Understanding is impossible. Sudden changes of mood and motive are what life is about. All laws of probability and physics are suspended.

Sartre's is probably the most optimistic statement associated with the movement. Man's *only* freedom is the exercise of his conscious mind. He is in a state of moral paralysis. There is no illusion or light left in the universe. There is only metaphysical anguish. (Absurd is used here in a broader, sadder sense than "ridiculous". It is derived from the original musical term for

> *"If man can recognize and accept the simultaneous existence of his absurdity and his responsibility to give himself definition through choice and action, there is hope."*
> JEAN PAUL SARTRE

"out of harmony.") Life has lost reason, logic, and propriety. Existence is useless and meandering. The laughter that may emerge comes from a deep state of pain. Laughter is a coping tool, often the *only* coping tool. It is difficult to communicate with others, so we need to fill time, as if life is spent in a waiting room with no inner office, by playing games, joking, dancing, singing, and indulging in silly routines or escapes. Space, linear time, and conventional structure are abandoned. Plots are often circular (everything that happens has happened before), with the play ending where it began, with the ever-expected explanation never arriving.

BACKGROUND

While the first plays are written in the 1940s, Beckett's *Waiting for Godot* (1953) is the first major success. World War II demonstrates the brutal fact that humanity is perfectly capable of destroying itself. Philosophers' Continental Europe has experienced the greatest devastation of this war, with massive human, economic, agricultural, and architectural loss everywhere. Fatigue and disillusionment are rampant. The idea of life as meaningful is suspect. Memories of the concentration camps and gas chambers are vivid. This is the canvas for absurdism.

Another major influence is the work of silent-film comedians (Buster Keaton, Charlie Chaplin, Keystone Cops, later Laurel and Hardy and the Marx brothers) who exist in an often-nightmarish, black and white world beyond their comprehension. Some writers point to Samuel Beckett's later short play, *Breath,* as the official end of absurdism, but absurdist elements are present today in some of the works of Sam Shepard, David Mamet, David Rabe, among many others.

IMAGES

Mind games—God is Dead—tackology —a roomful of beepers—toddler résumés—politics—quality time—Hiroshima—greedy evangelists—celebretantes—the comic strip *Life in Hell*—PBS fundraising —Zen vacuum —irrational man—*Le Néant*, the void—insurance.

SIGHT AND SOUND

Plays may be realistically mounted, so that absurdity comes out of setting up false expectations, or may be staged on a cartoonlike level. Since humans, animals, and objects are interchangeable in this world, they may be given each other's qualities. Characters may be complex or completely stereotyped. Casts are mostly small, and effects minimal. Speech is disconnected and rambling. People never seem to listen to each other. There are rushes of sound followed by sometimes interminable silences. The mood changes just as it appears to establish itself.

Figure 9.16

SKILLS

Actors need an ability to make rapidfire changes, produce massive variety, and come up with surprising use of pauses and silence. Movement demands may include acrobatics, silent-film technique, song and dance, vaudeville, circus tricks and quick breaks between presentational and non-presentational audience relationships, the capacity to be real and unreal in sharp juxtaposition. It is no accident that a major Broadway revival of *Waiting for Godot* featured three of the world's most brilliant clowns, Robin Williams, Steve Martin, and Bill Irwin. Can you comfortably launch into gibberish, a robot, a political dialectic, a catatonic trance, or high, ruthless rage, while doing a soft shoe shuffle? This may be your Ism.

WORKS

Albee, Edward	*The American Dream*
	The Sandbox
Beckett, Samuel	*Waiting for Godot*
	Krapp's Last Tape
	Happy Days
	Endgame
	Footfalls
Camus, Albert	*Caligula*
Genet, Jean	*The Maids*
	The Balcony
	Deathwatch
	The Blacks
Ionesco, Eugène	*The Bald Soprano*
	Rhinoceros,
	The Chairs
	The Lesson
Kopit, Arthur	*Oh Dad*
	Poor Dad
	Mama's Hung You in the Closet and I'm Feelin' So Sad
	The Day the Whores Came Out to Play Tennis
	Chamber Music
Pinter, Harold	*The Dumb Waiter*
	The Birthday Party
	The Caretaker
	No Man's Land
	Old Times
	The Homecoming
Pirandello, Luigi	*Six Characters in Search of an Author*

Sartre, Jean-Paul	*No Exit*
	The Flies
Shepard, Sam	*Buried Child*

FEMINISM

Theatre by, for, and about women.

MANIFESTO

Women have a voice, too long neglected and pushed inside, which must be released and heard. Drama has been dominated, to our great loss, by male perceptions. Invaluable insight and artistic expression come out of women's lives. Woman's experience must be considered in any future decisions for this art. Old plays need to be re-examined, and new works must be generated from a feminist perspective. Inadequate patriarchal forms must give way, through cultural revolution, to provide new forms to serve a new perspective. We must move from self-destructive misogyny to creative justice. Women must have freedom to decide their own life patterns. Theatre must reflect this freedom.

BACKGROUND

Roots are political rather than artistic. Out of the woman's suffrage movement of the nineteenth century grows the woman's liberation movement of the last half of the twentieth century. The early movement (with leaders Mary Wollstonecraft, Sarah M. Grimke, Lucretia Mott, Elizabeth Cady Stanton, Susan B. Anthony, and Lucy Stone) is associated with anti-slavery. The later movement takes inspiration from civil rights activism and is a recognition of subtler enslavement, in terms of economic and social rights. Feminism is precipitated by women filling the labor force, while experiencing job discrimination. Watershed years are 1963, with the publication of Betty Freidan's *The Feminine Mystique,* and 1970, with the publication of *Ms.* magazine. By the early 1970s, the term has entered general usage, and "consciousness raising" groups are widespread. Feminism has subsequently been co-opted, merged, redefined, and expanded beyond its essentialist origins, towards pluralism and diversity. Materialist (Marxist), ecological (environmentally based,), and radical (separatist) feminist movements now approach the issues from diverse perspectives.

Although many regard Nora in Ibsen's *A Doll's House* walking out the door and leaving her family as the first step for the movement in the theatre, there has been no clear playwrighting history, and issues are only beginning to be fully explored. Deconstructionist production, performance art, choral plays, and dramatic collages are the most common forms through which movement from disenfranchisement to empowerment is explored.

Figure 9.17

Rachel Rosenthal in performance in the 1990s. Photo by Martin Cohen

IMAGES

Affirmative action—comparable worth—National Organization for Women—the Equal Rights Amendment—fighting words: sex object— "Domesticity Deadens" —landmark titles: *A Vindication of the Rights of Women, Equality of the Sexes and the Condition of Woman, Our Bodies, Ourselves* —Simone de Beauvoir's *The Second Sex*—inclusive language—Sarah Daniels— Gloria Steinem—balance of power—Rachel Rosenthal's performance art—groundbreaking theatre troupes: Split Britches and At the Foot of the Mountain.

SIGHT AND SOUND

At the time of writing, more and more productions are carefully considering each of the issues above. Women are likely to look and sound stronger. There are likely to be more of them in any cast, as all roles are re-examined and alternative casting seriously considered. Most productions are simply mounted, with minimal technical effects and maximum feeling. The direct audience-address monolog is common, as is narration interspersed with episodes. Close attention is being paid to the natural rhythms of women's speech. Language is likely to be vernacular and associative. Like the early phases of naturalism, there is the laughter of recognition as moments in life appear on-stage, and we wonder why it took so long.

SPECIAL SKILLS

Ease with breaking the fourth wall. Capacity to play simultaneity and drop linearity. Ability to discover and enlarge creative, impassioned rituals. Capacity to work in communal, non-hierarchical collaboration. Flair for transformational playing with immediate embracing of new identities, contexts, and actions.

WORKS

| Churchill, Caryl | *Top Girls* |
| Cryer, Gretchen | *Getting My Act Together and Taking it on the Road* |

Fornes, Irene	*Fegu and Her Friends*
Kennedy, Adrienne	*Funny House of a Negro*
Lamb, Myrna	*Apple Pie*
Norman, Marsha	*Getting Out*
Shange, Ntozake	*for colored girls who have considered suicide when the rainbow is enuf*
Terry, Megan	*Transformations for Three Women*
Wolff, Ruth	*The Abdication*

> *"I found God in myself and I loved her. I loved her fiercely."*
> NTOZAKE SHANGE

POSTMODERNISM

New and old make . . .

> *"The post modern aesthetic is fundamentally theatrical . . . one form masks, disguises, hides itself within or behind another."*
> KARI TOEPFER

MANIFESTO

Play with the past, without nostalgia for it. See life with quotation marks around it. Place the new up against the old. The present sells, history is dead, ideals are illusion. Forget consistency, continuity, originality. Embrace splicing and blurring of forms, stances, moods, and cultural levels. Enshrine the discontinuous. Challenge all arbiters of good taste. Undermine seriousness with kitsch. Respect all uncertainties. See erosion as art. Theatricalize the mundane, politicize the theatrical. Replace declarations of faith with declarations of skepticism. Aspire to ambiguity. Avoid all systems.

> *"Postmodernism is a self-imposed, cultural anesthesia. It is anticipatory shell shock."*
> TODD GITLIN

BACKGROUND

Postmodernism first appeared in architecture, then painting, then dance as rebellions against modernism. The term was actually coined by J. Hudnut in 1949, and the first major work is Robert Venturi's *Complexity and Contradiction in Architecture*, followed by Susan Sontag's "Notes on Camp" (1964), and Charles Jencks' *The Language of Post-Modern Architecture* (1977). Modernism, roughly existing from 1450 to 1960, is based on production in the factory, society as capitalist, time as linear, orientation as nationalist, and culture as bourgeois. Postmodernism replaces each of the above with office, global, changing/cyclical, pluralist, and taste-centered. It is a reaction to the 1960s, where our collective belief in progress exploded, and old values were shattered, but none moved in to replace them.

IMAGES

Lite dog food—Radichio—Bill Irwin—Mabou Mines—David Byrne—music of Philip Glass—Fredric Jameson—the Global Village—ecological art—Julina Schnabel and Bad Painting—self-hypnosis—tanning clinics—Ariane Mnouchkine—Warhol's multiple screen images—Tom Wolfe—Twyla Tharp—Laurie Anderson—fiction by Bret Easton Ellis, Anne Beattie, Tama Jonowitz—David Letterman—Jennifer Blande's sculpture–photo blends—movies that use clips from old movies—photos of photographers.

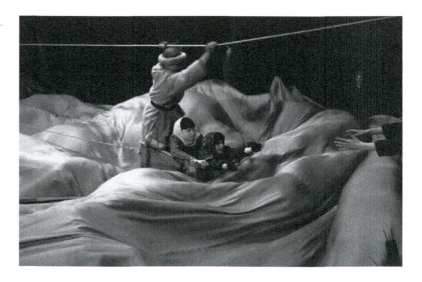

Figure 9.18

Ariane Mnouchkine's
Le Dernier Caravaserail

SIGHT

Designs are likely to evoke recognition of past and present simultaneously. A first impression will alter with extended viewing, through quirky, informed touches and sly insertions.

SOUND

Old sounds reverberating with new cadences. A blasé tone, exhausted, bemused, self-conscious. Helps to be a devastatingly accurate mimic of celebrities.

SKILLS

Capacity to express enthusiasm for any phenomenon while simultaneously mocking it, to ferret out humor and irony, and find political implications in every possible source. Balance the raucous and disrespectful with the bland and the meek. Strongly develop vocal technique, so as to convey a feeling and its alternatives.

LINGO

Reflexivity—authorial confession or intrusion into a work.
Intertextuality—mixing traditions, genres, texts.
Pastiche—ironic collage.
Appropriation—stealing or heavily modeling.
Androgyny—resistance to gender codes for normative behavior.
Neologism—an invented word that defies definition.
Deconstruction—reading against the grain, for what is latent or unsaid.

> *"I have forced myself to contradict myself in order to avoid conforming to my own taste."*
> MARCEL DUCHAMP

WORKS

Churchill, Caryl	*Cloud Nine*
Cogdan, Constance	*Tales of the Lost Formicans*
Durang, Christopher	*Laughing Wild*
Guare, John	*House of Blue Leaves*
Hwang, Henry David	*M. Butterfly*
Lapine, James and Steven Sondheim	*Sunday in the Park with George*
Lucas, Craig	*Reckless*
Mann, Emily	*Still Life*
Shepard, Sam	*Cowboy Mouth* *Angel City*
Wagner, Jane	*The Search for Signs of Intelligent Life in the Universe*

ISMOLOGY: Tacking qualifiers onto the Isms

Potentially confusing terms are often used in combination with *other* terms, which qualify, limit, expand, or distort original meaning:

Neo—new and different from (neo absurdism)
Retro—backward towards (retro absurdism)
Proto—first in time, the beginning of (proto absurdism)
Quasi—in some sense or degree (quasi absurdism), often a put down
Semi—partly or incompletely (semi absurdist)
Ultra —beyond the limit and then some (ultra absurdism)

Post—after, subsequent to (post absurdism)
Pre—earlier than, prior to (pre absurdist)
-Esque—in the manner or style of (absurdesque)

My advice: if a director starts talking about a neo absurdist expressionistic production with semi Dadaistic retro romantic elements, see if it's not too late to get out of town. Otherwise, talk to him and see how the concept affects you, the actor.

(Note: Group exercises exploring ideas in this chapter are located in Appendix I.)

10 PERSONAL STYLE
Creating reality

W**E USE** groups to define ourselves, but we are not just joiners. Those who are forces to be reckoned with are more than their memberships. Those who possess, master, transcend, create, or influence style find a personal signature to autograph the world. Group style is shared. Characterization gives distinct inner life. But *personal* style is how you leave your mark.

This chapter will help define your own style. It will explore ways of personalizing each style we have studied to carry some of that style into your life. Your personal style suits some periods and genres, just as it suits some groups and towns, better than others.

"What a man is, rather than what he knows, will at last determine his style."
E.B. WHITE

DEFINING YOUR OWN STYLE

To understand others, you must first know yourself. If you have experienced difficulty becoming Greek, Elizabethan, or Molièrian, it may be you are not clear about your own style habits. Look at your world-entering choices. Having studied style throughout this text, would your answers be different to questions first raised in Chapter 1? Has new information influenced how you see yourself? Remember that some of the most interesting style characteristics are those that fall short of perfection.

"Style reflects idiosyncrasies. Your personality is apt to show more to the degree that you did not solve the problem than to the degree that you did."
DESIGNER CHARLES EAMES

TIME

1. What is your own personal tempo/rhythm? How close or removed is it from those around you? Are you time-bound? Is there anything about you that has failed to evolve?
2. Have you ever felt you were born in the wrong time? Do you have a particular affinity for one bygone era, as if you lived there in another life?
3. Which time periods speak to you enough to influence your style choices? Which would you most love to visit?

SPACE

1. What is the size and flexibility of your personal bubble?
2. How do you connect with and use the space around you?
3. Do some rooms get too small for you as you suddenly realize that your are overbold and overloud? Does the reverse happen? How sensitive are you to the space needs of others?

PLACE

1. Do your attitudes, behaviors, vocal and physical lives reflect where you came from, no matter where you are? Are you place-bound? To what extent do you recognize and adapt to the place you are in?
2. What places do people associate with you, even if they are not part of your actual experience?
3. Where do you feel most at home? Most stimulated? Where do you really belong?

VALUES

1. Do you have beliefs not widely shared? Do some beliefs make you feel almost from another planet?
2. Which assumptions about right most strongly influence your interactions?
3. How clearly do you communicate your values through your presentation of self? How often are you misinterpreted? Do you bite your tongue and keep your own counsel, or do you impose your thoughts regularly?

STRUCTURE

1. What is your relationship to authority? How likely are you to accept, defy or manipulate the power of others? Where are you between rebel and conformist?
2. How easily do you move between social, economic, political, spiritual, cultural groups? How aware and flexible is your sense of appropriate behavior?
3. How do you impose structure on the lives of others?

BEAUTY

1. Where do you place yourself on the beauty scale and how have you responded to that? Are your own tastes or preferences outside the norm? Do you reveal this? Under what circumstances?
2. How do you change your looks to be seen by others? Where do you work hardest to adjust/improve yourself?
3. Other than theatre, what are your favored modes of artistic expression?

"Wouldn't this be a great world if insecurity and desperation made us more attractive?"
ALBERT BROOKS

SEX

1. Are you aware of what is sexually attractive about you? Of what is not? Do you exploit this in any way?
2. Do you emphasize, reveal, or hide parts of your body?
3. Do you express your sexuality? Are you embarrassed, intolerant, or defiant of "normal" courtship behavior?

RECREATION

1. Do you find things fun that others find boring or difficult?
2. Which of your pleasures are shared or unique? Are there "national pastimes" which you find impossible to comprehend? Are there some to which you are addicted?
3. Where are you on the doer/watcher, thinker/feeler, celebrant/meditator scales?

SIGHT AND SOUND

1. How do your vocal mannerisms help you or limit you? Where are you most bound?
2. How are the same factors true for your physical habits?
3. Does your speech or movement fit better into some genres or periods than others?

MUSIC AND DANCE

1. What is your theme song? Which is your dance?
2. Which style of music reflects you best?
3. To what extent do you use music and dance to express yourself?

IMAGES

This is where the abstract forms first introduced in Chapter 1 can be helpful:

1. Which answers jumped out at you the first time you saw the list and which have taken more time?
2. Where did you fear what others would choose? Which images do you really *wish* were associated with you?
3. Where do people's images of you most strongly disagree?

MASKING

1. Which are the faces you wear in public?
2. When does your façade drop most readily and when can it be counted on to appear?
3. Which of your masks work well for you? Which get in the way?

THE PERFECT AUDIENCE

1. Who admires you most? What kinds of audience response do you have the most trouble dealing with?
2. What kind of an audience are you? A good listener? Do you howl with laughter? Actively empathize? How generously do you respond?
3. Which members of your private audience are always present?

SOCIAL SUCCESS AND SUICIDE

"All styles are good, save the tiresome kind."
VOLTAIRE

1. What have been your greatest public triumphs and tragedies?
2. When you felt victorious and larger than life, why were you so good?
3. Is there a pattern of when you are hot and when you are not? Can you trace circumstances and signals that may help you to more success and less suicide in the future?

ANALYZING YOUR STYLE

Write a brief phrase in response to each of the three questions above in the categories of: time—space—place—values—structure—beauty—sex—recreation—sight—sound. Also, briefly summarize your style choices in these areas: images—masking—perfect audience—social success and suicide. Underline those answers you are comfortable with and highlight those you wish to do something about. Make some decisions about what to own, accept, develop, or change.

Don't rush to change. It is important to remember that very few styles were all that well received when they first appeared. Maybe you are a pioneer.

Figure 10.1

(Left to right) Pablo Ruiz Picasso, described as the most influential painter of the twentieth century © Bettmann/Corbis; Marlon Brando, widely considered as one of the greatest actors of all time © Bettmann/Corbis; Elvis Presley, "the King of Rock 'n' Roll," in his breakthrough year of 1956 © Michael Ochs Archives/Corbis; Lenny Bruce, the legendary and controversial comedian © Bettmann/Corbis

YOUR PERIOD STYLE SELF

Part of the joy of acting in classical plays is getting to live long ago and far away. Creating a whole new identity for yourself in another time and place is a great adventure. A period style alter ego can help you define yourself and serve as a path to playing a character in a play. Some actors are able to grow in a style if they can function as a character of their own creation, free of the constraints of text. Ask yourself what would be the Greek Me? Elizabethan Me? Restoration Me? Molière Moi? Georgian Me?

How would any of these personages answer these questions?

"My name is . . ." Note how names are formed. Pick one that still has some of your own in it. This helps symbolically keep some of the present you as part of the new you. Remember the Elizabethan guest dubbed me Bartonio? If I were Greek, I might be Baresius. Who are you?

"I was born in . . ." You were not necessarily born on this earth. You may be from an entirely imaginary kingdom, in an undiscovered province, or on a star. You need only choose.

"Original styles almost always look crude and excessive:

Picasso's in painting ("My three-year-old could draw better!"); Brando's in acting ("He's got marbles in his mouth!"); Elvis' in music ("Photograph him from the waist up!"); Lenny Bruce's in comedy ("Book him!").

In their first outrageousness, these artists seemed to signal the end of the world; instead they were heralding a new one."
MARY CRONIN

"My titles are . . ." If your twentieth-century origins are humble, don't necessarily buy into that for your period self. Who are you in your soul? Who were you *meant* to be?

"My primary possessions include . . ." You may own vast lands, fleets of ships, cities, magic potions, magic objects, and chests of jewels. You may own people. What gives you power and inspiration beyond your own drive?

"The people for whom I am responsible are . . ." Whose lives change because of your decisions? Do you have a primary advisor—a shaman, priestess, prime minister, or wizard? For how many and what kind of sheep are you the shepherd?

"A physical description of me would be . . ." Start with what you really look like. Adjust in your imagination. You may choose to square your jaw line, add more hair, grow a few inches, or make your coloring more striking. Keep the changes close enough that, as you walk around, you can believe that this is you, so that if you returned to your regular life you would not be unrecognizable.

"The most crucial event in my life up to now was . . ." Let your imagination soar. A profound experience or twist of fate could have changed your destiny. It could be an encounter with a god or a glimpse into the crystal ball. Who knows?

"Above all else, I believe . . ." Devise a statement that is a personal credo. It marks what you would fight to the death for, the point beyond which you will not be pushed. It guides you on life's adventure.

YOUR OTHER SELVES

Who would you be if you lived in the world created by the playwrights of other periods? If you had an ancestor, what would she have been like? If you are living there now, in a time warp, as you *also* live here, what kind of a creature are you? Devise a Greek, Elizabethan, Restoration, Molière, or Georgian persona. Create an alter ego for yourself in that world, based on what you know about that world. Approach it either as if you may have lived then or as if you still do. Test your knowledge of the period as seen by the playwright. What you are unsure of, make up. Remember that you know who you are better than anyone.

PERIOD STYLE DAYS

Create an event devoted to bringing one period to life. Your goal is to help all feel as if they have entered the world of the plays and briefly lived there, to have a personal experience with the style, experiencing sensuously information that can only be imagined in print. You are creating an educational theme party, which can be an actual social occasion, a rehearsal if you are working on a play, or a class period if you are part of a course. Initial considerations include:

OCCASION

What is the cause for gathering and celebration? Choose something that excites you, that you yourself would love to be invited to.

THE SENSES

How can sight, sound, smell, taste, and touch all take part?

1. How can you alter the space in terms of shape, light, and space?
2. What music or sound effects can serve as background and enhance mood? What kinds can get attention when you want it?
3. Are there aromas, perfumes, incense, scents, or food smells that might permeate the air?
4. What food and drink might you serve? How might this be ritualized?
5. What surfaces, fabrics, objects should be touched, or in which ways might people touch each other as part of the experience?

COSTUMES

What is the simplest, yet most evocative way for participants to dress, wear their hair, and look for the day? Review suggestions for rehearsal garments. How can each person change enough to feel like they live in this world? What personal props should actors carry?

IMAGES

Find picture books with examples of buildings, artwork, clothing, undergarments, furniture, and basic props. Find photos of actors playing key roles and paintings of the dominant personalities of the period. Use the Images section of each chapter to help with ideas. Consider setting these items up around the room as at a museum, fair, or festival, with the possibility of a slide show as well.

ADMISSION

How do people get in to this occasion? Must they show an invitation? A calling card to be dropped off? Must they bring an offering? Will only a weapon work? Or only a poem?

ACTIVITIES

Some energy devoted to each of these activities should be considered:

1. a warm-up (physical, vocal, and mental), helping participants let go and enter the world you are offering them;
2. family lies in this period: the simple three-character bigamy scenario from Chapter 2, but done with all the cultural assumptions and theatrical conventions of this particular style;
3. improvisations and sketches involving the checklist categories: select areas where "on your feet" exploration or theatre games will help the concept come to life;
4. lessons in success and failure in the worlds of the plays, including perhaps some masked activity;
5. some hints on ways to wear clothes and not let them wear you;
6. learning some basic steps for the most evocative dances of the time; keep it simple and avoid painstaking detail in favor of a quick feel for the dance as an expression of how people feel about being alive;
7. a chance to bow, pay obeisance, touch, and make contact in the period; set up a social interaction for these activities to be practiced automatically, rather than connected to problem-solving contexts;
8. experience in becoming the perfect audience, with side coaching and cheer-leading as encouragement.

GUIDELINES

In order to maintain the spirit of the day, agree to function within these basic rules:

1. The entire event is in the present tense and first person pronoun (i.e. "We worship Dionysus" not "They worshiped Dionysus").
2. Each person has a distinct identity different from her usual self, and, at some time, each person is presented or has the opportunity to introduce herself. Guests might be given name tags and brief character descriptions as they arrive.
3. Sacrifice historical accuracy in favor of the spirit of the plays.
4. All activities should involve tasks to be *accomplished*. We are not just here to honor a god: we are here to select the virgin to be sacrificed. This creates a dynamic.
5. Everyone should be given victories and made to feel valued and successful.
6. Have each participant encouraged to think of herself as from a province or precinct with its own customs. This way you can't do anything wrong. If you botch up a bow, it is because they bow differently where you come from. If you speak a strange word (such as "wow" or "O. K."), it is because that is a peculiar term used by your people. This will relax everyone and help free them from fear of failure.
7. Prepare a theatre program listing each interlude.

If you are not involved in a class or rehearsal and do not really feel up to planning a gala event, you can still give yourself many of these sensory experiences. This is basically dress-up and let's pretend. You are limited only by your own willingness and imagination.

> *"In matters of grave importance, style, not sincerity is the important thing."*
> OSCAR WILDE

YOUR ISM SELF

Which of the Isms speak most directly to your own sense of the world, to your vision of what art, music, and theatre should say and do?

1. What is your own manifesto? What do you tend to protest? What do you choose to advocate for the future?
2. How does your background lead you to your own convictions? Did your parents or ancestors espouse recognizable Isms that you are either evolving or defying?
3. Which special skills are necessary to perform you? What would others need to work on in order to be responsive to all your shifts of behavior and perspective?
4. Of the images you leave, are any reminiscent of an existing genre? Maybe you are a whole new Ism. Brechtian feminism? Postmodern naturalism? Dadaist romanticism? Now there's a thought.

(See Appendix J for events that might be part of an Isms day.)

ALTER EGOS EMPLOYED

Having found some other powerful selves in yourself, in what contexts might you use them?

1. Your Greek self could help you in a court of law, whenever you need to defend your position publicly and . . .
2. Your Elizabethan self can help you tap into your most romantic imagination when you want to win someone with music, verse, worship and . . .
3. Your Restoration self can help you get the dish, teach you how to get revenge and . . .
4. Your Molière self might show you how to prick the balloon of pretense, to recognize your own foolishness and . . .
5. Your Georgian self might allow you to be as gregarious, polite, and cheerful at that reception as your parents always wish you would be and . . .
6. Your Ism self might change you just enough to help you fit into a group you normally butt heads with and . . .

Miss Manner's suggestion for the best classic line to use when you disapprove of the style choice made by another:

"There is a time and a place for that sort of thing,"

the words "and this isn't it" being implied . . . It is particularly devastating to those who were trying to shock, because the "remark makes it clear that it is not the action itself that is being condemned, but the arena in which it has been performed."

Judith Martin

MODELS: Styling yourself on someone else

We all look to role models. Some influence us briefly and lightly, others long and hard. We may look and sound like their clones until we exorcise their influence and free ourselves. Imitation may be the most sincere form of flattery, but personal style models are still often overlooked for recognition. They are honored about as often as comic actors are at Oscar time. We easily forget our style inspirations. To help determine your own style, take time to honor those who have influenced it.

1. Go back in your own personal history and try to pick out the person you most often tried to be like during these ages: three to five, five to ten, ten to fifteen, fifteen to twenty-one, twenty-one to twenty-five (continue in four to five year cycles, depending on your own age).
2. Identify what you wore, said, moved, or in any other way changed in order to be like your model.
3. Who were the most emulated people you knew during those times?
4. Who are the people right now you would give anything to be? Whose personal style do you most admire? Whose do you emulate now?
5. When you think about yourself in the future and the kind of person into which you would like to develop, how is that different from what you are now? What about you would you love for others who follow you to try to emulate?

PRESENTATION CHOICES

Some people design themselves. They reinvent and create themselves top to bottom. They often begin by choosing a new name.

You may even have forgotten some of your own names.

1. Identify at least five names you have been called in your life, pet names, nicknames, or tease names others gave you. What were the circumstances? What

about your own choices in presentation of self may have caused the name to happen?

2. Identify any you gave yourself and tried to encourage others to use. Why? What were you trying to present?

3. If you had to change your name right now, because someone else in Actors' Equity had it or because some serial killer had it, what would you pick? Why? What would the new name put forth in the world that your old one does not?

Most of us do not change names. I have stuck with mine in spite of disliking it (Bob Barton sounds like a game show host), and most of us stay with what we have, fond of it or not. But whenever you even *think* about a change, you are considering a significant style choice. The name precedes you. It is the first message in your image statement. When people hear or read your name, what kind of person do you think they expect to own it?

Another way to gather information about your style is to ask others what they think of, when they think of you. What do you leave behind? The answer may be as literal as your keys (which you are notorious for losing) or as general as a lingering thought or impression or your leftovers:

1. What do you tend to leave behind for others to remember you by?

   • Food ? (Peanuts? Spilled coffee? Gum?)
   • Small objects? (Paper clips? Chocolate wrappers? Beer bottle caps?)
   • Scent? (Cologne? Mints? Body odor?)
   • Sound? (Welcome silence? Lingering rock music from your box? Screeching tires?)
   • Clothing? (Favored old shirt? Running shoes? Baseball cap? Earrings?)
   • Tracks? (Mud? Lipstick? Piles of laundry?)
   • Words? (Buzz words? Favored phrases? Lingering lingo?)

2. What do others most strongly associate with you when you aren't there?

   • Your book bag? Your car? Your dog? Your chatter? Your laugh?

3. Where do these images match and contradict your own sense of yourself?

Are there ways in which you never let others see you? Do you camouflage, enhance, or hide? Do you monitor language, moods, and vulnerability in order not to hurt or be hurt? Do you ever project something that is actually the exact opposite of how you feel or who you are? Have any of your masks become old habits, with no real protection value?

"When we see a natural style, we are surprised and delighted, for we expected to see an author and we find a man."
PASCAL

Here are some additional activities to help you define and develop your style:

UNMASKING

1. Make a list of circumstances and people with whom you mask.
2. Draw a cartoon of the mask itself or pick a symbol of what it represents.
3. Cross out those that are useless.
4. Put question marks next to those whose value you are going to investigate, with the idea of either removing or replacing.
5. See if you can put the symbolic act into actual practice.

YOUR PERSONAL COAT OF ARMS

Does your family have a coat of arms? If so, examine it to see if parts of it strike a responsive chord with you and feel right. If not, start from scratch.

1. Draw a circle, diamond, or a shield on a large sheet of paper.
2. Put on your coat of arms the images that reflect what you send out in the world. Don't feel any need to fit a heraldic mode. Yours may feature a can of beer and a Crayola box. Select as many as six visuals for the crest.
3. Explore what you want for color, decoration, and general adornment.
4. You may wish to do several drafts. Forget artistic ability. If you don't draw well, then *your* coat of arms *should* have stick figures.
5. Hang it on the wall and let yourself enjoy what it says.

MOTTO AND VOW

1. Devise a statement to go with your coat of arms, something that sums up your philosophy, your wisdom, your humor, in a nutshell. Let this be a statement that you would not at all mind emblazoned on your tomb, because you believe it down to your bones.
2. Pick another statement based on what you would like to be. Give yourself an identity that you know you can achieve, as anyone can tap the hero in him if he is truly called. Choose something possible but not easy, something you wish were always the case, and on good days *is* the case, but you would really like to reflect who you are all the time.

"You find your style by finding yourself and you make something of it by putting yourself on the line."
TRISH DEITCH
ROHRER

OLD MYTH/NEW MYTH

Review fairy tales, childhood stories, childhood heroes, comics, old wives tales, and myths that have influenced who you are. Which have always haunted you? Which images (such as ones about what a real man or woman should be) have plagued you, so that even when you decided mentally they were a crock, they still influenced how you presented yourself?

1. Pick the one that you feel is least helpful to you now. Revise the details into one you find nurturing, that serves you better.
2. Write a new fairy tale, stealing shamelessly from all those you like, but coming up with an adventure that is full of glory. Work with all the familiar terminology from the beginning: "Once upon a time, there was a handsome prince named Robert who woke up one day and . . ."
3. Let the revision and the new tale guide you.

"True style comes from flaunting our own limitations."
PATRICK FRALEY

ADAPTING VS ADOPTING

"Manners are a way to screw people over without their knowing it."
P.J. O'ROURKE IN
*MODERN MANNERS:
AN ETIQUETTE BOOK
FOR RUDE PEOPLE*

As an actor, you try to understand periods and genres for good style acting. You also try to develop an individual style, while communicating effectively with the group, being a good colleague, a supportive partner, an assertive and challenging co-worker. You try to become an ensemble player who can fly solo when the occasion demands it. Because theatre is shared art, we all need to learn to compromise, collaborate, and challenge. We need to master diplomacy while not letting others out of their responsibilities. This is a style challenge every bit as large and important as what occurs in front of the footlights. Many brilliant actors do not work much because their personal style is so abrasive that others cannot endure being around them. Others have modified their style choices to the point of complete wimp, never asserting themselves in order to grow, always in fear of being accused of having "attitude" and ending up never accused of having courage. Others manage playful compromises, both joining and remaining independent:

> "I liked to push the system at school. I did it through clothes. We had a regulation grey suit and I managed to get mine lined with gold or burgundy material. The school didn't like it—but I was wearing their suit so they couldn't do anything about it."
>
> Jeremy Irons

Acting style and personal style are connected. And growth in one may feed growth in the other.

> "As the charming person has a marked advantage in life over all others, even those with decidedly more important virtues, it is a skill worth honing. And the first requirement of charm is that the bearer of it appear to be alive."
>
> Judith Martin

STYLE FREEDOM

Know enough about what is going on to make informed *and* brave decisions. Your life is an adventure. You are constantly on safari. You explore the wilds. You unearth wonders, within yourself and all around you. Style is the parachute, submarine, or rocket by which you journey. It could be the three-wheeler, stroller, or skateboard. It can be the crystal ball, magic wand, or time capsule.

"Those who excel have 'kaleidoscopic' thinking. They can look at a routine, spin it around and suddenly put it in a different context."
ORGANIZATIONAL PSYCHOLOGIST ROBERT. GANDOSSY

The more you understand your own style, the better prepared you become to play other styles. The more understanding you have of other styles, the more options you have as you continue to develop your own. The more options you have, the less likely you are to be intimidated.

Acting in style plays can be a renewal of childhood Let's Pretend, with all its power and conviction intact. A journey of the imagination is possible any time, any place. The great period plays are awesome avenues by which we can journey past the mundane into the heroic. And the more of these plays you perform, the more wonder you discover—or rediscover. To play a modern factory worker in a child custody suit, concerned about car payments, has its own rewards, but the pleasure of playing a prince, a witch, a warrior, or a goddess wrestling with the future of the world, is unparalleled. Style work expands your horizons and unleashes your vision.

"We're born with biological hardware. But we can choose our cultural software."
PHILOSOPHER SAM KEEN

Personally, style education helps you extend your own playground. It frees you from cultural prisons. You discover more ways to create reality. You recognize events as neutral and contexts as chosen. You learn to see imperfections as loveable and ownable. You see more right ways to do things.

The relationship between the plays and the actor's life is subtle and complex. By acting those who are witty, powerful, and great, you unquestionably have a chance to tap into your own wit, power, and greatness. Understanding the styles of the world offers you both more masks and more chances to unmask. You gain the ability to present or protect whatever part of yourself you choose. Your own style is richer and more expressive for tasting others. Style gives you choice. It helps you act your own life better.

(Note: Group exercises exploring ideas in this chapter are located in Appendix J.)

APPENDICES

APPENDIX A
Group exercises for Chapter 1

EXERCISE 1.1 THE EUPHEMIZING OF LIFE

1. What euphemisms can your group add to the list on page 11?
2. The most euphemized subject in the world is the bathroom. How many terms can you think of for the place and what usually goes on in it?
3. Second place would go to the sexual act. How many can you come up with for it?
4. What instances can you identify where it is now in style to reverse the trend to a more blunt term (alcoholic instead of heavy drinker) in conversation?

EXERCISE 1.2 MISREAD SIGNALS

1. Sit in a circle on the floor.
2. Look at each person and recall your first impression.
3. Go around and identify how your first impression was off and how it has changed.
4. What signals does this person send off that give an impression other than the deeper one that comes later?
5. Stay free of judgment. Make sure there is consensus before moving on to the next person. This information is not necessarily given as a suggestion for change.

EXERCISE 1.3 CHANGING WORLDS

1. Each improvisation has three characters, two familiar with the world and one newcomer.

(a) A college student interviews for an executive business position requiring experience and maturity.

(b) An ardent feminist tries to make it to the Miss Universe finals without compromising her principles or offending the two key judges in the crucial interview.

(c) A journalist tries to pass as a member of a satanic cult in order to get the story.

(d) Working in threes, devise similar predicaments based on the sudden shifts that take place in *Rip Van Winkle, The Prince and the Pauper, Alice in Wonderland, A Connecticut Yankee in King Arthur's Court,* or other classic examples in literature or current news.

2. Discuss other struggles for survival you have experienced or observed.

EXERCISE 1.4 SONG STYLE

Pick a classic everyone can sing ("Row Your Boat," "Your Are My Sunshine," "I've Been Workin' on the Railroad," "Take Me Out to the Ballgame," " My Bonnie Lies Over the Ocean," "Happy Birthday").

1. Sing the song altogether, without any conscious style choice.
2. In groups of three, with ten minutes preparation, do the song in the style of: reggae, blues, country western, rap, opera, lounge singer pop, acid rock, musical theatre, others.
3. Draw again and present in the style of: Madonna, Mariah Carey, 50 Cent, Justin Timberlake, Elvis, Louis Armstrong, Willie Nelson, Celine Dion, others.

EXERCISE 1.5 SAME GAME

1. Work with partners, with half the class watching and half playing.
2. Agree on an imaginary physical game—shooting baskets, throwing and batting a ball, tennis, ping pong—anything two can mime.
3. After getting used to it, a side coach asks you to change your partner to:

   • the person you idolize most in the world;
   • someone you believe to be evil;
   • someone you want to love you;
   • your servant, who has not been working hard enough;
   • Your boss, whom you want to give you a raise
   • other suggestions.

4. Switch and have observers become players.
5. Discuss how the act changed by your attitude towards the other person involved.

EXERCISE 1.6 SAME STORY

1. Sit in a circle and begin to tell a familiar story, fairy tale, or legend everyone has heard many times.
2. When the teacher or a designated classmate calls out one genre (musical comedy, silent slapstick, reality show, sitcom, gothic romance, murder mystery, Sunday cartoon, network news broadcast, buddy movie, soap opera, slasher movie, masterpiece theatre, western, horror flick, documentary, game show), whoever is talking must change the way they tell the story without the actual plot details. For example, Cinderella might suddenly be refered to as a little filly, or the perpetrator, or contestant number three, but she still goes to the ball and gets the prince.
3. Variation—The "Die, die, die" game. A student who does not pick up the new style is "caught" by the rest of the class, who shout the line "die, die, die!" This student must then drop out of the circle by dying the appropriate death of someone living in that style.
4. Discuss circumstances under which you felt most and least secure with the challenge of keeping plot identical, but not style.

EXERCISE 1.7 STYLE IN A NUTSHELL

1. Draw names for classmates.
2. Between one class and the next, find a short phrase (no more than five words total) that captures the style of this person.
3. Check with others who know her to gauge the accuracy of your own impression.
4. Try to predict how someone else will summarize your style.
5. Gather in a circle and share the results.
6. Note when you are most and least surprised.
7. How did you feel about your style nutshell? What does it say about what you send out?

EXERCISE 1.8 STYLE SIGNALS

Write a one to three word response to each of these words as they relate to impressions you leave.

1. Sight
2. Sound
3. Ritual
4. Lifestyle
5. Group membership

Turn in your answers. Every class period read two or three sheets without the names. As a group, try to guess who it is.

EXERCISE 1.9 STYLE ABSTRACT

1. Analyze yourself first, attempting to predict the responses of your classmates.
2. Fill out the form for everyone in class, turned in stages, but not returned to the subject until the last week of the term.
3. Look for trends, noting particularly where there is either uniformity or remarkable diversity.

1.	fabric
2.	animal
3.	bird
4.	beverage
5.	transportation mode
6.	city
7.	tree/vegetation
8.	color
9.	show
10.	scent
11.	type of day
12.	decade or era
13.	song
14.	myth/fantasy figure
15.	landmark/building
16.	snack
17.	spice/flavor
18.	musical instrument
19.	painting/photo
20.	toy

APPENDIX B
Group exercises for Chapter 2

For some of the exercises below, here are images from decades that may be outside your experience:

THE 1950s

Jitterbug, hula hoop, Sputnik, TV dinners and TV trays, low slung,"blonde" furniture, the baby boom, Norman Rockwell, cars with fins, Eisenhower, Elvis, poodle skirts, pony tails, duck tails, jello, beatniks, bowling, "the Hit Parade," Howdy Doody.

THE 1960s

Free love, Vietnam, love beads, communes, acid rock, bell bottoms, the Beatles, the Kennedys, tie dying, folk music, Haight Ashbury, *Easy Rider*, "Laugh-In," mod, mini skirts, psychedelia, op art, roach clips, munchies, black power, peace symbols, the generation gap.

THE 1970s

Self-help, personal space, the Me Decade, the women's movement, Watergate, disco, homemade anything, gas lines, the Bees Gees, logo T-shirts, designer jeans, stir fry, jiggle, cults, vegetarianism, environmentalism, running shoes, quiche, *Saturday Night Live*, *Saturday Night Fever*, white wine, cults.

THE 1980s

Surrogate mothers, prenuptial agreements, designer water, yuppies, stress, insider trading, Glasnost and Perestroika, self-esteem, aerobics, greed, homelessness, trickle down, personal computers, Nintendo, Aids, Tex Mex, co-dependency, fiber.

EXERCISE 2.1 CHANGE TIME

1. Imagine the same act performed in different times reflecting different views of the world. Agree on a simple, everyday activity such as setting the table for your family dinner.
2. In pairs, perform the event as if you are living in the 50s—60s—70s—80s—90s—00s—cave persons' pre history—*Star Wars* or intergalactic science fiction future.

EXERCISE 2.2 SAME PLOT, DIFFERENT TIME

1. In teams of three (with at least one member of the opposite sex in each group), draw one of the times above.
2. With ten minutes' preparation time, present a proposal of marriage and an acceptance. The third actor may be a character involved, inanimate object, narrator, pet, any key third element.
3. With the same preparation time, go back and present the proposal with a refusal.
4. Discuss comparative values in the scenes and in the two versions.
5. Try these two variations: a woman announces she is going to have a baby. In version 1, the news is received joyfully. In 2, it is received as bad news.

EXERCISE 2.3 CHANGE PLACE

1. Pick a simple activity and in pairs perform it as if you are: French, Iraqi, Russian, Italian, German, Southern, Irish, a native New Yorker, in the nearest big city.
2. Take the same plot elements for the "Same plot, different time exercise," and apply it.

EXERCISE 2.4 VALUE CEREMONY

1. Work in teams of three.
2. Each team take one of the following and arbitrarily pick a shared value for your society: ideals—family—mood—idols—sin—attention—money—God—humor —fear.
3. What kind of a culture emerges? Can you begin to act these people?
4. What ritual or ceremony would be most meaningful to this group? Enact it for the class. See how close they come to guessing the values behind the act.

EXERCISE 2.5 CHANGE GROUP

1. Pick a simple activity or encounter and in pairs perform it as if you are: army—evangelical fundamentalists (God squad)—bikers—surfers—Mafia—skinheads—slackers—street people—theatre people.
2. Take the same plot elements for the "Same plot, different time" exercise, and apply them.

EXERCISE 2.6 CHANGE GENRE

Pick a simple plot (example: coming out to your parents) and perform it as: musical comedy—silent movie slapstick—sitcom—gothic romance—reality show—Agatha Christie-type murder mystery—Sunday cartoon—network news broadcast—buddy movie—soap opera—masterpiece theatre—western—horror flick—martial arts film—foreign film—documentary—game show.

EXERCISE 2.7 BEAUTY CONTEST

1. Select a panel of three judges. Everyone else competes and/or tries to influence the judges.
2. There will be five quick contests from these eras: the 50s, 60s, 70s, 80s, 90s, and 00s.
3. When a judge calls out the new era, everyone has 30 seconds to change yourself into what you consider the ideal of that time. Parade around the room. Judges may ask questions, but each contest is no more than 5 minutes long.
4. When all six winners are chosen (someone may win more than once), they should tell why they think they won. How does everyone else feel?

EXERCISE 2.8 SEX ROLES

The class becomes a society that is:

1. bisexual, with women as aggressors;
2. women like experienced, knowledgeable women and chaste, virginal men; many prefer one of each for a *ménage à trois*;
3. elbows and eyebrows are considered hot;
4. women are supposed to brag and strut; men are supposed to be relatively silent, appreciative audiences;
5. everyone is horny, and it is last call;

6. when everyone has a partner or gives up, the game is over;
7. discuss how it felt to exist in this world.

EXERCISE 2.9 ULTIMATES

1. Divide into teams of two. Determine what would be, in your department, the ultimate compliment and insult for each of the eras worked earlier.
2. How would the line be phrased, who would say it and where? Who would be listening?
3. The first group to feel you have the compliment, pipe up. Everyone share what you have come up with.
4. Then do the same with the insult.
5. What do the two lines say about life in your department?

EXERCISE 2.10 FAMILY LIES

This exercise combines all the questions into a single acting experience in familiar styles. In order to make the story true, each of the issues above needs to contribute to the lives of the characters. Since the basic story line is set, the creative space is all style.

Place—France, Russia, Italy, Spain, Ireland, southern US, New York, your town.

Time—1950s, 60s, 70s, 80s, 90s, 2000s, prehistory, the future.

Group—army, God squad, bikers, surfers, Mafia, skinheads, street people, theatre people.

Genres—musical comedy, silent slapstick sitcom, gothic romance, murder mystery, cartoon, soap opera.

Draw from two different categories. Work on the story out of class for a few hours.

Scene involves three actors, with both sexes represented:

1. A is at home, exercising and fixing dinner. (What is "home?" How is the nest defined? What value is placed on exercise and what is popular as a way of staying fit? What foods are valued and what kinds of rituals of preparation are involved?)
2. B arrives (they do not know each other) with something that has been mistakenly delivered to the wrong address. (How do strangers approach each other? How is the sanctity of the home invaded? What is a hospitable response to unexpected visitors?)
3. A and B discover they are both married to (or living with) C, who has been keeping two separate households, across town. (How much of one's shock, rage,

hurt can be shared appropriately with someone you've just met? How do these people deal with wild, primary emotions at this moment? What is considered civilized behavior?)

4. A and B resolve to confront C (who is expected momentarily) and to force C to make a choice. (How easy or difficult is confrontation, how much a part of life? How fearful are they of losing C altogether? How solid or tentative is this joining of forces?)

5. C arrives, is shocked at being found out, gets the ultimatum, but then presents another solution. (How strong is guilt a factor at this moment? How humbled is the offender likely to be? What proportion of threat and charm tactics are likely to be employed?)

6. Some kind of resolution occurs that may please all, some, one or none of the above. (Who leaves? Who stays? Three people going their separate ways? A *ménage à trois*? Something in between these extremes?)

APPENDIX C
Group exercises for Chapter 3

EXERCISE 3.1 CLASSICS VS CONTEMPORARIES

After selecting your own A and B list performers:

1. Compare lists with others in class. Are there names that emerge with regularity on each list? Discuss these.
2. Are there some actors who appear on *both* lists, for different classmates? Why?

EXERCISE 3.2 CLASSICAL WARM-UP

This exercise is meant to supplement or be integrated with a standard physical and vocal warm-up that already works for you.

1. Sit in a kneeling position. Bring your head forward so that your forehead touches the ground in front of you, while moving your arms straight backwards so they rest at your side, pressed against your legs with your palms facing upwards. The position will feel like total supplication.
2. Breathe into the spine and let it relax and stretch comfortably in this position.
3. Rise to a standing position very slowly. Move arms in half circle forward across the floor, then turns palm downward and move them close to your knees to support you and rock back onto your heels as the soles of your feet touch the floor. Keep your head low and back rounded, in a fetal position. Again, breathe and release the spine.
4. Move into a puppet or rag doll position, but raising the tailbone so that it is the highest part of your body off the ground. Let your knees bend slightly. Test the freedom of your upper body by swinging your arms and head back and forth, left and right, like an ape or a prehistoric human.

5. Feel a pull at your tail bone and at each vertebra along your spine as you very slowly stand. With each small rise, move through an evolutionary phase, growing brighter, quicker, deeper, and more confident. Pass through the stage at which you consider your real self now and move beyond into a heroic mode you rarely allow yourself. By the time you are fully upright, feel that you have evolved into a powerful classic personage.

6. From a standing position, look up at the ceiling and beyond to the sky. Raise your arms above you and reach as far as possible with one, release it slightly, then with the other, alternating, in a gentle tugging stretch. Believe you can touch the stars and clouds with each reach.

7. Look in front of you and drop you arms and shoulders. Feel tall, aligned, and open.

8. Begin to make giant circles with both arms, with the motion coming from the shoulder joint. First move both arms to the right, then the left, then to the center, then outside. Visualize gestures emanating from your center, which is strong, into a large space that you command.

9. Spread legs apart and lean to the right, with that leg bent and the other straight, feeling a stretch in the hip joint and letting the arms do circles to the right. Do the same with your left side.

10. Return to a neutral stance and breathe deep into the small of the back while doing arm circles, first inward, then outward.

11. Stand still. Begin humming. Turn the hum into a roller coaster of pitch, moving comfortably higher and lower in your range.

12. Let your voice turn into an elevator or a magic chariot plunging down a mountainside over and over, so that it explores the bottom notes of your register. Do a big yawn, which turns into a hum, and then let the hum drop lower, lower, lower, lower and get off the chariot and into a vast hidden valley, speaking a few lines from your favorite role.

13. Repeat point 12 three times until you are actually comfortable using these bottom notes, adding them to the others available to you.

14. Alternate arm circling and leaning in opposite directions. As you move, repeat the B list words and cast the ones you don't want away from you as you speak them forcefully: "limited—rough—low-class—conventional—shallow—comedic —crude—small—light-ethnic—informal—slow—contemporary—insensitive— weak—subdued—simple-monotonous—internal—awkward."

15. Develop your own pattern of circles that feels like you are beckoning or taking on qualities, which you will *own*, from the A list as you speak the words: "poise—grace—class—power—sophistication—presence—versatility—voice— boldness—size—sensitivity—eloquence—depth—control—command—stature —intensity—focus—clarity—majesty."

16. Speak either a speech that always makes you feel powerful or move into one of the warm-ups for feeling Greek, Elizabethan, Restoration, Molièrian, or Georgian in subsequent chapters.

EXERCISE 3.3 CLASSICIZING

1. Work in pairs. Take any four lines of dialogue from a classical play or make up an encounter that seem vaguely classical.
2. Each couple demonstrate one or more of the of the concepts below through the dialogue:

perching	focus
descent/ascent	clasp
asymmetry	full extension
lifting	energized arms
punctuation	breath under arms
stillness	clarify in space
head float	ceremony
taller than others	unfolding gestures

3. First present the scene in as "inappropriate" or contemporary a way possible, really having fun with it.
4. Metamorphose into a classicist and re-do the scene.
5. Discuss both how each scene looked and how it felt.

EXERCISE 3.4 CLASSIC VOWELS

Work with a partner, ideally someone with whom you are already partnered on a scene assignment. Draw slips of paper with the following categories:

flat vowels
aspiration
honoring each sound
diphthong substitutions
vowel substitutions
relaxed jaw
liquid U
euphonic choices.

1. Again work with a short excerpt or invented scenes.
2. Present it in the least classical way possible, almost anti-classical, playing into the problematic vowels fully.
3. Present it as phoney and affected as you worry about sounding sometimes.
4. Find the golden mean where you use the technique for both clarity and truth.

EXERCISE 3.5 COMMERCIAL CLASSICAL THEATRE

1. Work in groups of five. Each team come up with a list of ten slogans or lines from commercials, political mottos, public service announcements, lines that are heard frequently in broadcast.
2. A pair of actors from each team should go up, and each is handed the list of a team they are not on. These contain your lines.
3. Perform a scene with a situation suggested by the audience, such as a pick-up in a singles bar or a parent waiting up for a late son or daughter.
4. Discuss what you had to do to make it work and how the line often had a life of its own. This exercise makes you think. There are many lines in classical theatre that the audience has heard before, but that mean little to them beyond the familiar words. Your task is to place the line in its context with enough conviction to drive it home.

EXERCISE 3.6 SCANSION AND FREEDOM

Here is the vocabulary of verse. Consider these tools that can build your performance:

Blank verse—Language formalized into lines of equal (or nearly equal) length, but not into rhyme. The most common form is **iambic pentameter** (ten syllables, five feet, each foot consisting of an unstressed followed by a stressed syllable). Middle ground speech—more elevated than normal speech, but less so than some other verse forms. The rhythm in blank verse approximates the beating of the human heart.

Catalectic—Line with some syllables deliberately dropped for emphasis, to indicate an entrance, an exit, or a reaction. Response time is within the verse.

Compensation—Repairing metrical omissions in a line of verse by speaking a vowel that would normally remain silent to get the line to reach ten syllables in speech. Most common types: *-ed* ending (remembered—remember*ed*), *-ier* ending (soldier—sol*jeeer*), *-ion* ending (indignation–indigna*sheeun*).

Couplet—Two rhymed lines of verse that become a single expressive unit. Shakespeare uses couplets to call attention to an important point within a speech or to provide a striking ending to a speech or scene.

Distributed stress—Effect produced when two consecutive syllables share the stress, instead of one being heavily accented while the other is barely touched. The emphasis is distributed equally between the two. Instead of da DUM, you may have Da Dum, neither being hit all that soft or all that hard.

Elision—Omitting a syllable in order to conform a line to a metrical scheme. Examples: o'er for over, th'incestuous for the incestuous, 'gainst for against, on't for on it.

Endings—The last syllable in a line of verse may be stressed—strong (traditionally masculine) or unstressed—weak (traditionally feminine). A weak ending is usually accomplished by an added eleventh syllable in blank verse. A strong ending is the more common form. It may help to deal with the obvious sexist nature of these terms to regard a "feminine" line as very powerful, because it forces the reader into the next line and does not allow any lingering over the line just spoken.

Foot—The basic unit of measure in verse, usually two or three syllables in length, with various stresses. In a phrase describing verse, the first word will identify feet, as in *iambic pentameter*. The four most common feet are iamb (unstress–stress), trochee (stress–unstress), anapest (unstress–unstress–stress), and dactyl (stress–unstress–unstress).

Metre—The number of feet in a line of verse, by which a line is parceled into divisions of time. The second word in a phrase describing verse will indicate metre: monometer—one, dimeter—two, trimeter—three, tetrameter—four, pentameter—five, hexameter—six, septenary—seven.

Metrical pause—Actor tendency to stop at the end of a line of verse, even though there is no punctuation to indicate a pause. Also called *end stopping*, this understandable but irritating habit will prevent builds in a speech and interfere with an audience's capacity to hear a lengthy sentence as a single unit.

Personification—Common practice, in verse, of giving human characteristics to objects, emotions, or abstractions, so that they appear to have a life and a will of their own. Standard choices are Love, Fortune, Reason, Nature, and Time.

Poetry—Use of elements from both speech and song to express feeling, ideas, and imagination. Language full of imaginative power and evocative phrases. Too often mistakenly used interchangeably with verse. Poetry is an imaginative use of language that may or may not be formalized, while the formalization, if it exists, is called verse.

Pronominal mode—Use of "thee" or "you" to address another. "Thee" most often indicates familiarity, while "you" is more likely to occur in situations involving anger, coldness, unfamiliarity, high regard, or simple formality. The distinction is like the French use of *"tu"* or *"vous"* in showing the degree of intimacy the speaker shares with his listener.

Rhyme—Repetition of the same or similar sounds for emphasis. Historical rhyme refers to words that used to be pronounced the same, but usage of one of them has changed with time (for example, Dumaine from *Love's Labour's Lost*: "Through the velvet leaves the wind, All unseen can passage find.")

Rhythm—Recurrence of any beat with enough regularity that time intervals seem equal and the impression is one of balance. Rhythm causes the audience to maintain a sense of pulse and the actor to keep the play moving along in a lively manner.

Scansion—Close analysis of the metrical pattern of lines of verse in order to figure out how they should be read aloud.

Split line—More than one character speaks, but so briefly that a single line of verse is the result. Example:

First Lord:	Was't you, sirrah?
Second Lord:	Not I.
Third Lord:	Nay, it was I.

This is an indication from the playwright that no pause should occur at all, that the lines should come just as quickly as if they had all three been spoken by one person.

Stress—Intensity of emphasis placed on an individual syllable. In a perfect iambic pentameter line, the second, fourth, sixth, eighth, and tenth syllables will be stressed, while the odd-numbered syllables are unstressed. Also called *accent*.

Tempo—Speed of delivery. While verse makes strong rhythmic requirements of actors, they are comparatively free to manipulate tempo, which can be a great help in keeping rhythm from seeming tedious.

Verse—Arrangement of language into formalized structure, usually iambic pentameter. It is sometimes said that verse is the grammar of the speech, while poetry is its soul.

Take a verse speech and analyze or apply each of the terms above to it.

EXERCISE 3.7 CLASSICAL SPEECH

1. Sit in a circle with the terms above before each person.
2. Go around the room reading out loud in your best possible classical speech.
3. Let each reader complete a term. Then tell him both what seemed genuinely classical to you and what you lost, in terms of vowels, consonants, sounds, and phrasing.
4. When everyone has read, summarize the major successes and difficulties of this particular group. Agree to listen closely for these last items so you can all help each other.

EXERCISE 3.8 SWINGING THE PENDULUM

1. Work with a drum or something that can stand in for one.
2. Speak the speech in as laborious and throbbing a way as you can.
3. Go back and pretend it is prose.
4. Sit down and discuss what you like from each attack and what might help the scene fly.
5. Try to blend all that you have learned.

EXERCISE 3.9 THE MIGHTY HUMAN IAMBIC PENTAMETER LINE

1. Ten actors go up in front of the class, with two others waiting in the wings stage left.
2. Observers suggest very famous lines from Shakespeare.
3. When the group gets the line, it tries to physicalize it, with each person becoming a stressed or unstressed syllable by standing or kneeling. So "If music be the food of love play on" might have the odd-numbered actors kneeling and the even-numbered standing, with no need for the back-up team, because there are only ten syllables, not eleven or twelve. Discuss how stresses might vary. A syllable with very low stress might crawl down into a fetal position. A strong stress might jump in the air. A strong stress with an exclamation point might leap in the air with arms thrust high above him. If elision is needed, the actor might scrunch in as if he had been hit in the stomach.
4. Do the line with each person speaking and physicalizing his syllable, first for a straight scanning for stressed and unstressed syllables. Then repeat for a more refined line reading, acknowledging other factors in the vocabulary list. Accept suggestions from the audience.

EXERCISE 3.10 SHIFTING INTO HIGHER GEAR

1. Four volunteers. Walk on-stage as if you have just come out of a public building to return to your vehicle and find that:

   (a) your three speed has fallen over and landed in a puddle;
   (b) your battered VW bug has gotten another scratch in the side;
   (c) your Volvo has a dent on the front bumper;
   (d) your BMW has been totaled.

2. Class suggest two other series of escalating disasters with a theme to connect them.
3. Discuss the differences in behavior. The moral is: do not play as if you have a muddy three speed when you have a totaled BMW. In the classics, particularly tragedy, discoveries are often earth shattering and monumental, requiring a reaction plane much larger than most of us use.

EXERCISE 3.11 MAKE IT INTO A MUSICAL

1. Agree on one of the following events:

   • the Family Lies scenario;
   • a current news story;

- the plot of a popular film;
- a great historical event;
- a classical myth or legend.

2. Working in threes, convert it into a musical of no more than five minutes length. Use known popular songs to fit in where the moment is right. Change the lyrics slightly if necessary.

3. Consider the full range of musical conventions and styles available—a Gilbert and Sullivan operetta, a Busby Berkely tap show, a Rogers and Hammerstein, a Stephen Sondheim, or British "high concept" musical.

4. You may wish to simply describe some of the events instead of acting them all out, the way composers might pitch a show to potential backers. Narrate some passages and show others.

APPENDIX D
Group exercises for Chapter 4

EXERCISE 4.1 GOD MEETING

1. Members of the class will play the gods in this exercise. You might choose to discuss who you feel is right to play each god or just draw and go for it.
2. Each find a spot in the room according to your station. Arguing and negotiating are fine.
3. Those left over and undeified should come as supplicants before the gods with a request. Keep it simple, something you really would like, such as an A in the class or glorious weather for the weekend.
4. Gods should discuss the request and whether it should be granted, who should become the patron of this supplicant, how each might contribute to bringing it about.

EXERCISE 4.2 HOMAGE TO THE DEAD

1. Select someone no longer living whom you admire, a custom or courtesy no longer practiced, or some quality of life that is missing.
2. Between one class and the next, devise a simple offering and statement honoring the dead. Ask for the care and protection of Dionysus, Apollo, or any other god of your choice.
3. In a circle, each person should perform the ritual of honor. Don't make any effort to sound Greek. Just speak simply and from the heart.

EXERCISE 4.3 MOVEMENT CYCLES

1. With everyone up, but focused internally, explore basic movement for acts of survival.
2. With a designated side coach calling out the event, mime it and interpret it into a simple, rhythmic move. Events may include planting the seed, nurturing, harvesting, anything that all people at all times have done.
3. At a signal from the coach, look around you at the different movements and silently agree as a group on a fusion, so that everyone is doing the same move.
4. Move on to another and several more cycles.
5. Go back and attempt to repeat the entire set of cycles, as the coach repeats the basic acts.

EXERCISE 4.4 CHORAL INTERPRETATION

1. Take the basic idea for the exercise above, but use a choral passage from a script instead.
2. Each person should take a line and add a distinct move.
3. Go back and repeat, with everyone now joining in on the moves and repeating or echoing key words.

Variation: Do the same with the Greek warm-up.

EXERCISE 4.5 MASK DAY

1. Wear neutral masks as you arrive to class and go about normal class business for at least a full half-hour.
2. Perform familiar tasks, such as a well-known warm-up or critique session.
3. Discuss the effect on bearing and sound coming from the mask.
4. Sit in small circles of five or six people. Each person should pick up an imaginary mask in front of him, and while everyone watches, demonstrate it and put it back down.
5. Next, pass each mask around the circle. Everyone's mask should be worn by everyone else.

EXERCISE 4.6 STADIUM PLAY

1. Organize a trip to a football stadium. Approximate the space that would be used in a classical Greek production.

2. Using one end of the stadium, have some performers down on the field and others spread around the audience.

3. Start with a simple discussion, class announcements, questions about an upcoming assignment, with this amount of space to be filled between you.

4. If Greek scenes or speeches are being worked on, let those actors present in the space. Repeat the choral exercise above, with each actor having the opportunity to speak and move in the space, as well as watch and listen.

EXERCISE 4.7 SHE WHO IS MOST BEAUTIFUL

1. After Eris was rejected from Mount Olympus, she supposedly caused the Trojan War by sending a golden apple there inscribed "For the most beautiful." Hera, Athena, and Aphrodite all claimed it, and Paris, son of the king of Troy, was chosen to act as judge in the dispute. He ultimately chose Aphrodite, because she promised him Helen, the most beautiful woman in the world.

2. Cast the five roles and enact the story in ritualized manner, with improvised dialogue. If you are Athena or Hera, really try to get it to end differently this time. If you are Paris, consider all arguments carefully.

APPENDIX E
Group exercises for Chapter 5

EXERCISE 5.1 SONNET FOR A SOVEREIGN

1. Cast a classmate as Queen Elizabeth I. Everyone else has two class periods to choose a poem in honor of the queen's coronation.
2. Poems may be sonnets from Elizabethan poets or others, including you!
3. Each classmate stands before the court, pays obeisance to the queen, and then reads her offering.
4. Discuss what it felt like to be honored and to honor.

EXERCISE 5.2 INVENT LANGUAGE

1. Each actor is responsible for coming up with two entirely new terms not presently in the language.
2. One term can be silly (such as *nairs*—for nose hairs) and the other more serious and useful (such as *forback* for the feeling you have sometimes of wanting to move on and retreat at the same time: "I feel *forback*").
3. Unveil your terms to the class and try very hard to use them during the next few weeks, both in and out of class.
4. Some special reward or recognition should be given to the person who employs the largest number of new terms and to the actor who came up with the one everyone finds most useful.

EXERCISE 5.3 TRIBUTE FOR TWO

1. Draw the name of a classmate of the opposite sex.
2. Create a tribute to that person, by either:

    (a) writing and presenting a poem;
    (b) composing and singing a song;
    (c) performing some heroic public deed.

3. Keep the particular nature of the tribute secret until its unveiling in class. While there may be some humor in the works, there is no roasting or satire. It is a genuine tribute and gift.

EXERCISE 5.4 TOP AND BOTTOM HALVES

1. Present a speech stressing just music, then just earth, then pessimism, then optimism.
2. Let the pendulum swing wildly in each direction. Then go back and repeat, allowing each of the four a voice in the final product.

EXERCISE 5.5 SHAKESPEAREAN SPAT

1. With a partner, devise a scene of some disagreement between you, with each of you using at least one term from each category (greeting, good-byes, disagreement, agreement, and so on).
2. Present your work with the idea of owning the terms.

EXERCISE 5.6 DANGER GAMES

These Elizabethan party games all have an element of risk and a high potential for losing dignity.

1. Pass the orange—must be passed under the chin, no hands allowed, preferably down a line and back, with competing teams.
2. Jingling—blindfolded in a circle, players try to catch the one unblindfolded person present, who continuously rings a bell.
3. Stool ball—A player in the center tries to hit others with a ball as they run from stool to stool. If you get hit, you are it.
4. Jousting—two men, carrying rolled-up newspapers, riding on the backs of two others, try to knock each other off.

5. Cock fighting—two men in a circle try to push each out with their chests.
6. Shark island—like King of the mountain, but played in the center of a circle.

EXERCISE 5.7 PRAISE AND INSULTS

1. Divide the class into two teams, one called the Suns and the other the Moons.
2. Devise a competition to see which team is the superior deliverer of Elizabethan praise, then insults.
3. Either draw the phrases above or have an uninvolved party point to the remark you are to speak just before you deliver it.
4. Have a team of judges call each encounter between two insulters or two praisers, so that the score is known as the competition continues.
5. Discuss what means of delivery, beyond the words themselves, causes a victory in this type of exchange.

EXERCISE 5.8 OPEN SCENES

1. Devise two strongly contracting encounters within the world you have just learned.
2. Take one scene into verse and discuss the difference in challenge.

APPENDIX F
Group exercises for Chapter 6

EXERCISE 6.1 CHECK ME OUT

1. Each actor in class takes a turn standing in the center.
2. Everyone else should get up and walk around him and examine him, not by touching, but still very curiously.
3. Revel in the attention. You are a world-class model, and they should be eating their hearts out.
4. Shift your position occasionally to show yourself off to better advantage or to give them a little peek.
5. Discuss when you were tempted to feel intimidated and what helped you get past it.

EXERCISE 6.2 PROMENADE

1. Work in couples, with appropriate music from the period playing in the background.
2. Calling on your impressions of ballet moves, men offer women your arm, and the two of your promenade around the room as if you are ballet stars on curtain call.
3. Assume you are the most dazzling couple, but acknowledge the others as you pass. Give yourself plenty of room and focus on jointly executed curves and other graceful maneuvers.

EXERCISE 6.3 MESSING WITH MOTHER NATURE

1. Keeping in the mode above, go outside with your partner for fifteen minutes.
2. Your task is to find as many things as possible that can be improved on nature in order to fit your Restoration sensibilities.
3. Return to class and share your findings.

EXERCISE 6.4 CHIC IT OUT

1. Everyone should come to class one day dressed in what you consider your most sensational, knock-out outfit.
2. Take turns parading around for applause and approval.
3. At an agreed-upon break, go out and change, this time so that the body part or parts that you feel most proud of are exposed or emphasized.
4. Come back and repeat the exercise, with the idea of showing off what a phenomenal specimen you are.

EXERCISE 6.5 DOUBLE DISH

1. Agree on a task that the whole class can accomplish, such as cleaning up the classroom or rearranging the furniture.
2. Someone designated will start a rumor that no one should get caught spreading.
3. Each person should arrange an assignation with someone and also not get caught by others doing so.
4. You have a three-part task: the group activity, the gossip, the assignation agreement.
5. When someone thinks they are the first to achieve all the tasks, stop the action.

EXERCISE 6.6 ENTENDRE

Sit in a circle. Have a group discussion where every remark made can be taken two ways. Load each statement and employ all of the techniques discussed. Agree on a topic or agenda that you are motivated to discuss, so that your effort is not on keeping the conversation going, but keeping both the literal and the innuendo planes functioning.

APPENDIX G
Group exercises for Chapter 7

EXERCISE 7.1 *COMMEDIA* VS COURT

Take any twenty lines of dialogue. Any period of script will do, as long as two actors know the lines well enough to play with them.

1. Discuss and demonstrate the lazzi described on page 178.
2. Present the script, finding every opportunity to perform the traditional *Commedia* business.
3. Go back and remember decorum. Perform the script with an aristocratic sense of precision and purpose.
4. Attack the scene a third time, combining the elements of points 2 and 3. Shoot for grandeur and then shoot that grandeur down, then aspire to it again. Find the tension between decorum and slapstick.
5. Discuss and analyze how the seemingly disparate elements might blend.

EXERCISE 7.2 CREATING *COMMEDIA*

1. Using the list of *Commedia* types as a starting point, identify what you consider modern parallels. Which of these types exist in our world and popular entertainment. Put the new list on the board.
2. Create contemporary *lazzi* or comic situations. Which funny encounters happen often enough to be classics?
3. Cast two or three of the scenes and, with no more than five minutes preparation, present them for the class.

EXERCISE 7.3 ACCEPTING THE MIDDLE CLASS

1. Half the class are old-school aristocrats, and half the middle class.
2. You are meeting for the first time because the aristocrats need the middle class's money and help, and the middle class wants culture and status.
3. Negotiate.

EXERCISE 7.4 CONTRASTS

1. Work in threes in front of the class.
2. Discuss a topic the audience gives you.
3. Each time you speak or react, do so in a dignified and intelligent way, followed by some whooper-cushion, lower-level response. So you might say something terribly polite and then stick your tongue out behind the other person's back.
4. Try not to get caught in the low-life pranks by your two partners.
5. Discuss the contrasts and concentration necessary.

EXERCISE 7.5 FENCING WORDS

Take an actual set of foils, if you have the protective gear, or any other gentler battling items such as foam bats. Have an improvised spat, where you tap your partner each time you make a point. Then move on to actual dialogue, letting the weapon sharpen your delivery.

EXERCISE 7.6 FAMILY REUNION

1. Delegate two representatives of the Restoration, Georgian and Molière cultures. Everyone else is the cheering squad for one of the three delegations.
2. You are actually family members. The Molièrians are the uncle and aunt of the Restorations, who are the parents or grandparents of the Georgians. The topic of discussion is "What is the proper way to behave?".
3. Debate, discuss, and attempt to compromise.
4. Alternative topic—"What is the best way for us to conduct our next family reunion?"

EXERCISE 7.7 FAMILIAL INDISCRETIONS

1. Start with the basic premise of the Family lies exercise (Chapter 2), one of the other encounters set up earlier between the sexes, or a new one invented by the group.

2. Any number can participate, but probably three in a group is a good number.

3. Place the story in the Restoration, as written by Molière, and in the Georgian period. Begin by discussing with your group what will be exactly the same and what will have to be different.

4. Start with names. These may be either based on your own names or on personal characteristics, or both. For example, some recent class choices:

   • Restoration names with clear innuendo:

   —Sir Wellington Worthit (a potential lover, slow to coax, but ultimately highly satisfying)
   —Mistress Quickly-Compromised (no explanation necessary)
   —Sir Randy Rutting (no explanation necessary)

   • Molière names based on current social stereotypes:

   —Bimbette de Florette (an actress known to space out)
   —Madame Demande (someone who always gets what she wants)
   —Walkmande (an actor always accompanied by his personal cassette player and off in his own world)
   —alternative: French versions of actual names, such as Barbie, which imply certain personality traits.

   • Georgian, names based on more exaggerated, less sly or overtly sexual qualities than in the Restoration:

   —Lady Snickersnort (actress with an unusual snorting laugh)
   —Mrs Buxombounty (actress with enormous breasts)
   —Sir Joshua Sloshedalot (played by an actor known to drink more than a little)
   —alternative: combined with Georgian-type names, may be simple, plain ones for unaffected characters of character.

5. Proceed through a basic analysis of the customs and rewarded behavior to devise the details of the scenario.

6. Create your text by referring to actual scripts from each style for syntax, word choices, and rhythms.

7. After presenting the work in class, discuss in greater depth the areas where the three seem to intersect and where they are, in fact, worlds apart.

EXERCISE 7.8 KEYS TO THESE WORLDS

Given your cumulative knowledge of each era, invent specific answers for these world entering ideas:

1. Social success and suicide—Molière and Georgian.
2. Ultimate Compliment and Insult—Molière and Georgian.
3. Ideal audience—Molière and Georgian.

Discuss, as a group, ideas for point 1; then work in pairs demonstrating point 2, while the class attempts to respond as point 3.

APPENDIX H
Group exercises for Chapter 8

EXERCISE 8.1 PERSUADE THE PLAYWRIGHT

This exercise gives you the chance to improvise within the mind set of a character.

TWO VERSIONS

(a) All actors are characters in the same play, which has yet to be written (and could end up quite different from the one the actors know).

(b) Actors are from different plays, vying for their stories to be told.

CASTING

Director, teacher, or other staff member—William Shakespeare.

Others on staff—Members of Shakespeare's acting company (Burbage, Condell, Hemming, and so on).

Everyone else—The characters they are performing in the show or in their scene assignments. The highest authority figure in the play(s) chairs the event.

SITUATION

Version (a)

Word of the event itself has reached the world's greatest playwright, who appears as an honored guest. He has expressed interest in writing a script based on the event. It is six months after the end of the story. All participants have agreed to meet in a neutral space (including those returning from the grave) to share their versions of what occurred. Shakespeare has sent word that he is intrigued with the story, but is puzzled by individual motives, unclear as to where he should place primary and secondary focus in his play, and uncertain how serious or light the treatment should be. Since the play has yet to be written, there is great potential for *change* and high stakes for each participant. All are motivated to make certain they are accurately represented.

EXAMPLE

In *Romeo and Juliet*:

- Tybalt's role could be greatly expanded; or
- the entire story could be focused on the Prince and his troubles ruling Verona; or
- it could emerge as largely Lady Capulet's personal tragedy; or
- Benvolio's struggles to be a good Montague; or
- the story of the Friar's experiments with potions.

and the title itself could naturally change as well.

Version (b)

Delegations from different plays compete to capture the author's imagination and become his next script. The action is the same as above, except that actors are not competing simply for the portrayal of truth as their character sees it, but also for their story to be regarded as more immediately worthy or compelling than others in the eyes of the writer.

Variation: The characters persuade a director to stage their play as his next production. In this version, actors performing scenes from a variety of periods may compete, arguing not only the value of their play but also their period.

EXERCISE 8.2 THEATRE SPORTS PERIOD DRAMA

1. Using the standard format for Theatre Sports competitions, working in teams of four or five, select one of the major categories: Greek, Elizabethan, Restoration, Molière, or Georgian.
2. Audience call out and suggest a place, an object, and a situation.
3. The team immediately creates a scene in the style in question, combining the three elements and attempting to resolve the problem.

EXERCISE 8.3 THIRTY STEPS TO CLASSICAL ACTING

The steps are summarized here for you to use as a checklist. Take a scene or monolog and determine how long you have before the material is to be presented in class or performance. If you have a month, work with one classical step each day between now and then. If you have two weeks, work with two each day.

1. Scansion—honor the meter
2. Stanislavski-based character analysis—unearth circumstances and motives.
3. Record while reading from manuscript—memorize and review.
4. Reference room research—multiple and contradictory meanings.
5. Regular taping and playback—gain permission to do more.
6. Antitheses—try to overdo.
7. Key words—punch up even more in long passages.
8. Adjectives—give them value, let them modify, qualify, change nouns.
9. Metaphors—put in quotations, underline, or place in capital letters.
10. Coining—refuse summaries or generalizations.
11. Alliteration—try to overdo matching letters or sounds.
12. Verbs—punch up and relish.
13. Humor and irony—unearth all kinds, add quickness.
14. Audience relationship—confide in them.
15. First time—expect the opposite of what you get.
16. Interruptions—speak as if you may be stopped.
17. Exits—speak as if audience or listeners may leave.
18. Bottom out—mumble naturalistic, scratch and itch delivery.
19. Over the top—old-fashioned oratorical delivery, full of bombast and over-playing.
20. Speed through—race it, earn each pause.
21. Music—sing it like an original musical or opera.
22. Changes—shifts in mood, tactic, and attack.
23. Layering—give shape to the performance.
24. Onomatopoeia—coloring your words.
25. Apprehension—understanding beyond simple comprehension.
26. Contemporary paraphrase—clarify work in modern idiom.
27. Rhymes—say them with extra pride and relish your own cleverness.
28. Monosyllabic lines—need air, never rush them.
29. Ambiguities and contradictions—look for them and play them.
30. Truth + poetry + character = good classical acting—all three balls need to be in the air.

APPENDIX I
Group exercises for Chapter 9

EXERCISE 9.1 ISM TABLEAUX

Working in groups of five or six, draw one of the Isms above.

1. Without any talk, arrange yourselves into a pattern that you feel captures the Ism visually.
2. Discuss the manifesto and collaborate on a more sophisticated tableau agreed on by all.
3. Return to class and present both. Discuss the differences.

EXERCISE 9.2 BIG MOMENTS

Working in small groups, draw an Ism. Meet briefly, then present:

1. a marriage ceremony;
2. a brief death scene.

How does the major event alter because of the genre?

What was the crucial difference between the happy and sad events?

EXERCISE 9.3 GENRE LINGO

1. Agree as a class on the relationship between two characters and a topic of discussion that will be the same in all scenes.

2. Between one class and the next come up with a short stretch of dialogue, no longer than an opening scene, that captures your Ism.
3. Discuss the differences in presentations and your own feelings about the feasibility of this Ism being revived in the future or being used as part of a production concept.

EXERCISE 9.4 ISM VISUALIZATION

Work in teams of three.

1. Each person should find a photo, sketch, cartoon, painting, etching, or ad. that pulls together some of the Ism's ideas. Bring these to class and arrange them as a collage.
2. Set up a museum time when everyone circulates without speaking.
3. Gather in a circle and guess each Ism. Discuss those where there was some disagreement.

EXERCISE 9.5 BERLITZ MANIFESTO

Work in groups of three. Draw an Ism.

1. Each member should write a one-sentence version of the manifesto that will speak to today's audience.
2. Compare sentences; pick the best or a new blend.
3. Stage the line so that you make a statement with words and action.

EXERCISE 9.6 MEETING OF THE MINDS

Draw an Ism. Either assume the identity of its most famous spokesperson or invent a new identity for yourself.

1. You are the most adamant proponent of this theatrical concept.
2. Come to class and debate your ideas with other Ismologists.
3. Discuss which most easily dominated and what it felt like to assume a position not necessarily your own.

EXERCISE 9.7 REALISM ISMS

Within our predominant Ism, we tend to subdivide.

1. Take either a contemporary realistic scene in progress or one devised through improvisation in which actors are cast close to age and type. Change it so that it could be called a:

   comedy
   drama
   farce
   tragedy
   tragicomedy
   dramedy
   political drama.

   Discuss the changes, particularly where the scene became less "realistic."

2. Try it again with the scene becoming a:

   fantasy
   melodrama
   satire
   burlesque.

   Discuss the Isms outside realism that were touched when the scene entered these realms.

APPENDIX J
Group exercises for Chapter 10

EXERCISE 10.1 OTHER SELVES

1. Complete the statements on pp. 279–80: My name is . . . I was born in . . . My titles are . . . My possession include . . . The people for whom I am responsible are . . . A description of me is . . . My most crucial life event was . . . and above all else I believe . . .
2. Introduce yourself to the class or cast, sharing crucial information from the list above.
3. Let them ask you questions and trust yourself to respond.

VARIATION

1. Repeat the exercise as a character from a play.
2. Characters from different plays might be interviewed by the class. It helps if they share something, such as all kings, all wanting revenge, or all unfaithful.

EXERCISE 10.2 ALTER EGO INTO CHARACTER

1. If you are showcasing scene work, consider having created characters introduce real ones as a conduit.
2. Enter as your alter egos, set up the scene, enter the characters, then return to your alter egos to bow.

EXERCISE 10.3 PERIOD STYLE DAY

Draw from the checklist below left those activities you wish to plan and assign a specific time period for each.

Checklist	Principles
1. Warm up	1. Present tense
2. Family lies	2. Distinct identities
(or variations such as	3. Time outs allowed
proposals or pregnancy	4. Spirit over accuracy
announcements)	5. Purposeful activities
3. Music, slides, and food—senses work	6. Combined tasks best
4. Improvisations	7. Many possible victories
5. Social success and failure lessons	8. All are experts from their region
6. Clothing suggestions	9. Program for clarity and structure
7. Dance steps	
8. Bows	
9. Perfect audience coaching	
10. Translation readings	

EXERCISE 10.4 ISM DAY

This project works particularly well with pairs of actors each drawing two Isms, and if the class all dress black and then change just one element for each section.

1. Go through the list chronologically, with five minute time limit per presentation.
2. Have the audience change location and configuration to suit the genre. Instruct them how they should respond. Have fun with who gets to sit or stand and when people should howl support or sit on their hands.
3. Find music or series of sound effects that most supports the movement, and al least one backdrop.
4. Act out a pregnancy announcement, with the appropriate outcome for that genre.
5. Find a food image to show and, if edible, to share.
6. Share five abstract images that capture the essence.

EXERCISE 10.5 ALTER EGOS UNLEASHED

1. Pick one of the characters you have created for yourself as a Greek, Elizabethan, Restoration, Georgian, or Ism.
2. Take this creation into the twenty-first century for a four-hour period, staying in character and responding in kind.
3. You may work with a partner or a small group, as long as you are all from the same period or genre.
4. Make sure that the excursion involves some interaction with contemporary people and that you give yourself the gift of viewing the peculiarities of our society from another's perspective.
5. Report to the class, as your alter ego, about your journey, what you learned and found most peculiar about the time journey.
6. Bring an object back to the class from the modern age that your compatriots in history would find particularly miraculous, peculiar, or horrifying.

This exercise takes some courage and only works if you stay in character. But it can also give you a sense of confidence and power.

EXERCISE 10.6 FACULTY STYLES

The models examined in this exercise are not necessarily ones you have attempted to be like. In fact, the exact opposite may be true. You have, however, observed them at some length in class, rehearsal, production meetings, student conferences, coaching sessions, working in the shop, supervising others, lecturing, at receptions and parties. You see them in enough situations to be able to conjecture their style choices in other imaginary situations.

The "recipients" here are graduate students. If there is no graduate program in your department, any level of student will work, with minor adjustments. Working in teams of three, each team draws the name of one of your own theatre faculty.

SITUATION A

The graduate student's thesis or dissertation has been selected for publication, and she has been asked by a major repertory company to do a year's residence exploring the theories in the document. The teachers sought this award on the sly and are about to announce the good news to the lucky student.

1. Each of the three "teachers" has decided to adopt the style of a particular faculty member (imagine that, at one time in your life, you decided that the way this person presented himself in the world was so admirable that he served as a

genuine role model for you). The trick is that this is not a simple imitation. You are not trying to *be* the faculty member, just to adapt their *style* of presentation and communication.

2. Questions to consider:

Time—How likely would the person be to prolong the announcement, even teasing as opposed to popping right out with it? How anxious is she to get on to other business?

Place—Where would this person choose to break the news? A shop, office, conference room, hallway, auditorium, lobby, or some place off campus?

Space—To what degree would physical contact or distance be employed?

Beauty and sex—Do these factors enter into this encounter in any way? To what extent are they always or never present in conferences with this person?

Recreation—How close to fun or just business as usual is this meeting?

Structure—How formal/informal would the basic situation be? How official does it seem?

Values—Are there particular truths that these faculty members embrace which may or may not be shared by the recipient?

Sight and sound—How do the above express themselves in the range of choices, from ways of sitting and eye contact to tone of voice and choice of images?

SITUATION B

The graduate student has been caught plagiarizing on his thesis or dissertation, and the proof is absolute. As if this were not bad enough, the graduate student has been caught naked in one of the faculty lounges with a Freshman student of indeterminate sex. The faculty "team" has got to break the news that the graduate student will be expelled, and there may even be a lawsuit.

Present both versions and discuss the style decisions made. Which stylistic choices seemed most and least on-the-money as likely selections for great admirers or emulators of this faculty member?

EXERCISE 10.7 PERSONAL STYLE DAY

The group should decide what it would like this day to be. Here are some possibilities:

1. **Pictures from the past**: Each person brings two photos—a baby or early childhood picture and the worst photograph ever taken of you in your life. Place these around the room. Have a guessing game.

2. **Style extremes show**: Each person brings two items reflecting how different or varied she can be in public. Two recent examples: A woman brought two red

shoes—one a spike-heeled slide for her "babe" self, the other a high top for her more funky side. An actor brought a comic book and a *Complete Works of Shakespeare*, the two things he was most often seen reading in the green room. Write up a commentary, just like in a real fashion show, to be read by the hosts. Get up and parade around, showing off your extremes while the narrative is read to music you have chosen.

3. **Style ritual**: Write down on a slip of paper the one abstract image that you would really like to lose, or at least to put on a back burner. This is not how you want to present yourself in the world. Pick the image that you like the most and would like to be worthy of in the future. Set up the room with a waste basket on-stage and a very nice basket with little paper wishing stars or some other symbolic objects in it. With everyone watching, go up and read the word of the dumping image, tear it up, and throw it in the waste basket. Take the wishing star and announce your commitment to your second image, after which the class will give you tumultuous applause.

4. **Theme songs and leftovers**: Everyone is to bring a leftover of theirs and put it on a table when no one is really looking. Someone who really feels they know your classmates is to volunteer to guess whose each is.

5. **Stage names**: Each person gets up and quickly shares the five names of the past and then, to drum roll or fanfare, announces the name he would choose if he got to choose or had to join Equity.

EXERCISE 10.8 STYLE GROWTH

Consider your own status in the following categories. If time allows, draw the name of a classmate to analyze:

Acting style:

> evidence of progress;
> need for growth.

Personal style:

> evidence of progress;
> need for growth.

1. Interview those who have worked with this person, particularly scene partners and directors, to get their ideas.
2. Check your own impressions with those of others in the class. Make certain that your conclusions are based on evidence and shared opinion.

3. Write out a list under each of the four categories.
4. Share in class a brief summary of what you have learned. Be sure to speak to the actor in question. Make sure your suggestions are stated in positive and future-oriented terms.

INDEX